Property of Linda McDermott

Library of Congress Catalog Card Number 87-83580
ISBN 0-9619924-0-9

RECOLLECTIONS OF A HIGH SCHOOL DISTRICT 1893-1968

An Informal History of the Kern County Union High School and Junior College District

J.S. WALLACE, AUTHOR

TABLE OF CONTENTS

	Page
DEDICATION	i
PREFACE	iii
CHAPTER I:	
THE BEGINNINGS – 1893 – 1908	1
Birth Pangs of Kern County High School	1
The Community Served by the School	5
The First Graduation	7
Politics and the Operation of the School	9
Early Classroom Experiences	11
A Famous Graduate is Remembers	15
Students in a Frontier Town	17
The Curriculum is Broadened	19
The Peckham Incident	20
School Activities	24
The Origins of the District in Summary	34
References	39
CHAPTER II:	
THE EARLY BOOM YEARS – 1908–1916	46
Kern County and Oil	46
Kern County High School Grows with the Boom	48
Student Life at the Beginnings of the Century	50

	Page
Chapter II (Continued):	
A Junior College Program is Added	52
Governance of the District Changes	56
School Days Cirea 1916	58
1908 - 1916 in Review	63

CHAPTER III:
WORLD WAR I AND THE TWENTIES — 75

The War and Kern County — 75
    The School During the War Years

Post War Education in the District — 79
    The Curriculum in 1918
    A Transportation System is Begun
    Student Activities after World War I
    Athletics
    The Night School is Born

The Roaring Twenties — 87
    Tragedy Strikes
    The Instructional Program in the Twenties
    Programs of Special Interest
    A Counseling Program is Organized
    Athletics in the Twenties
    Other Activities

The Junior College in this Decade — 108

Two New District Institutions — 111
    McFarland High School
    Shafter High School

The District at the End of the Twenties — 116

CHAPTER IV:
THE THIRTIES AND WORLD WAR II — 126

Facing the Depression — 126

District Activities During this Decade — 128

Staff Related Problems — 130

	Page

Chapter IV - Continued:

School Programs and Activities
    Instruction
    Athletics and Other Activities
	133

Two New Campuses are Established
    East Bakersfield
    A Campus in the Kern River Valley
	142

Other Expansion Plans
    North of the River
    Arvin and West Bakersfield sites
	156

The "Outlying" Campuses
    Shafter
    McFarland
	157

The Junior College in the Thirties	161
Other District Programs	163

The District Moves Ahead
    The Auditorium
    The End of an Era
	163

World War II and the District
    A New Campus is Born Out of
       Military Activity
	167

CHAPTER V:
THE END OF WORLD WAR II AND THE
POST-WAR YEARS 179

The Return of World War II Servicemen	179

District Concerns
    Bond Election of 1947
    A Public Information Program
    Completion of the Auditorium
	181

Schools in the Post-War Era
    Bakersfield College
    Bakersfield High School
    East Bakersfield High School
    Shafter High School
    The Kern River Valley School
    A High School on a Naval Base
    The Adult Evening School
    A New School Opens and Another
       on the Drawing Boards
    North of the River
	186

Page

Chapter V - Continued:

    The West Campus
    Planning for Growth
    The Earthquake Hits

Following the Earthquake   199
    New College Takes Shape
    Other Post-Earthquake Building
    North of the River High School
    South High School
    New Administration Offices
    Bakersfield High School
    Further Changes
    Relocation of Burroughs

School Operations in Post-War Day   207
    Recruitment Program
    Improvement of Instruction
    Personnel Changes in the 1950's

District Moves into the Sixties   212
    New School on Morning Drive
    The College Becomes a Separate
      District
    Retirements and Other Personnel
      Matters
    Another Bond Election Needed
    A New School in the West
    Tax Proposals and Voter Resistance
    Building Funds Secured
    Other District Considerations
    Continuation School
    Special Education
    Employment Concerns
    Meanwhile - At The Schools

Benchmark Events of the 1960's   228
    Retirements at the Top
    New Administrative Regime
    New School on the Horizon

References   234

APPENDICES:

    BOARDS OF TRUSTEES - HIGH SCHOOL
      DISTRICT   240

    SUPERINTENDENTS - HIGH SCHOOL
      DISTRICT   253

	Page
HIGH SCHOOLS AND PRINCIPALS	257
CHANCELLORS, PRESIDENTS AND BOARDS OF TRUSTEES - Kern Community College District	264

EARLY EXAMINATIONS:

Grammar School Graduation Questions	267
High School Graduation Examination Questions	269
County Teachers Examinations	272
LIST OF TAPED INTERVIEWS	274
CHRONOLOGY OF EVENTS, 1968-1980	277

Alfred Harrell
"The Father of the Kern County Union High School District"

Justly called "the father of the Kern County Union High School District", Alfred Harrell, was Kern County Superintendent of Schools in 1893 when the District was originated. He had circulated the petition the previous fall which gave rise to the election approving the establishment of the District. Until 1916 the District was operated by the Kern County Board of Education.

Theron and Hazel McCuen

DEDICATION

This story of the Kern County Union High School and Junior College District is affectionately dedicated to Hazel and Theron McCuen. They were both teachers at Kern County High School in the fall of 1929, fresh from the campus of Stanford University, where they were casual acquaintances. Hazel Kelley was assigned to English, history, and public speaking classes, and after school, debate coaching. As an undergraduate student at the College of the Pacific, she debated with notable success, having been a team member there with Leonard McKaig, later a long-time Bakersfield College forensics instructor. During that first year, Theron taught engineering drawing and their friendship at Stanford was renewed to the extent that, before the next fall, they were married. Because of District policy, it was necessary for Hazel to resign, but she continued to substitute in the Adult Evening School, in various high schools, and at Bakersfield College. From 1964 to 1968 she returned to teach full time at several of the District schools, filling in various emergency vacancies which occurred at the beginning of the school terms.

Mr. McCuen's career is chronicled in this volume from 1929 to his retirement in 1968, having served as teacher of drawing, the first Business Manager, and Superintendent. During the years between 1945 and 1968 the McCuens are well remembered for the welcome given at receptions in their home each year to countless teachers who came from disparate sections of the country. Their concern for personnel in the District and their participation in community affairs made important contributions to the District and the community it served.

PREFACE

This early retirement project began at the end of the 1979-80 school year at the suggestion of Dr. Gerald S. DeGrow, then Superintendent of the Kern High School District. He believed that a school district as distinguished as this one should have a written history.

I envisioned a rather brief account of the beginnings of high school education in Kern County encompassing a modest thirty or forty pages. But as the effort got underway, with the encouragement of Dr. DeGrow and the current Superintendent Don Murfin, the concept expanded to take on the dimension of oral history. This seemed a way to breathe life into the rather colorless factual accounts contained in the official minutes of the Board and other such references.

Beginning with a few of the earliest available graduates of Kern County High School, the list of persons interviewed was expanded to include other graduates, former staff members, and Board members who had a story to tell about life in the District, particularly in the early days.

The account may be criticized for the attention given to the first schools, i.e. Bakersfield, McFarland, Shafter, East Bakersfield, Kern Valley High Schools, and Bakersfield College. The only excuse offered is that as time moves on, the incidents surrounding these events, particularly the personal accounts, may be lost. In fact, as of this date, eight of the thirty-six persons interviewed since 1980 have passed away.

One problem encountered in recording the origins of the schools constructed since World War II is their rate of proliferation. It is hoped that a story of the genesis of each of the schools will be written in detail -- perhaps modeled after that of West High School, written as an early retirement project by Edwin DeMello.

Many persons deserve appreciation for their assistance and encouragement. A few will be mentioned here with the recognition that some significant omissions may inadvertantly occur. All of the persons interviewed and taped should be recognized, but particularly noteworthy are the three elder graduates, the late Marianna

Bohna (1906), Lawrence Weill (1906), and Mary Ann Ashe (1908), who gave depth and insight to the early days. Unselfish with their time, they submitted to numerous interviews and inquiries. The late Harold Brewer, great-grandson of Col. Thomas Baker and a graduate of the class of 1929, provided the viewpoint of a former student as well as historical dimension to the account.

A debt is owed to three former superintendents as well: Dr. Gerald S. DeGrow for his suggestion to write the account; Theron L. McCuen for contributing to the content and for reading the entire text and making a valuable contribution to its accuracy; and Dr. John W. Eckhardt, particularly for the story of teacher recruitment in the late Fifties and Sixties. Dr. Edward C. Simonsen, former Chancellor of the Kern Community College District, was also most helpful in giving the college perspective.

In addition, well known Kern County historian Dr. W. Harland Boyd read most of the content, making many helpful editorial and historial suggestions. My special thanks, too, goes to Beverly Banks, District Writing Proficiency Chairperson, for her editorial and proof writing assistance, making my often rough hewn prose more smooth and readable. Superintendent Don Murfin has been very supportive in the entire project, as well as his office staff of Vida McMillen, Becky Shipley and former staff member Dina Elliott. The latter three introduced this writer to the magical world of word processing. Librarian Mary Louise Sikola and her staff gave me and my research material a home during the last months of the writing effort, and are due my thanks.

Finally, my warmest gratitude goes to my wife, Dorothy, who gave invaluable suggestions, read the script, and was always optimistic about the outcome!

Apologies perhaps should be expressed to a number of the present and former District staff members for the omission of academic titles, particularly the doctorate, in the use of quotes and other references. However, in the interests of fairness to all concerned, since it was difficult to determine in some cases who had which degrees, titles of this nature were arbitrarily deleted in the narrative.

J. S. Wallace

CHAPTER I
THE BEGINNINGS - 1893 - 1908

The origin of almost any institution is the result of many diverse factors which arise from the circumstances of that particular era. The beginnings of the Kern High School District in the form of Kern County High School certainly illustrate this maxim. By the year 1892, the City of Bakersfield, California, and the County of Kern were ready for the organization of a secondary school. The nearest high school was located in Visalia, and it had just been organized, while another one in Fresno had opened some three years previously in 1889.[1]

The Caminetti Act of 1887 permitted elementary students to attend postgraduate schools established by the elementary districts in order to prepare them for entrance to the University of California. However, this arrangement proved to be unsatisfactory for several reasons, primarily monetary, since this advanced schooling was to be paid for out of the budgets of the elementary districts.[2]

In 1891, corrective legislation was passed to allow county and city high schools to be established.[3] These were to operate as entirely separate units and to provide, in one distinct institution, schooling primarily aimed at preparing students for college and university work.

Birth Pangs of Kern County High School

A man of vision who headed the schools in Kern County provided the motivational spark for the organizing of the Kern County High School. In the fall of 1892, Mr. Alfred Harrell, who had formerly been a first grade teacher at the Railroad Avenue School in Bakersfield and was then Kern

County School Superintendent, saw the need to establish a high school in the county. In fact, according to Glendon Rodgers:

> A high school became his pet project. As a result, he combed the county for students, persuading the parents to send their children to the proposed high school at Bakersfield rather than away. Following this informal survey of possible high school students, he had circulated a petition, requesting the County Board of Supervisors to submit the question of establishing a county high school to the voters.[4]

This petition was required by the Caminetti Bill, and it was filed with the Board of Supervisors on October 3, 1892. A few days later the following action occurred in a meeting of the Board of Supervisors:

> In the matter of the County High School, a petition having been heretofore filed with this Board praying the establishment of a County High School in and for Kern County. Upon motion of E.A. McGee, seconded by J. Fontaine, it is ordered that the question of the establishment and maintenance of said County High School at the expense of said Kern County be, and same is hereby ordered to be submitted to the qualified electors of said County at the General Election to be held therein on the Eighth day of November, 1892.[5]

A general election had already been set for Tuesday, November 8, 1892, and this matter was added to the county-wide ballot to go before the electors at that time. The issue of the proposed new high school received strong support from the local press as is evidenced by an excerpt from the November 5, 1892, Weekly Californian:

> Do not forget as you go to vote that it requires a majority of all votes cast to obtain a high school for Kern County. Everyone who has school and county interests favors the establishment of a school where higher grades can be taught, but there is a danger that many will neglect at the poles. Voters of Kern County, do not neglect such an important matter as this. It will not be an expensive matter, as the building can be had, suitable for such a school until such time as necessity will require something more extensive.

That the voters did not neglect this important matter was shown when the official returns from the election were verified on November 18. The count showed 1,274 votes for a high school and 286 against. This was considerably more than the two-thirds favorable vote required. Now the new high school was virtually assured to serve the County of Kern, whose population at this time totalled just short of 10,000 persons.

The Board of Supervisors was quick to follow the mandate of the public, and on December 6, the supervisors ordered the County Superintendent of Schools to purchase

> ...fifty high school desks No. 2; two recitation settees, (long benches placed in front of the teacher for recitation purposes); two revolving chairs, two teachers' desks, and four common chairs. C. F. Bennett and E. A. Morgan were appointed as a committee from the Board to confer with the Board of Trustees of the Bakersfield district as to the possibilities of using an old elementary school building as a high school building.[6]

The Board of Supervisors' education committee was successful in its negotiations with the Bakersfield School District and secured the use of a school building referred to in the supervisors' board minutes as "an old school house opposite the court house in Bakersfield." This was the Railroad Avenue School on the street that is now Truxtun Avenue, located on the site where Emerson Junior High School stood for many years. The building was vacant because the city school district had recently built the six-room Bryant School on land facing 21st and G Streets.[7] The first site of Kern County High School, then, was two rooms in the upstairs of the old Railroad Avenue School. While the county Board of Supervisors had the responsibility for financing and passing on the business aspects of the new school, the day-to-day operation of the school was in the hands of the county Board of Education. It followed then that the county superintendent was the head official for the administration of the high school; this man was Alfred Harrell, who more than any one person deserves the appellation "father of the Kern High School District."

Minutes of the county Board of Education show that the school was authorized to begin on January 9, 1893. Apparently, however, for some unknown reason, the school actually did not get underway until three days later on January 12.[8] In a special December session, the Board had established entrance requirements, the basic curriculum and adopted text books. The school was to be opened to all students holding diplomas of graduation from the public schools of Kern County, and there were two branches of study to be followed in the curriculum: scientific and literary. Since a number of students had already had postgraduate work following their eighth grade graduations, it was decided that, for the time being, the first and second years would be combined into one grade to be known as the advanced grade.[9]

After due consideration, the following basic textbooks were adopted: Robinson's High School Arithmetic, Robinson's Algebra, Steel's Philosophy and Cathart's Literary Reader. An additional course in civil government using the State series of textbooks was also established.[10]

The new school was to have three staff members: Philip Eden was selected as principal for a term not to exceed five months at a salary of $125 per month. His assistant was a young lady named Kitty M. Crusoe, and she was selected under the same circumstances with a salary of $100 per month. The third staff member was to be a janitor who was to be selected by the secretary of the board. With the new high school now securely underway, a rather smug and self-satisfied attitude was projected by this quotation from The Daily Californian:

>   The new county high school is well in the fourth week of its existence and is no longer an experiment. Thirty-two students are regularly enrolled and pursuing the adopted courses, and there are several pupils doing work along special lines. The maintenance of this institution means more to the educational interests of the county than appears at first thought. To gain admission to it will soon come to be the legitimate aim of pupils enrolled in the grammar schools of the

county. It furnishes the needed incentive to these students to pursue their grade work to its completion and places a higher education within the reach of all...[11]

When first established, the Kern County High School, as the name indicated, served the entire county of Kern. Such was to be the case until 1911, when the Delano Union High School District was formed in the northern part of the county.

The Community Served by the School

Just before the turn of the century, the county's economy was largely that of agriculture and livestock, since mining had declined in importance since 1870. The importance of oil was yet on the horizon, but it would play a vital role in the economy in the early decades of the Twentieth Century.[12] Just thirty years prior to the establishment of Kern County High School, Colonel Thomas Baker arrived at Kern Island along the lower reaches of the Kern River and saw the possibilities of future development for this area. Colonel Baker had been a state senator and an assemblyman in Tulare County and had obtained reclamation rights to the swamp and overflow lands in the Kern area.[13]

Several years after Col. Baker's death, his wife, who was by then Mrs. Ferdinand A. Tracy, read a paper before the Woman's Club of Bakersfield which was published in one of the local newspapers. She noted that the Kern River pioneers lived primitively and the closest house that could justly be called by that name was at Porterville, some three days journey away over mountain trails. "An old shanty built of poles planted in the ground and thatched with tules or cattail flags, windowless, doorless and floorless must be our home for the time being. We moved our belongings into the one room and then built on a brush shed to serve as a kitchen and dining room." This dwelling had been built a few years previously by one of the earliest white settlers in the area, Christian Bohna.

It was a hundred miles to the nearest store, and the provisions came by way of a mule team and spring wagon. The freight wagon came from Los Angeles, a trip which took weeks at that time. There was no post office, and it was weeks before word came from the outside world regarding important events. In fact, the families on Kern Island learned of the assassination of President Lincoln from a Mexican who swam his horse across the Kern River and said that the President had been killed. They thought he meant the president of Mexico until belated bundles of newspapers arrived some time later. But Colonel Baker was a man of prophetic vision. He is reported to have said about this country when he first glimpsed it: "This is God's country! Some day it will be filled with happy homes. The largest town south of Stockton will have its site here. Three or four lines of railroads will come through those mountain passes and center here. The place is rich in future possibilities."[14]

The year 1874 was a propitious one for Kern County. During this year, the first railroad arrived; and even though its terminus was not in Bakersfield, but in Sumner, some two miles away, the importance of this event cannot be overstated. The railroad furnished a reliable and regular method of transporting products to market and, thus, gave impetus to the growth of agriculture as a economic boon to the area. It was during this same year that Bakersfield finally became the county seat after a hotly contested election that was not settled until litigation occurred. Since the creation of Kern County in 1866 the county seat had been located at the mountain town of Havilah, and the mining interests and others who favored this location were loath to see it moved to the valley area, which was infested with mosquitoes and malaria.

According to De Mello:

> The census of 1880 showed the county with a population of 5,601. Ten years later the count stood at 9,808. This growth, while considerable for the times, was not tremendous. Even with the railroad to transport the products to market, that the development of the area was not more

rapid is attributed in part to the uncertainty prevalent because of the great legal battles over water rights which were not finally resolved until 1888.[15]

One recurrent theme of history is that progress is made in a positive manner only when leaders are available who have vision, a vision which transcends the mundane environment and looks towards a more promising future. Colonel Thomas Baker and School Superintendent Alfred Harrell were certainly examples of this kind of leadership in the county. But the question of education and its demand for additional public expenditure had also received an early "yes" vote from the people of the community. That they were somewhat reluctant to burden themselves with public debt is evidenced from the fact that several of the issues on the November 1882 ballot did not pass. On the same ticket with the school question was a bond issue for the purpose of constructing a hall of records, county hospital and jail, and this proposal went down to defeat.[16]

The First Graduation

At the end of the first high school term in May, 1893, Principal Philip Eden left at the expiration of his five months' contract, and E. F. Goodyear was elected to succeed him. Kitty Crusoe remained as the assistant, and the salaries remained the same as they were the previous year. Speaking of financial matters, the secretary of the Board of Education provided the Board of Supervisors with an estimate of the expenses for operating a high school for 1893-94 school year. It totalled $2,500. Curiously, this estimate was not provided until the September board meeting just as the new school year was getting underway, which seems to indicate that there was little concern, either on the part of the Board of Education or the Board of Supervisors, about finances needed to operate the school.[17]

At the conclusion of the first school year in May, 1894, the first commencement exercises were held. Three young ladies had the distinction of being the first graduates. They were May Stark, Ella Fay and Adaline Nicholson. The <u>Californian</u> noted that there was more than ordinary interest in these three young ladies who were "the first fruits of this most beneficent enterprise."

It is enlightening to look at this first graduation ceremony and compare it with a modern counterpart. Superintendent Harrell spoke, commenting on the "opportunities, possibilities and advantages of opening the high school to the youth of this county." Principal Goodyear presented the graduates, asserting that they were "like caravels with which Columbus set out to discover, set out over unknown paths, seeking prosperity and happiness." The president of the Board of Education, J. H. Berry, presented the diplomas, and there was music by the Kern City String Band as well as instrumental and vocal solos. However, the piece de resistance of the graduation ceremony came from the graduates themselves in the form of essays which they had written and which were read to the audience. May Stark's contribution was entitled "Character Building," and that by Ella Fay, "Present Possibilities," commenting on the past and present role of womanhood. Adaline Nicholson's reading was entitled, "Among the Heights". It gave an account of the traveler who scales the mountain tops as he attempts to reach higher and higher ideals. All in all, the ceremony was a most auspicious conclusion to the first full year of operation of the Kern County High School.[18]

The reader may wonder how these three young ladies were able to graduate and receive credit for a four-year high school course when the school had only been in operation a year and a half. The answer is that they were given credit for postgraduate work, which all three had taken after the conclusion of their grammar school course, before the new high school had come into being. Provisions for accommodating such students were laid down by the Board of Education when the school was started.

Politics and the Operation of the School

Earlier in this account, in discussing the basic administrative organization of the high school district, it was noted that the county Board of Supervisors had the financial obligation to provide for the school, while the county Board of Education was in charge of day-to-day operation. The fact that the county school superintendents ran for election as members of particular political parties added to the partisan flavor of education in those early days. Another factor in this political arena was that the Board of Supervisors appointed members of the county Board of Education, and then, just to add to the partisan turmoil was the fact that at the turn of the century the two leading newspapers in the community, The Daily Californian and The Morning Echo, represented different political points of view and were usually on the sides of opposite candidates for the position of county superintendent of schools.[19]

In 1899, a new superintendent of schools took office, and there was a change in the politics of the office. This man was W. C. Doub, who took over after twelve years from Alfred Harrell. Mr. Doub was a Republican, and his politics were strongly supported by the The Morning Echo. Two years previously, Mr. Harrell had purchased The Daily Californian, and he decided not to run for office when his term expired in 1899, in order to devote his full attention to the operation of the newspaper. With a publisher such as Mr. Harrell in charge of The Daily Californian, it could be assumed that school affairs would be featured prominently in the pages of the newspaper; this was true throughout Mr. Harrell's tenure as publisher and the policy has been continued into modern time.

Two incidents reflect the active political life which centered around the operation of the school affairs, and they are recounted by Edwin De Mello in his monograph on the early history of the district.[20]

A prominent member of the Board of Education in those days was Mr. Leo G. Pauly, who had been on the Board since

1896. In 1902, Mr. Pauly was contacted by the chairman of the Board of Supervisors who explained that it was politically necessary for him to give up his position on the school board. He promised Pauly personally that he would be reappointed at a later date. Thus, Mr. Pauly was off the Board for some two years but was reappointed and continued to serve until 1918. The reason for this action was to keep some balance in the political alignment on the Board of Education.

The second anecdote concerning politics in education during the time occurred during the campaign for the superintendency in 1902. Robert L. Stockton, a prominent rancher and farmer in the area and a member of the Board of Education, had decided to challenge Doub for the position. It was reported in The Daily Californian that Superintendent Doub and his friends had charged that Mr. Stockton was not educationally qualified to fill the office. Stockton, as a member of the Board, had been critical of the fact that a number of textbooks written by Superintendent Doub were required to be used in the high school, and this concern, along with the general interest in educational matters, apparently had prompted him to run for the Board. After the charge that he was not educationally qualified, Mr. Stockton offered "to submit to a competitive examination in all subjects required to be taught in the public schools." According to the local newspaper account, Stockton offered to leave the contest for the superintendency if he did not score higher on this examination than his opponent. The examination was to be given and monitored by neutral parties. For whatever reason, Mr. Doub declined this challenge, and the result was that Mr. Stockton won by approximately a two to one majority.

Whether or not partisan politics was an unfavorable factor in the operation of education at the time is open to question. De Mello was able to interview Leo G. Pauly, the man who was forced to withhold his application for reappointment to the Board for political reasons. Mr. Pauly felt that

10

the politics of the time was not a negative factor in the operation of the school district. He believed that, once the appointments were made, the board members were able to put aside their political beliefs and carry out the operation of the school district in the best interest of the students. He quoted as substantiation for this belief the fact that except for this one interruption, he had served on the school board for more than twenty years, and more often than not, he was not of the political party in power in the county at the time.[21]

Early Classroom Experiences

As has already been noted, the courses of high school studies had been established as scientific and literary. The actual subjects taught included Latin, English, history, mathematics and science, and chemistry as a special science subject. The field of English included literature and composition, while political science and government were added to the history field. These were all subjects, of course, which were considered acceptable towards entrance to the University of California, and the curriculum was generally aimed in that direction. As early as 1896, however, proposals were made to establish a commercial course for those students who did not plan to go on to the university and might find their future in the world of business. However, this was not accomplished until 1899.

Fortunately, some early graduates of the school have been willing to discuss with the author their remembrances of their life at Kern County High School. Two of them, Marianna Bohna and Lawrence Weill, are graduates of the Class of 1906, and entered the school in 1902, some ten years after the school was actually founded. The third, Mary Ann Ashe, is a graduate of the Class of 1908. These three persons were interviewed at length and generously shared their recollections to help provide a better understanding of school life in those early days.[22]

Marianna Bohna is a granddaughter of Christian Bohna, one of the earliest settlers on Kern Island. Mr. Bohna actually came to Kern in 1859 and built a cabin which was later to be occupied by Colonel Thomas Baker. Later, the Bohna family moved to the Woody area and continued to live there since it was a healthier climate than the lowlands of Kern Island. Miss Bohna began her high school work in Banning, staying with a friend there in the fall of 1902, and came to Kern County High School in midyear. She describes her entrance into the school in these words:

> ...When I went to the high school I was just actually very timid because we'd hardly been around the city at all...Down in Banning the whole school was forty children and here were sixty piled in that one room. Then when Mr. Childress came in I don't know but what the first thing he did was to take some big boy by the shoulders and mop the floor with him.

She recalls taking history, English, mathematics and Latin, and remembers with particular pleasure her classes in Latin, not only because of the value of the subject matter, but also because of the excellent tutelage and sympathetic understanding of the teacher, Mrs. Helen S. Craig. As Miss Bohna recalls:

> ...Dear Mrs. Craig she was worth her weight in gold to me. I took Latin from Mrs. Craig. She was an elderly lady, quite gray haired and very meticulous, the old style and a very darling person. A number of students were scared of her, but I wasn't a bit afraid of her... she really knew how to teach...

The basic curriculum was still literary and scientific, although by this time the commercial course had been added, and students in these courses were on campus and involved in a two-year course which was not considered the educational equivalent of the academic course. Miss Bohna remembers particularly the hours spent on homework to prepare herself for her classes, and recalls, with a great deal of pride, that the principal at the time, C. C. Childress "...was good enough to write him [Miss Bohna's father] a little note which meant a thousand dollars to him. In one place it says I was the second best in the class which made him feel very happy." Grades were given in percentages, and 75 percent was established as a passing grade. (The facsimile of Miss Bohna's report card is reproduced elsewhere in this document to indicate the differences in grade reporting then and now.)

To achieve academically was important then for such reasons as pride of accomplishment, feelings of self-worth, admission to college, family prestige, progress toward becoming an educated person, and the ability to pass the examinations required for graduation. Examination questions were frequently published in the newspapers of the community, presumably after they had been administered. According to the May 29, 1904, issue of the Morning Echo graduates were required to answer questions in the subject areas of Latin, English, trigonometry, physics, and United States civil government.

The Latin examination included translations of Vergil's Aeneid, as well as critical questions about this classic. Criticism of literary selections from Browning, Shelley, Wordsworth along with quotations to explain and identify made up the English section. Specific problems, solutions and proofs were required in the trigonometry section, while detailed questions on the nature of physical laws were contained in that part of the examination. Specific knowledge of state and federal government relationships were required to answer the government questions. Without doubt, detailed knowledge of a concrete body of knowledge was expected of Kern County High School graduates in 1904.

It should be noted that passing a formal examination was also required before graduating from the eighth grade. In 1904, the subject areas of spelling, arithmetic, history, geography, bookkeeping, reading and language were included.

Teachers' examination questions were also published in the local newspapers. Questions, mostly essay-type, were asked of credential applicants in the areas of English and

American literature, arithmetic, physics, history, geography, physiology and hygiene, drawing, penmanship, vocal music and bookkeeping.[23]

Lawrence Weill remembers the two courses, literary and scientific, and that all students were required to take physics in their fourth year. He also recalls, with a great deal of appreciation, the affection that students had for Mrs. Helen Craig, even though another teacher particularly stands out in his memory. This was the man who really got athletics going for the high school. He came to the school in 1901, fresh from Stanford University to take charge of the science program, as well as all athletics. His name was Fayette Birtch, and he left a lasting impression upon the students in those early days.

Mary Ann Ashe entered the school in 1904, and describes herself as being "scared to death coming in from the country." She grew up in the Panama area and felt that at least some of the teachers in the school doubted her ability to pursue the academic course because she came from the country. She was able, as a result of long hours of study, to be successful in her school subjects and recalls with a special appreciation, Mabel Chubb, her history teacher, Mrs. Craig, the Latin teacher, and with somewhat reluctant appreciation, C. C. Childress, who in addition to being principal, taught mathematics. Mr. Childress, called "C Cube" by the youngsters for obvious reasons, had come to the school in 1897 and was a strict disciplinarian following a long line of early schoolmasters who expected and saw to it that students behaved according to rigid principles of law and order.

Miss Ashe recalls an incident told to her by the janitor, a Mr. Duty, illustrating the extent to which the principal would go to ensure discipline:

> One time, the custodian who was old Mr. Duty, was outside by the bicycle rack. Mr. Duty talked to himself and he turned around to find Mr. Childress creeping up on his hands and

knees, expecting to find some students cutting class. He was quite surprised to see Mr. Duty, so he got up and brushed the dust off his knees, and said "OK, its you Mr. Duty!" Mr. Duty agreed with him that it was he.

On another occasion a classmate of Miss Ashe's was expelled from the school by Mr. Childress for accidentally hitting one of the teachers with an eraser. As far as was known, this particular student left the school and never returned.

A Famous Graduate is Remembered

Miss Ashe had the good fortune to be a fellow classmate with perhaps the most famous of all Kern County High School graduates, Earl Warren, later to be Governor of the State of California and Chief Justice of the United States Supreme Court. According to Miss Ashe:

> In our senior year (1907-1908) Earl Warren, who was one of my classmates and Reginald Stoner, another, were in the class play. The last night of rehearsal their coach kept them until after midnight. Well, Earl lived over on Niles Street east of Baker Street and he had to walk home because the street cars had all quit running and Reginald lived on Chester near 14th Street. Their mothers let them sleep in the next morning knowing that they were graduating that night...
> ...When they came to school late in the morning Mr. Childress expelled them. He thought they were just taking advantage of the situation.

Apparently, members of the Board of Education intervened in this case, and the boys were later reinstated, but this is another illustration of the severity with which rules and regulations were enforced by the principal in those early days.

Miss Ashe also recalls with relish an occurrence related to Earl Warren in their physics lab class. She and several students, including Warren, worked together on experiments in the lab class and, on occasion, Earl left before the experiment was concluded because he had a job as call boy for the Southern Pacific Railroad. He would ask the others in his lab group, all girls, to finish the experiment for him since he had to go to work. Many years later, when Miss Ashe reminded him of this incident, "...he looked up in surprise and said, 'Why, I didn't have to work.' I said, 'Well you certainly convinced Ethel and me that you had to--the way you pulled out of that classroom.'"

Fifty years after graduation at the anniversary of the graduating class, Miss Ashe remembers with great satisfaction the fact that both Earl Warren and Reginald Stoner, who had become a high official in the Standard Oil Company, appeared and addressed those members of the graduating class in attendance.

Another of Earl Warren's classmates, Omar Cavins, in an interview conducted for an oral history completed about Mr. Warren by the University of California, recalls an incident indirectly involving Warren. It also illustrates the severity of school discipline in those days.

> Well, there's one thing that happened to Earl Warren when I was there. I was sitting up toward the front. Stoner was sitting ahead of me. C Cube went back to tell Earl Warren, who was, judiciously, I suppose you'd call it, sitting in the back (he wasn't much of a student, seriously, particularly)--he went back through the aisle to tell Earl something. There was no fuss until C Cube started back to the front of the room and Stoner turned around, and as he turned to see what was going on, he kicked old C Cube in the shins. C Cube grabbed Stoner by the back of the coat and just banged his head up and down on the desk. They'd hang principals for doing that nowadays.[24]

Interestingly enough, Warren is not remembered by his classmates as being an outstanding student; neither was he particularly active in social activities or athletics, although Cavins remembers that he did try out for the high school baseball team, but "I beat him out for right field."[25] Undoubtedly his job as call boy for the railroad and the fact that he spent a good deal of time delivering newspapers, including The Daily Californian, had something to do with his lack of participation in school activities.

Francis E. Vaughan, another classmate of Earl Warren, recollects that the latter came from Kern, which was the name given at that time to the separate community of East Bakersfield, and traveled to school "by the PT&L (Power, Transit & Light Company) streetcar everyday of his life." As a matter of fact, some of the students of those days commuted by Southern Pacific from Delano and other points along the railroad route according to Mr. Vaughan.[26]

Students In A Frontier Town

Bakersfield, in those days, had a well earned reputation as being a rough, tough frontier town, and it is interesting to speculate on the effect of the mores of the community on high school students. Mr. Vaughan recalls that there was a definite distinction made in the student body between the "drinkers and nondrinkers." "There was a lot of drinking in high school, and I was a nondrinker. A total abstainer. That marked me as an outcast by certain groups... I was frequently reminded that I was a 'baby, drinking milk, instead of a man's drink'."[27]

Lawrence Weill remembers distinctly the prominence which the red light district had in the community. It was no surprise to him that Bakersfield had such an area. As he says:

> ...I grew up with the understanding that a "red light" district was just as important to a town and as necessary as a City hall. Every town that I ever visited had its "red light" district, big and small. San Francisco's was remarkable."

The crib district was located in an area between "L" and "M" from 20th to 22nd Streets, and Mr. Weill recalls particularly three dance halls - the largest one being called, "The Palace." Young men from the high school would often meet at one of the bars and "go down the line," that is, walk by the cribs, talk with the girls, and go into the dance halls. They knew that the patrons of these places were often fleeced of their money, but accepted this as one of the vicissitudes of life.

Mr. Weill also remembers with clarity the famous shoot-out at one of the Chinese joss houses which is the subject of Joseph E. Doctor's book, <u>Shotguns on Sunday</u>. The central character was described as one of the last bad men of the West, a man named James McKinney, who after killing two police officers in Bakersfield, was himself shot to death in this joss house. As a footnote, one of the officers killed in the shoot out was W. E. Tibbett, the father of Lawrence Tibbett, later to become an internationally famous member of the New York Metropolitan Opera Company.

In 1986 the Bakersfield Chapter of LINKS, Inc. honored the first Black graduate of Kern County Union High School. Henry Edward Simpson was in the senior class of 1900 along with four other graduates - all girls. According to the information made available at this occasion, he was valedictorian of the class - certainly quite an accomplishment considering that he was in competition with four female students. He and his family had migrated to Bakersfield from his birthplace in South Carolina by way of Arkansas, arriving here in 1890.

According to the program publicity:

> ...around this period of time he (Simpson) played in a "colored" band known as the Kern Valley Band along with another Black Kern Pioneer, William Pinkney.
> In 1913 the Blacks of Kern County organized their first political club, The Kern County Political Committee. Henry was one of the first leaders of this movement. Through the efforts of this club, in 1916, Kern County received its first two Black public servants, Joe Pinkney and Clarence Boswell."

Probably the Pinckney mentioned here is actually William Henry Pinckney who worked for the City of Bakersfield Street Department from 1916 until his retirement in 1945.

The Curriculum is Broadened

In its beginning, the Kern County High School was primarily a college preparatory institution with its classical curriculum offerings in the two areas: literary and scientific. However, during the summer of 1899, the Board of Education approved a change that was to set the new school on the road to becoming a true "comprehensive high school."

The new course of study was described as follows:

> All pupils who are residents of Kern County and are prepared to do the work will be permitted to take the commercial course even if they do not hold the proper credentials entitling them to take up the regular high school work, and at the discretion of the principal, pupils may be permitted to take part of the work only, if they desire.[28]

Actually the need to establish such a course of study had been felt some three years earlier and board action had taken place to establish the studies, but for some reason nothing had come of it until this time. Two teachers were employed to teach commercial subjects in typewriting and shorthand. A strict distinction was maintained between the commercial courses and the academic courses. Mary Ann Ashe recollects that Principal Childress did not allow academic students to become involved with the commercial courses. In fact, during the plans being made for graduation exercises for the class of 1901, the academic group rebelled at the idea of being on the same stage with the commercial students for the commencement exercises. Superintendent W. C. Doub had to come in and resolve the situation so that the program could proceed. It was arranged that while the two groups would be on the same stage, they would be seated separately. Graduation pictures taken during this time always separated the two groups, and students of that era tended to think of their classmates as being associated with a particular course, either academic or commercial.[29] It should be recognized that by this time the academic course was a full four-year program and, in the beginning days, at least the commercial course was only a two-year program. The time requirement, no doubt, contributed to some extent to the separation between the two programs of studies.

By 1904, the commercial department had made great strides from a few basic courses in commercial subjects in typewriting and shorthand, which were established in 1899. An article in the January 29, 1904, <u>Morning Echo</u> is headlined "Business Deals at the High School." It describes the commercial department at the high school as "one of the most active business centers in the city." Thirty-one girls and sixteen boys were at that time enrolled, and the department had been set up to simulate organized businesses in the particular areas of banking, railroading, and commission houses. In the classrooms, tables had been fitted with drawers to keep ledgers, journals, passbooks, checks, receipt bills, deeds, insurance policies and mortgages. Small "pasteboard slips" were kept with the names of merchandise, such as "six dozen cases of eggs, dress gingham and steel rails." Students were encouraged to buy and sell to each other with proper records being kept. Interchanges were maintained with business schools elsewhere. Merchandise was "shipped" back and forth on "college railways." According to the newspaper article, conservative business methods were followed and accurate records were kept of profits and losses experienced by the students. This was certainly a realistic forerunner of modern day merchandising and commercial business programs.

During the same summer (1899) that the Board approved the commercial courses, action was taken to broaden the offerings in the academic areas with history and political science courses being added to the two original branches of learning: literary and scientific. And, it was at this time that the academic course of study was extended to a full four years.[30]

The Peckham Incident

During the 1902-03 school year, an incident occurred which shook the school to its very foundations. It was undoubtedly a primary topic of discussion in the community and was even aired nationally in an Associated Press story. According to the latter, as reprinted in the December 20, 1902, issue of the Morning Echo, "An open mutiny broke out in Kern County High School today and resulted in the summary suspension of thirteen boys."

The "rebellion" was against a rule promulgated by Principal Leroy Bliss Peckham, which required that when dismissed, students would leave separately by sexes – the boys going first, the girls following. This was supposed to discourage promiscuous consorting of the sexes between classes and to assist in maintaining a more serious attitude towards scholarship at the school. Prior to this, Principal Peckham had made himself unpopular by suspending two senior boys, prominent members of the football team. When they enrolled at arch-rival Tulare, their loss was directly attributed to the principal by most students. The revolt started with the sophomore boys, and apparently, was abetted and fostered by some of the older students. The initial action consisted of the sophomore boys' refusing to leave class ahead of the girls. The principal was called in by the teacher, and he summarily suspended all thirteen boys involved. The matter was fully reported in the local newspapers. The Morning Echo expected that the whole matter would be closed very quickly and that the boys "would" apologize gracefully and that their action, heedless and ridiculuous, will be condoned and that there will be no further breaches of harmony."[31]

However, this was not to be the case. The matter simmered during the Christmas holidays, and when school reconvened in January, 1903, action broke out anew. County Superintendent Robert L. Stockton had just taken office, and one of his first official duties was to settle the matter of the revolt against Principal Peckham. The Bakersfield Californian reported on the matter of the suspension of the football players as follows:

> Another matter that has exercised the students not a little is that of the Football game

with Tulare tomorrow. It appears that two of the
boys on the Bakersfield team are among those who
are under suspension and acting upon a section
of the by-laws of the Athletic League, Principal
Peckham notified Tulare that these boys were not
eligible to play in the contest. Without them
Bakersfield could not go onto the field at all, as
they had practiced with the team and are a part
of the machine. A number of leading citizens of
the city have become interested in the matter and
yesterday waited upon Mr. Peckham in view of
adjusting the differences that have arisen.[32]

Although Bakersfield did field a team, it lost the game, and this certainly did not add to Peckham's popularity. The Board of Trustees was in a somewhat embarrassing situation on this matter. Up to now, the Board had been supportive of the principal, even though a great deal of pressure had been exerted, not only because of the debacle of the football game, but also because the general sentiment that the principal had been guilty of lack of good judgment in dealing with students. Finally, the Board of Education made its position known in a newspaper article, and the spokesman was quoted as follows:

> We were loath to move in this high school
> difficulty and refrained from doing so until we
> were satisfied that the usefulness of the school
> had been impaired. It became evident in the last
> month of the last year that the school was
> becoming demoralized and that the friction
> between Mr. Peckham on the one hand and the
> students and teachers on the other hand had
> grown to such an extent that it would be
> impossible to continue through the term under
> existing conditions. Even then we attempted to
> sustain the authority of the principal and as late
> as November we served written notice that Mr.
> Peckham's authority must not be questioned...
> However, our efforts on behalf of the school were
> without avail for we were practically told by the
> principal that he was supreme in authority and
> that the serious nature of the suspension of the
> boys did not concern the Board.
> In the meantime, the public had lost patience
> and the patrons of the school, or a large and
> influential part of them, petitioned this Board to
> remove Mr. Peckham...

> We chose ... to give him a month notice called for under our contract and the action of the Board now is in accordance with our notice of January 3 dispensing with his services.[33]

It was at this juncture that the superintendent moved in, reinstated the students after proper apologies had been made, and put Mrs. Craig in charge. Principal Peckham was reassigned to the history classroom and given thirty-day's notice as required in contracts with teachers at that time. However, a Morning Echo story dated January 6, 1903, was headlined "Mr. Peckham Won't Give Up." The account went on to say that Peckham, acting probably on the theory that the Board had upheld him in the supervision of students up to this time, refused to be relieved saying that he would stay until the completion of his contract at the end of the school year. The Board and the superintendent were not to be deterred, however, and they authorized Janitor Duty to affix a "Yale lock" to the principal's office to keep him on the outside. Thirty days later, President of the Board Leo G. Pauly and County Superintendent R. L. Stockton went to the school and visited all the classes, informing the students that Mr. Peckham was no longer associated with the school, even as a history teacher. The former principal asked that he might accompany the delegation and was allowed to come along to see the effects of the news on the students.

The man sought for the principalship was not "new." He was, in fact, the former principal, none other than the inimitable "C Cube", who had gone to Hanford after resigning his position with Kern County High School in the spring of 1901. After some negotiations with the Board, Mr. Childress did return, decided he wanted no part of this problem situation, and returned to Kings County - away from "the smoke of the battle." However, after Mr. Peckham was finally deposed, "C Cube" was prevailed upon to reconsider and return to finish out the school year bringing a semblance of order out of the chaos that had engulfed the school.

Former Principal Peckham continued to seek financial remuneration from the district, and the Board minutes of

September 10, 1903, indicate that he was successful. The Board agreed to his demands and paid him the grand total of $18.50 including $15.00 for three days' pay and $3.50 for cash advanced by him for purchase of a stove. This is the last official notice taken of Mr. Peckham. However, the incident remains in the memories of at least one student of that time - Lawrence Weill. He recalls clearly the events of the student protest and understandably looks at it all from the student's point of view.

School Activities

The school activity program of Kern County High School in the early years appears to be lean and spare in comparison with that of a modern high school. During the first half year of its operation, the school organized a literary society which captured the interest of students and townspeople alike. A local newspaper gave this report on the nature of this activity shortly after the opening of the school:

> ...Their first entertainment was given yesterday at the high school when a fine programme was rendered to whit: "Opening Address" by Mae Stark; Recitation, "Lady of The Lake," by Mattie Freeman; Selection, "Necessities of Education," by Leroy Rankin; Recitation, "How to be Happy," by Mabel Swisher; Essay, "Silver Lining to a Cloud," by Ella Fay; Recitation, "Decleptomania," by Lulu Norris; "Biographical Sketch of Ben Butler," by Bert Tibbett; Selection, "Lady of the Lake," by George Brundage; Recitation, "Unbelief," by Bertella Fergusson.
>
> The entertainment was highly enjoyable, and the selections were delivered in a very bright and effective manner by the members who participated in the exercises, who displayed a very clear conception of expression and delivery that reflects credit upon their instruction...[34]

Apparently a number of the boys organized a debating society during the next school year, but the first issue of the <u>Oracle</u> in October of 1902, bemoaned the lack of the debating society since the "demise of the Goodyear debating club in 1900." An editorial in the school publication goes on to say, "Is there any side of school life more pleasant or instructive than the afternoons or evenings spent in such societies?"[35]

By 1902, Professor George W. Taylor had arrived on the scene to conduct the school's music program. This same first copy of The Oracle notes that the chorus work under Professor Taylor had the entire school singing together with each class receiving forty-five minutes of musical instruction each week. In addition, a high school mandolin club had been organized under the tutelage of Professor Taylor. However, the music instruction during these days was sporadic at best, and a thorough-going music program awaited the arrival of another staff member several years later.

A mention of this school publication, of course, brings to our attention another school activity - that of journalism. The Oracle, however, was the not first journalistic effort of students of the high school. In fact, mention is made in the first issue of The Oracle of the ill-fated publication, The Hermes, that met its demise because of financial problems. Volume I, Number 1 of The Hermes dated May, 1897, is still available in the Bakersfield High School library. It is a thin volume containing poems, vignettes, jokes, a history of the original Hermes, social comments, a list of the senior class officers, and an account of the debate conducted in the high school literary society. Staff was composed of Nora Moss, editress in chief; Lena Brower, society editress; Roscoe Maples, athletic editor; Maurice Hershfeld, business manager; Ralph Frisselle and Claude Collins, associate business managers. With the beginning of The Oracle in the fall of 1902, the students started a publication which was to extend until this day. In the early years, it was a combination newspaper, yearbook, and anthology of creative writing. The copies of The Oracle, of which the Bakersfield High School library has an almost complete file, serves as the best continuous source of information regarding the history of the school during the early years.

One of the premiere school activities, developed shortly after the turn of the century, was the senior high school play. As has already been recounted, Earl Warren and one of his classmates were almost expelled because of their tardiness to class resulting from time spent in rehearsing the play to be presented as the highlight of the 1908 graduation season. This play was entitled, "What Became of Parker?" However, the senior class play tradition had actually begun as early as 1901, and Lawrence Weill remembers vividly playing the role of Bassanio in his senior class play - "The Modernized Merchant of Venice" as part of the graduation activities in 1906.

Thus, by the end of the first fifteen years of the school's operation, dramatics and forensics were entrenched, and social activities evolved around such activities as literary clubs. In conversation with some of the graduates of this era, frequent mention was made of school dances. There were, of course, dances held during these years, primarily at the Woman's Club of Bakersfield, located on 'H' Street, but they were not sponsored by the school at this time. In fact, student attempts to conduct dances during the early years in the old Railroad Avenue School were squelched by teacher Kitty Crusoe, who felt that it was improper for students to dance on school premises. Some of the students had informally organized the dancing group which met at noon in the lower portion of the building, occupied then by a private kindergarten school.

According to an article in a Founders' Day Edition of the Blue and White, Bakersfield High School newspaper, the student body and the four classes elected officers in September, 1902. Student body government began to function in the spring of that year. A female student, Ruth Blodgett, has the distinction of being the first student body president. She was a sophomore when elected to this post and succeeded herself as president the following year, according to the Blue and White article. First class presidents were William Robinson, freshman; (Miss) Douglas McMurdo, sophomore; (Miss) Lou White, junior; and Hugh Allen, senior. Of the first five "chief executives," then, three were women.[36]

What about athletics? Glendon Rodgers, for years the "historian in residence" at Bakersfield High School, states that the first football game was held shortly after the school opened on February 22, 1893. The high school boys pitted themselves against the elementary school team, and the high school won easily. Apparently football was played on an informal basis during the first few years of the school's organization as was baseball. The first record of a football game against another school was in October, 1899, when a football team was organized to play Fresno. The initial interscholastic football contest was on December 25, 1899, when Kern County High School fielded a team against powerful Tulare and was outclassed 90 - 0. The first record of a high school win was during the next school year, 1900 - 1901, when Kern County High School defeated a Visalia team by the score of 11 - 10. This game was followed by a banquet and a social event.[37]

Mention has already been made of coach and science teacher, Fayette Birtch, who arrived at KCHS in the Fall of 1901. Fresh from Stanford and active in athletics on that campus, Mr. Birtch was instrumental in 1902 in organizing the Central California Academic Athletic Association, which included Visalia, Hanford, Bakersfield, Tulare and Porterville. Eventually the association sponsored three sports: football, field sports, and baseball; basketball was soon to be added for the young ladies.

During the first year of its operation the CCAAA sponsored six football games, including the four teams from the four-member schools. According to the October, 1902, Oracle, each team actually played three games, and the games for KCHS were scheduled on November 27, December 6, and December 25, 1902. An annual field day was organized, the first one in the spring of 1902; and in 1903, The Oracle notes that tennis was added as a sport for girls and played among the girls who were members of the Girls' Athletic Club. The commencement addition of The Oracle in 1903, has this summary of the athletics for the year: "Most successful year in athletic career of the school. . .since the beginning of inter-academic matches in the Valley." It went on to say that during the second year of the Central California Academic Athletic Association, the school was third in football (there was a tie between Tulare and Visalia for first place), third in track (first was Visalia; second - Hanford), and the school won the baseball championship, being defeated only by Hanford. The October 1903 Oracle has this interesting quotation regarding one sport: "Basketball is a neat little game, and no girl need be backward in enlisting as a devotee."

By March 1904, however, The Oracle was able to boast "KCHS is established as the champion of amateur athletics in Central California." Kern County High School athletes were fresh from a field day win in Hanford, having beaten that school in this all-day match by one-half point. Track star, John O. Miller had himself accounted for 28 1/2 of the 44 points needed to win the match. In the fall, the football team had triumphed over Tulare by a 5 - 0 score and was declared the champion even though it suffered a tie with Porterville in a game played on New Year's Day. The team had, on Christmas Day, beaten a Los Angeles commercial high school football squad by a score of 28-0. During the previous spring (1903), KCHS had one the baseball championship, although the team was not successful in repeating in the spring of 1904.

After the 1903-1904 school year, Coach Birtch left his position at Kern County High School to return to medical school in the Bay Area. The Oracle bemoans his loss with this statement: "Before he became a member of the faculty our boys very seldom knew what it was like to win a single game, but look at us now. We are the whole thing in athletics..."[38] Lawrence Weill remembers clearly the influence of Coach Birtch and credits him with having a positive affect on the lives of many students during those years. In his own words:

> He was very much beloved. He was studying medicine at Stanford. He had to work because he did not have enough money to complete his course and so he taught for several years here. He was very popular -- we thought the world of him.

He recalls after Mr. Birtch had returned to Stanford medical school, several of his classmates paid him a visit. According to Mr. Weill:

> He asked us if we wouldn't like to go around the laboratory where he was doing his work. The corpses were there, and were covered with a towel or wrap and Mr. Birtch said, "Now this is mine where I do my experimental work." He pulled that cloth off the cavity of the stomach. He looked in there and jumped back horrified and said, "Geez, somebody stole my liver!"

The May, 1907, issue of The Oracle happily notes that Mr. Birtch had completed his degree in medicine at Cooper's College and took further particular delight in the fact that he completed the four year course in three years. His contributions to the school and athletics as an excellent teacher and as a friend of the students were noted with appreciation.

Mr. Weill played on the football team while in high school, and his recollection is that his contribution was slight, primarily because he was small in stature. However, in the December, 1905, Oracle, an article reviewing the game with Porterville gives a different perspective. Attention was called to the performance of the linemen's making holes for the men with the ball: "This position is held by Lawrence Weill, who, though weighing but a hundred and thirty-five pounds, proved himself able to handle a man much larger than himself." The game ended in a 5-5 tie.

Track champion John O. Miller was supported financially by the student body in tryouts to represent the United States in the World's Fair after his graduation in 1904. A letter to The Oracle expresses his appreciation. He may have been the first high school student to break the five-minute mile, although verification of this is not available in written records. In Lawrence Weill's words, "He [Miller] was a splendid all-around athlete, particularly in track--a distance man, and in football."

During the years that followed until the fall of 1908, the athletic fortunes of the Kern County High School were somewhat unsteady; although during that time, they did manage to collect another track championship at the field day in Hanford and a baseball championship. Significantly, during this period, girls' interscholastic basketball became recognized as a outstanding athletic event. In fact, the commencement issue of The Oracle in 1908 comments that the only bright spot in the whole athletic picture during the year was the basketball pennant brought home by the girls. The 1907 basketball season was the beginning of a domination in this sport for several years for the KCHS girls' team. It is interesting to note that interscholastic competition for girls in basketball was discontinued in 1916. The reason given for this action in the January, 1916, Oracle was that it had been determined to be too violent and injurious to the health of the girls involved. Furthermore, it was contended that coaches encouraged girls to go beyond the limits of their strength and a campaign "beginning in the East" was successful in eliminating interscholastic girls' basketball, at least in California. For a period of some sixty years, basketball was not played interscholastically by the girls in the district.

Another competitive sport taken up by girls during this period was tennis. This apparently was a part of the track and field day program for a while until it gained enough momentum to stand on its own as an individual sport.

The Oracle was not adverse to dealing in plain language with athletic officials who aroused the displeasure of the KCHS fans; i.e., the commencement, 1907, edition, in reviewing the school year as far as athletics was concerned, was particularly critical of the officials in a key baseball game at Tulare. The editorial comment was that, with assistance of "dirty work" from the umpire, Tulare won the game. After commending the efforts of pitcher, Will Forker, and catcher, Reginald Stoner, (who both later went to the University of California and appeared in these same positions on the University baseball team) the article closed with the remark "And now, let Tulare play the game over with us, with a fair umpire up, and then our boys will show her how it feels to be licked."[39]

With the gloomy appraisal of the athletic fortunes of KCHS in the commencement, 1908, <u>Oracle</u>, the stage was set for the arrival of a man who established the school as one of the best known secondary institutions athletically in the state. This, of course, was Dwight M. Griffith, whose personality and athletic coaching skills are almost legendary.

Facilities

During the first fifteen years of the history of the Kern High School District, two separate buildings were constructed because of the growth of the school. This is testimony to a tradition long a part of the Kern High School District - that when the needs are presented to the public for facilities, as well as operation, generally support has been available. The two rooms leased from the City School District in old Railroad Avenue School were not adequate for long. By 1895, plans had been solidified to build a new school, and after some indecision and searching about the community, the old hospital site on 14th and "G" Street was established as the place for building the first Kern County High School building. Superintendent Alfred Harrell reviewed the status of the school in 1895, saying "the progress of the school has been most satisfactory to those interested in its welfare. Already it has been accredited to the State University in part, and it is believed that within the next year, with the increased advantage that the new building will offer--the Institution at Berkeley will accept our graduates in full and without examination." So the new building then was, in the superintendent's opinion, an important part of the program of the school, particularly in its relationship to the university.[40]

During 1895, the new building was constructed by contractor F. W. Hickox, for the cost of approximately $14,000. The building contained four classrooms and an assembly hall; and, while it was accepted by the Board of Supervisors in October, 1895, it apparently was not occupied by high school students until 1896.[41] The location of the new high school was that of the old county hospital -- a frame building which had been torn down with the construction of the new county hospital on 19th Street at Oak Street. Eugene Burmeister notes that bones from arms and legs removed by amputations which took place in the old county hospital were unearthed when the foundation was excavated for the new building. Apparently the basement was the disposal site for these left overs.[42] This building became known as the "Commercial Building" because, after the construction of the second high school building across "G" Street, it was occupied by students from the commercial classes. In fact, it's even referred to in some of the writings as the "Polytechnic High School." The cornerstone ceremony of the new building was conducted by the Grand Lodge of California Masons, beginning a tradition of such ceremonies carried through into modern times.

In less than ten years, the high school had expanded to such an extent that thought was again given to building new facilities. At first a decision was made to enlarge the present building after a study by a San Francisco firm of architects determined that the building could be enlarged and remodeled at a cost not to exceed $25,000.[43] However, in November, 1905, the Board of Education had a change in thinking, as indicated by this memorandum transmitted to the Board of Supervisors:

> It is the opinion of this Board that the contemplated plans for making alterations and additions to the present high school building are

> adequate to the demands of the school for a few years only. When these plans were recommended to your honorable body, the Board of Education understood that not more than twenty-five thousand dollars were available...
> Being informed... that sufficient funds can be raised for a new high school building without being a burden to the taxpayers of the county, this Board respectfully recommends that a new building site be purchased and a new high school, modern in every feature, be erected thereon; the new structure to cost not less than seventy-five thousand dollars exclusive of the building site and furnishings...[44]

Actually the cost of a new structure was $56,000, and it was located on "F" Street, just west of the old building. Even though the Board showed that it was farsighted in determining that a new building should be built instead of additions made to the old one, this clairvoyance did not extend far enough into the future to predict that these two buildings would accommodate the high school for a period of only five years.

The new building is vividly described in an article on education in Bakersfield written by David W. Nelson, City Superintendent in 1908. He notes that the new building was 65' x 150' and made of white sandstone brick. Its contents were an assembly hall, with a capacity of 300 students, ten recitation rooms, four laboratories, one lecture room, a large gymnasium with baths, drawing rooms and offices and private rooms for teachers. The entrance is depicted as having a marble base with a tile floor, 200 steel lockers available for use by the students, and the rooms automatically furnished with air at 70 degrees Farenheit, changed every twenty minutes by the modern ventilation system.[45]

Financing of the schools, while given scant attention in the literature up to this time, began to be more of a concern of the Board of Trustees when it was decided that it was necessary to levy a special tax of ten cents to provide necessary funds for the construction of the new school building. During the 1905-1906 year, the levy for operating expenses for the high school was established at four and one-half cents, and the total county rate was $1.60. De Mello states that "the Board would have preferred to issue bonds for the high school building, but it was found that there was no law permitting a county high school governing board to submit such a proposal to the voters.[46]

During the 1903-1904 school year, Superintendent Stockton submitted a budget just in excess of $13,000. Of that, teachers salaries accounted for approximately $9,000; janitors salaries, $900, and current expenses, $3,000. It was about this time that the principal received an all time high of $2,000 per year, and teacher's salaries ranged from $1,000 to $1,250 yearly primarily based upon the length of service to the district.[47]

The Origins of the District in Summary

At the close of the first fifteen years of operation of Kern County High School it seems appropriate to comment upon some of some of the concerns expressed regarding the future of the high school in the local press and otherwise.

As might be expected, former Superintendent of Schools Alfred Harrell, now publisher of The Daily Californian, maintained close watch over the progress of the schools and was not loath to express his concern in the pages of the newspaper. During 1904-1905, the paper dealt with the fact that salaries of teachers were too low in comparison to workers in other fields. Particular concern was expressed that local taxation was not adequate to support the expenses of the schools, and it was recommended that the state law be amended so as to increase the amount of money returned to local school systems from the State Treasurer.[48]

Another concern frequently voiced by educators was whether or not the schools of the nation actually were meeting the needs of students, particularly as represented by the local curriculum in the high school. As early as 1903, The Californian had quoted an exchange editorial characterizing the strong feelings held by certain people that the University of California dominated the curriculum of the high schools throughout the state to such an extent that they were forced to cater to the needs of a minority of students rather than to those of the majority.

> ... A fault of our school system in general is that it is arranged mainly for the benefit of the pupils that intend to enter college. There is no course of education made up for the boy who must leave school at sixteen. From the receiving class, the grammar, and the high school, the grade rating is done with an eye on the requirements for admission to college. The boy who cannot go through the university must be content to go as far in that direction as he can."

The Californian was in complete agreement with this opinion, adding one of its own:

> ... that institution has absolute control over the curricula of the high schools. The aim of every such school is to be on the accredited list of the university and to do so it must conform exactly to the requirements of the university.

The 1905 class history of the school, normally a rather playful inane document, contained some statements that precipitated some controversy in the community as reflected in the pages of The Californian. The class historian, Ruth Blodgett, had noted that of the group of 55 who had enrolled in the school as freshmen, only 10 received their diplomas. A letter to The Californian written by C. C. Childress, principal of the high school, and David W. Nelson of the Board of Education, reported a study of this situation and the following findings and conclusions in the matter:

> ... Inasmuch as the statement made by Miss Ruth Blodgett, the class historian of the present graduating class to the effect that out of a membership of fifty-five students that entered the academic course of the high school four years ago only ten of that number received their diplomas of graduation at the close of this year, has excited considerable editorial comment throughout the state, we beg to submit the following facts concerning each of the individuals constituting the original membership of the class...

35

1. Ten graduated this year. 2. Seven are still in the academic course and will doubtless graduate later. 3. Five have changed to the commercial department. 4. Eight lost their membership in the class by moving away. 5. Five are attending school elsewhere. 6. Eleven left school on account of ill-health. 7. Seven girls are married. 8. Two members of the class are deceased.

The writers commented further that the university required that there be but one course in a high school leading to college entrance, but that "Under the law, the boards of education have the power to establish whatever courses of study for the high school the public sentiment of a community may demand..." The educators tried to make the point that there was latitude for the community to influence the direction of the school curriculum.[50]

The response of The Californian was that since a small number of the students starting school actually finished, the courses of study, not only in the local high school, but in those throughout the State of California, do not appeal to a great many students "who have their lives before them and must make ready to take their places in the busy world..."[51] More than 80 years later the issue of deciding how to make the course of study relevant to all the students is still under discussion.

An ebullient description of the school in 1908 is contained in the article by D. W. Nelson quoted earlier. Kern County High School had two modern buildings valued at $100,000, with an enrollment of more than 200 pupils. Its curriculum contained two departments, academic and commercial, with the academic branches in three directions: literary, scientific and engineering, any of which led to enrollment in the University of California. According to City Superintendent Nelson, the school had a core of ten teachers from such institutions as the University of California; Stanford; Ann Arbor, Michigan; Monmouth College, Illinois; the University of Missouri; and "other prominent colleges."

It had an excellent library and equally superior laboratories and scientific apparatus.

The commercial department contained two courses: bookkeeping and shorthand, of two years each, which could be completed in three years in combination. A department of manual training was being established to include courses in wood and iron work for boys; sewing and cookery for girls. The new manual training building, which was in the planning stages, when complete, would offer a complete course in manual training "as thorough as that offered by any other polytechnic high school in California."

And what kind of community did this school serve in the year 1908?

> Bakersfield is located 170 miles north of Los Angeles, and 300 miles south of San Francisco. She has the greatest oil fields in the world, the finest alfalfa and orange lands in this state, and is a cosmopolitan city in every sense of the word. Bakersfield can boast of as fine stores as will be found in the larger cities of the state. She has paved streets, electric lights, gas, electric street car system, telephone exchange, an elegant water system, public library, fine hotels, banks, opera houses, two transcontinental railroads, flouring mills, brickyards, railroad shops, wholesale and retail stores, two daily newspapers, etc. She depends not upon the outside world for her support, and prospers as no other city in the great state of California upon our own resources. She has a climate second to none in the world, and a few short weeks of really warm weather, which brings the sugar into the growing fruits, are a necessity. The nights are always cool, and a sun prostration is an unknown quantity.[52]

In a final note regarding the school in the early years, several people involved intimately with the operation of the school appear to have had a strong influence on determining its progress and made a positive imprint on the lives of the students involved. Making this kind of a statement is certainly dangerous since it involves the possibility of overlooking persons who should also be recognized; however, it appears to this writer that it is incumbent upon one telling the story of an institution to point out those persons whose influences are remembered through the years. Certainly no one would question the singling out of Alfred Harrell as one whose vision and commitment to education provided leadership for the opening of the school. Robert L. Stockton, as County Superintendent, continued the strong administrative leadership in directing the Board of Education and influencing the Board of Supervisors to make sure that the school's needs were attended to. C. C. Childress, whose service as principal extended over a period of some ten of the first fifteen years, certainly should be designated as a formative influence in the early years. While severe and strict in his discipline, he was recognized by students as one who could be depended upon to make sure that the basic principles of a good education were maintained. And he did return to give strong leadership after the Peckham episode. Mrs. Helen S. Craig, teacher of Latin, was recognized by students as an outstanding teacher and a friend of the students. The man who really began the school's athletic program, Fayette Birtch, should also be noted. He so captured the affection and respect of students that his progress through medical school after leaving KCHS was recorded in the school's yearbook publication.

Thus, in the early days of KCHS, it was true -- and it remains true today -- that people make the difference in outstanding educational programs.

REFERENCES
CHAPTER I – THE BEGINNINGS 1893-1908

1. Rodgers, Glendon J., The Bakersfield High School Story, 1893-1962 (unpublished manuscript) p.3.

2. DeMello, Edwin, Kern High School District The Early Years, 1893-1908 (unpublished Ms., 1974) pp.3-4.

3. Ibid., P.4.

4. Rodgers, p.2.

5. Minutes, Board of Supervisors, Kern County, California (Bakersfield, 1892) ledger p.523.

6. Rodgers, p.9.

7. Ibid., p.10.

8. DeMello, p.6.

9. Ibid., p. 5.

10. Rodgers, p.12.

11. The Daily Californian, January 31, 1893, p.1.

12. DeMello, p.6.

13. DeMello, p. 7.

14. The Morning Echo, January 27, 1904.

15. DeMello, p.8.

16. Ibid., p.8.

17. Rodgers, pp.17-18.

18. The Daily Californian, May 19, 1894.

19. DeMello, p.14.

20. Ibid., pp.15-17.

21. Ibid., pp.35-37.

22. Reference here is to four of a number of interviews conducted by the author as a part of the research for this document. The four used in this chapter are referenced as follows: Ashe, Mary Ann (Bakersfield, CA, 1981); Bohna, Marianna (Bakersfield, CA, 1981); Weill, Lawrence (Bakersfield, CA 1980 and 1982).

References - Chapter I (Continued)

23. See issues of The Morning Echo, May 4, 6 and 9, 1904.

24. Earl Warren's Bakersfield (Berkeley, CA: University of California Regional Oral History Office, Bancroft Library, 1981), p.18.

25. Weaver, John D. Warren, the Man, the Court, the Era (Boston: Little, Brown, and Co., 1967), p.26.

26. Earl Warren's Bakersfield (Berkeley, CA: University of California Regional Oral History Office, Bancroft Library, 1981), p.24.

27. Ibid., p.50.

28. Minutes, Kern County Board of Education (Kern County, CA: July 8, 1899).

29. Rodgers, pp.55-56.

30. DeMello, p.13.

31. The Morning Echo, December 21, 1902.

32. The Bakersfield Californian, December 29, 1902, p.1.

33. Ibid., p.4. Also see The Oracle, 1903, Commencement Issue, for student view of this incident.

34. The Weekly Californian, January 28, 1893, p.1.

35. The Oracle, October, 1902.

36. The Oracle, Commencement issue, 1904.

37. Rodgers, Glendon J. Footnote on Athletics (Bakersfield High School football program, November 11, 1960).

38. The Oracle, Commencement issue, 1904.

39. Ibid., Commencement issue, 1907, p.45.

40. Harrell, Alfred, A Brief History of the Kern County High School (Bakersfield, CA: unpublished manuscript, July 3, 1895).

41. The Oracle, October, 1902.

42. Burmeister, Eugene, The Golden Kern County, California (Beverly Hills, CA: Autograph Press, 1977) p.100.

43. DeMello, p.20.

44. Minutes, County Board of Education, Kern County, California (Bakersfield) November 11, 1905.

References - Chapter I (Continued)

45. The Spirit of Bakersfield and Kern County (Kern County, CA: 1908) unpaged.

46. DeMello, p.23.

47. Minutes, County Board of Education, Kern County, California (Bakersfield) August 5, 1903, and July 2, 1906.

48. Californian, December 8, 1904, P.3.

49. Ibid, May 23, 1903, P.2.

50. Ibid, June 10, 1905, p.6.

51. Ibid, June 12, 1905, p.5.

52. The Spirit of Bakersfield in Kern County (Kern County, CA: 1908) unpaged.

Railroad Avenue School, later Emerson, located at Truxtun and L. Kern Union High School District classes began in two rooms of the second story in January, 1893.

Courtesy of Public Information Office, Bakersfield City Schools.

Seniors of 1894 — the first graduates of Kern County Union High School: Ella Fay, Addie Nicholson, and May Stark.

Photo courtesy of the Kern County Museum.

First Kern County Union High School District building built in 1895 in the center of what is now Elm Grove on the Bakersfield High School campus. The building cost between $14,000 and $15,000. Later it was called the Commercial Building.

Photo courtesy of the Kern County Museum.

Football was played on an unscheduled basis as early as February, 1893, the second month of the school's operation. The first interscholastic football game was played against Tulare in December of 1899; the score: Tulare 90 -KCUHS - 0. The next year, 1900-1901, the high school team defeated Visalia 11 - 10 — this **may** be that team, or it may be a team which represented the City of Bakersfield in those early years.
Photo courtesy of the Kern County Museum.

The staff in 1904 pictured on the steps of the first high school building.
Left to right: Donald Ross, teacher of drawing; T. W. Miles, head of the commercial division; Miss May White, history; Mrs. Kate Rardon, shorthand and typewriting; C.C. Childress, Principal and mathematics ("C" Cubed); Mrs. H.S. Craig, Latin; Miss M. Pauline Scott, English; Fayette Birtch, science and coaching; and George W. Taylor, music.
Photo courtesy of the Bakersfield High School Library

Auto mechanics in the early days. The date that appears on the caption of the picture is 1903-04. It may actually have been taken after the construction of the first Manual Arts Building in 1911.

Photo courtesy of the Kern County Museum.

In the beginning there were report cards at Kern County Union High School. Marianna Bohna was particularly proud of this one and so was her father.

The academic graduates of 1906. Two contributors to this volume were members of this class; Marianna Bohna at the lower right corner and Lawrence Weill at the opposite corner.
Top row: (L-R) Lawrence Weill, Edward Benson, Odin Bickerdike, Mark Said, John Shannonhouse, George Work, and Albert Cuneo.
Middle row: (L-R) Marian Blodgett, Clyde Nybert, Jeanne Alexander, Elinor Merritt, Bessie Houghton and Hattie English.
Front row: (L-R) Ruth Robesky, Lelia Wells, Alice Reynolds, Wilma Scodie, Hannah Biggs and Marianna Bohna.

Coach Dwight W. Griffith's first football squad pictured in the **Oracle** published in October, 1908. (I.D. shown in picture). The coach began his winning ways early, as this first team won the championship of the old Central California Academic Athletic League. This picture, labeled in this manner, hung in the Robesky store for many years.
Top row: (L-R) L. Stroud, J. Stroud, Dennen, Grandy, Wegis, Forker, McKinley, Wieman, Rankin.
Middle row: (L-R) Brown, Curtis, Wirt, Tilton, Newell, Baker, O'Hare, Fugitt, Stiern.
Lower row: (L-R) West, Robinson, Ogden, Stockton, Macmurdo, Garner, Coach Griffith.

Basketball was played competitively by girls against other schools during the early years. The championship team of 1908 is pictured. Interscholastic competition for girls in this sport was terminated in the 1915-16 school year.
Top row: (L-R) Rachel Smith, Kate Grenville, Ardis Hare, Mollie Harris.
Middle row: (L-R) Alice Eyraud, Coach F.B. Gainer, Beulah Eagan, and Elsie Slater.
Bottom row: (L-R) Claire Bender and Ethel Robesky.

The District's most prestigious graduate, Earl Warren, with his graduating class of 1908.
Top row: (L-R) Helen Campbell, Ruth Smith, Dorrit Smith, Amy Boettler, Ethel Said.
Middle row: (L-R) Nona White, Hazel Grandy, Ethel Robesky, Lottie Blodgett, Mary Ann Ashe, Minnie Robinson.
Bottom row: (L-R) Reginald Stoner, Frank Vaughn, Earl Warren, William Forker, Omar Cavins, Denton Stockton.

CHAPTER II

THE EARLY BOOM - 1908 - 1916

Kern County and Oil

Actually, Kern County was well into the oil business prior to 1909. In fact, there had been some oil industry as far back as 1864, when the Buena Vista Petroleum Company was established in the Temblor area. In 1877, the Columbian Oil Company drilled two wells near McKittrick. But primarily for two reasons, the oil industry did not flourish until the beginning of the Twentieth Century. At first the crude oil, which was mined, was thought to be too heavy for general use, and it was found to be more profitable to refine asphalt. As a matter of fact, an early name of the community of McKittrick was actually Asphalto.[1]

The second problem was transportation costs. The early oil production industry could not compete with that in the East because of this problem. In fact at one time the cost of transportation was $1.00 per barrel, which was the same price oil was being sold for at that time.[2]

The year 1899 is one of the landmarks in the oil industry because it was then that the so called "discovery well" was found on the north bank of the Kern River, some seven miles northeast of Bakersfield. On lands owned by James and Jonathan Elwood, a driller named Milton McWhorter struck oil and "the Kern River field came into existence, the first of the fields that made history in Kern County which today contributes one-fourth of California's total oil production."[3] This statistic dates back to 1961, but there is no question of the importance of the pioneer well. Nearby another well, which became really the first commercial area in Kern County, was brought in by McWhorter's son, Horace.

In spite of all this activity, the big gushers of 1909 and 1910, brought the greatest oil boom to Kern County. Oil contributed to the population growth of the county in a way that could not have been predicted by those who planned for the schools prior to the Twentieth Century. According to Glendon Rodgers, "names of gushers like Santa Fe, Honolulu, St. Lawrence, Crandall, Mays and finally Lakeview all sent newspapermen looking for new descriptive adjectives."[4] The greatest of them all, Lakeview, came in during March, 1910, and it firmly established Kern County as one of the oil capitals of the world. Towns sprung up overnight. Maricopa, called "Mother City of the West Side"; Taft, "Miracle City of the West Side." Fellows, Ford City, and McKittrick all followed a similar growth pattern of the gold mining camps in the mountains of an earlier era. These settlements established themselves quickly as population centers, whose sustenance depended on the new gushers of black gold.[5]

According to Thelma Miller, "From 1910 to 1914, California produced forty percent of the total output of petroleum in the United States, and Kern County produced over fifty-eight percent of that total..." This author makes an interesting comparison to the production of gold ore. During the same time, in 1912 for example, $19,000,000 worth of gold was taken from all of California, while during the same year, $20,000,000 worth of petroleum was mined in Kern County alone.[6]

According to a publication dated February 28, 1911,

> "the invasion of the locators [oil locators] was followed by a rush of teamsters, rig builders, land brokers, promoters, drillers, superintendents and stockholders eagerly hoping for large rewards from their investments, large or small. Hotel facilities of Bakersfield, Taft and Maricopa were completely swamped, lumber yards of the county were exhausted quickly, and the state supply of timber suitable for building derricks was taxed severely.... The oil boom of the early part of 1910 rivaled any mining or oil excitement that the West has ever known."

Then, according to this same article, came a "stately procession of gushers" that had its climax in Lakeview "The Permanent Wonder of the Oil World."[7]

It was also in the year 1910 that the natural gas industry got its start, and the combination of oil gushers and gas outbursts was unbelievable. The result naturally was population growth which was unexpected and unrivaled up to that time. From 1890 to 1900, the county population grew from 9,808 to 16,480, and from the years 1900 to 1910, it more than doubled from 16,480 to 37,715.[8]

KCHS Grows With The Boom

In the Fall of 1908 the first copy of The Oracle that year was dedicated to the football squad. It contained an article on football by the new coach, one Dwight M. Griffith. He stressed that athletics was only one of the many branches of school life. "We believe that the primary purpose of the educational institution is to develope[sic] the student mentally, morally, socially and physically and that if any one of these is neglected, the student must suffer as a consequence of a one-sided development." Coach Griffith went on to comment on the importance of training and discipline, stating that a strong, healthy body was necessary for a strong, well-balanced mind. He expressed guarded optimism regarding the new season stating that 28 students were out for the squad.[9]

Another newcomer to the campus, C. T. Conger, the new principal, replacing "C Cube," was also quoted in this Oracle. His article contained an account of the Olympic games of 1908 which were held in England. He noted that there was some bitterness because of the vagueness of the rules, and that the pervading concern throughout on the part of the British was that participants would go by the rules and keep the sport clean. The implication for the school athletic program and for school activities, in general, was obvious. A "Calendar of Information of the KCHS" for that year, which was found loose in that issue of The Oracle. It lists the faculty members and studies they taught, giving some idea of the breadth of the school program, developed since the beginning years.

In addition to a new principal, F. B. Gainer was listed as vice principal and teacher of science. Mrs. Helen S. Craig was still on campus teaching Latin, as were M. Pauline Scott, English; Mabel Chubb, history; Lois Jameson, mathematics, drawing and French; Dwight M. Griffith, mathematics and director of athletics; J. E. Dyer, commercial branches; William L. Mason, shorthand and typewriting; Charles Cottle, manual training; Estelle Story, domestic science and art. Subjects new to the curriculum were manual training and domestic science, with the former program soon to be housed in a new building, still in the planning stage. George H. Taylor instructed in music, apparently on a part-time basis, but for some reason was not listed in the "calendar."

Other evidence indicates that agricultural instruction may have already been a part of the program. A circular published a few years previously by the University of California, College of Agriculture, states that:

> "In the year 1905-1906, the Kern County Union High School of Bakersfield became the first district high school in California to make a beginning in agricultural instruction. A. G. Grant, the instructor, taught general science, soil and crops, physics and chemistry. Three years later the Kern County High School engaged H. F. Dout, a graduate of the class of 1906 of the California Polytechnic School, to teach agriculture and manual training."[10]

In an article written by County Superintendent of Schools, Robert L. Stockton, featured in a special edition of The Bakersfield Californian published in 1912, it was noted that thirty teachers were employed and the enrollment was 392 students. In addition, the district was just completing a new manual arts building, which cost some $10,000, and had purchased a school farm the following year at the cost of $16,000. This land was located on approximately 25th and "M" Streets and was called "Hudnut Park" or the "Hudnut

Place." Superintendent Stockton noted that it was... "the largest high school farm in the State of California now worth at least double that amount." He further asserted that in addition to university preparatory courses, vocational subjects were being stressed at the school to the extent that "... expert farmers, accountants, surveyors, assayers, stenographers and mechanics are being turned out."[11]

Student Life at the Beginning of the 20th Century

Mrs. Frances Veon (nee Getchell) graduated with the Class of 1915, having entered Kern County High School in 1911. She remembers vividly her life as a high school student, the subjects she took - English, science, agriculture and Latin, in particular. Her memories of Dwight M. Griffith are positive: "He was my best teacher and I took four years of math from him... He taught all my children." She followed the football team because her husband-to-be (Roland J. "Boots" Veon) was a member of the team. There were no stadiums at that time, and the crowd stood at the games. She remembers that it was a thrill for the students to drink out of the sponge that the team players used. Her social life was full and satisfying:

> We had school dances but not in conjunction with the school. We had two fraternities and they gave big formal dances twice a year, one was at Christmas time and the other in the spring. These were not regular school dances... they were given independently of the school. We had school plays, senior proms, junior-senior banquets and all of that which everybody in the class attended.

Other activities included student government (she was freshman class president), hayrides, riding the tallyho (horse carriage) to the power plant grounds in Kern Canyon, parties at houses and attending the new form of entertainment, motion pictures, which cost all of five cents admission. Kern Canyon was a particular source of social pleasure for picnics and swimming, although most of the swimming parties were held at the Standard Oil swimming pool. Dances were sometimes held on tennis courts to the music of an organ.[12]

School activities during the 1914-15 year were enlivened by a dramatic presentation written and directed by a KCHS staff member. The commencement issue, 1915, of The Oracle gives an account of the production of "Pop's Choice," an "extravaganza" written and directed by Clarence Cullimore, teacher of drafting. In fact, this issue of the yearbook was warmly dedicated to the teacher - playwright. The author of "Pop's Choice" is also remembered as the architect of many of Bakersfield's most notable homes.

In the Fall of 1915, Mrs. Christine Summers (then Christine Noriega) entered Kern County High School. Because she lived in East Bakersfield, she was forced to ride the street car to high school. This mode of transportation, the Kern County Railroad, provided a connecting link between the Southern Pacific Depot and the Santa Fe Depot, which was on the edge of the Kern County High School campus. Christine Noriega was actually born in the Iberia Hotel built by her father, Faustino Noriega, and she lived at the hotel for the first years of her life. When his children became school age, Mr. Noriega felt that the hotel atmosphere was not suitable for their upbringing, and he built the Noriega home across the street from the Baker Street School, currently the site of the Bakersfield City Schools administration offices. The hotel, now called the Noriega Hotel, was headquarters for Basque people who had come to this country primarily to herd sheep.

Mrs. Summers was, to an extent, bilingual when she entered school, her family having spoken Spanish at home as well as English, and she became active in the Spanish program and remembers with particular pleasure a play in Spanish put on by the Spanish classes, in which she had a starring role. Her Spanish instructor was Ysabel Forker. In addition to class activities, Mrs. Summers remembers especially school activities, such as sewing clubs, which were prestigious organizations for girls, hayrides in Kern Canyon, and particularly an interest in politics. As a matter of fact, she became president of her sophomore class and enjoyed the hurly-burly of the election campaign.

Football was an important part of school life in her recollection:

> The football games used to be out at the end of 19th Street and, of course, then we didn't have bleachers like they have now. So we used to run up and down the fields right along with the football team and follow the ball. We never missed a game... They were always played in the afternoon and then the boys would have a truck or a big car in which they picked up the football team. Everybody else who had cars or transportation would follow the football teams back to the school and get dressed.

KCHS had by this time established itself in a prestige position athletically throughout the state by winning several state championships.

Beginning her educational career at the high school in the commercial course with O. W. Rister, she changed to the academic division because her vocational goal was to become a Spanish teacher. Although this goal was not realized, she did stay in education to spend, in later life, a long career with the Kern County Superintendent of Schools office. Her son, Paul D. Summers, has carried on in his mother's tradition at the county school office where he is currently an administrator.

A Junior College Program Is Added

The first reference to junior college instruction in the minutes of the Kern County Board of Education is by inference only in this cryptic statement, dated October 20, 1913: "Contract for Junior College Books Awarded to Book Shop. Contract Price $8,788.97, List Complete F.O.B. Kern County High School Building." It was not until the summer of 1914 that there is any kind of direct reference to advanced instruction in the minutes. On July 1, 1914, the Board authorized B. S. Gowen, then Principal of Kern County High School... "to arrange for second year Junior College work on account of having seven who wish to take the work."[13] Certainly these are humble beginnings for the junior college system which actually dates from the fall of 1913 and has the distinction of being the junior college system with the longest history of continuous operation in the State of California. Fresno junior college instruction began in 1910, but its operation was interrupted for a period during World War I. The college program at Fresno was followed by instruction in Santa Barbara and Hollywood in 1911, Los Angeles in 1912, and Kern County, Fullerton, and Long Beach during 1913. For various reasons, six of the seven closed their doors for periods of time during the early years, and only the Kern County school has continuously remained open.[14]

The beginnings of the Kern County Junior College program illustrate that this system of education in California sprang from the high school. For a considerable period of time, the program was considered to be postgraduate, similar to the beginnings of the high school programs as after-graduation adjuncts to the elementary schools. Although the graduate course of studies began in 1913, the KCHS Oracle, the most faithful chronicle of events of the school, did not take notice of junior college students until the January, 1915, issue. In a section called "Class Notes", the editor took up the cudgel for the junior college students, saying that they should have the right to take part in student affairs, at least to the extent of having the right to vote. So it would appear that these students, staying on to continue work for which they were receiving college credit, were in a sense disenfranchised from the rest of the student body and thus suffered a similar fate to many who take part in a pioneer venture.[15]

Midyear in the 1915-1916 school year, junior college students numbered about twenty and had organized themselves into classes. The student body organization had officers. Basil Herman was president; Arthur McManus, vice president; Ainsley Coates, secretary/treasurer; and the class colors were gold and white. According to The Oracle article,

53

one lesson in college was equal to two high school lessons, so rugged was the academic discipline. The boys were getting up a basketball team; also track, baseball, debating, journalism and social activities were being planned. Correspondence had already taken place with Fresno Junior College to develop an "interclass", looking toward interscholastic, competition.[16]

A commencement issue of this student publication for 1916 gave a complete summary of the junior college work at the end of its first three years of existence. At that time it was noted that the enrollment was 27, and 20 courses, including the first two years of university work, were offered. A series of facts for those expecting to enroll gave further particulars. It was stressed that the school was not a separate institution since students would receive instruction in the high school rooms by high school faculty. A student might take five subjects per semester and earn sixteen units. After two years of successful schooling and sixteen units of work, students would be entitled to "the Junior Certificate."

The Oracle account indicated two aims for the junior college program. (1) Vocational training: here it was indicated that some "vocations" would need additional university work. Apparently included in this branch of instruction were students who planned to go on to university work or to enter some other vocation that might not need advanced college credit. (2) Improvement of social efficiency for those not going on to school: This latter objective appears to have a modern ring, perhaps unexpected for education in 1916. Two particular advantages were noted for the new program. The first was that it would relieve the university of a heavy load of lower classmen, and secondly that it reduced expenses for the participant. In summary, the writer noted that "This last item is an all important factor, and it alone would seem to justify the existence of a Junior College."[17] Apparently, at this stage of its operation, the junior college program received no specialized direction from a single staff member who had the sole responsibility for the operation of the program, although Paul VanderEike, Vice Principal of the high school, supervised the new program as one of his duties. Rather, the program was really a special high school with offerings aimed at the particular needs of students in the community.

A circular published by the Kern County High School in September 1915, gives a more complete description of the junior college program. It indicates that ". . . since the Universities of California and Stanford give full credit for work done in the Junior College, students may take the first two years work here and the last two at the university, and thus save half the expense of a college course." It is further noted that the program had been planned after consultation with the authorities at the University of California and would attempt to parallel student requirements there. Courses would be offered in English, history, mathematics, economics, foreign languages and several of the sciences. "In other words, there will be a number of normal courses, including work in psychology, pedagogy, history of education, methods, etc. As far as possible classes will be organized for the review of public school subjects."

Then a complete course of study is listed, including the following: Advanced English - two years; Advanced Latin - two years; Advanced French - two years; Advanced German - two years; European History - one year; General Chemistry, Inorganic and Qualitative - one year; Organic Chemistry - one year; General Geology - one-half year; Minerology - one year; Economic Geography - one-half year; Economics - one year; Physical Geography - one-half year; Botany - two years; Psychology - one year; Pedagogy - one year; History of Education - one year; Analytical Geometry - one-half year; Calculus - one-half year.[18] Certainly this represents a breadth of subject matter materials and courses for a student body of approximately twenty students.

Governance of the District Changes

Since its founding in 1892, the high school had been operated by the Kern County Board of Education, the members of which were appointed by the Kern County Board of Supervisors. An editorial in The Bakersfield Californian on March 10, 1916, pointed to a change in the law which was, according to the editor, "seemingly, a very foolish one." From now on voters of the county would be called upon to elect a Board of Trustees for the county high school, with the first election scheduled in May, 1916. The editorial went on to point out that under the direction of the county Board of Education, appointed by the Board of Supervisors, the high school had become "one of the best known and one of the most progressive institutions of its kind in the state, its efficiency being recognized everywhere in school circles." It was suggested that it might be a mistake to transfer authority over the school to others inexperienced with the conduct of school affairs and that, perhaps, present members of the Board should consent to stand for election.[19]

Another positive aspect of that situation was that the school board worked in harmony with the Board of Supervisors in matters affecting the welfare of the school, particularly financial ones. Apparently in preparation for a change in the laws, in February, 1916, the Board organized itself into a high school division and the minutes beginning in February 7, 1916, are entitled "Office of Kern County Union High School Board." Leo G. Pauly had been elected president of this new division of the County Board on this February 7th meeting. Other members included J. E. Dyer, clerk; F. S. Benson; E. W. Owen, and Mrs. Jean A. Durnal.[20]

In spite of the disapproval of The Bakersfield Californian, the election took place on April 7th, and these same board members were elected. A new organizational meeting took place on May 6th with the same results as the previous one in February. Thus, Leo G. Pauly officially became the first president of the Kern County Union High School Board.

Even though the label "county" remained in the title of the district, by this time the high school in Bakersfield was not the only such school serving Kern County. In 1911, a high school district was established at Delano, thus breaking up the monopoly of Kern County High School over the whole of the county area. In Taft, Conelly High School was started in 1915. That same year high schools were organized in Maricopa and Wasco.[21]

During 1916, a high school district called Southern Kern County Union High School District was established. It included elementary districts in the eastern part of Kern County. This district encompassed Mojave, Muroc, Randsburg, Inyokern, Tehachapi, Rosemond, among others and, in fact, included all of the districts east of the mountains except one small elementary district. Apparently this latter district in its original form had a short life for it lapsed two years later. For several years these eastern county elementary districts were not a part of a high school district until new high school districts were formed to which they were annexed.[22]

Actually the Kern County High School had established branch high school programs in various areas outside of Bakersfield prior to this time. Reference was made to a class of some 50 pupils doing freshmen high school work in McFarland in 1910.[23] Branches were also established at Taft, Fellows and Delano during this period of time.

Although the minutes and other records of a high school do not show marked changes in the way in which the school was operated, 1916 is an important legal landmark. From that year on, the organization was on its own as an entity separate from the Office of Kern County Superintendent of Schools. Curiously enough, however, the school district did not have a superintendent until a number of years later. The head official continued to be the principal.

School Days CIRCA 1916

With the close of the school year 1915-1916, it was evident that the institution had come a long way from its beginnings in 1893, a period of less than 25 years. Enrollment of the school had risen to nearly 600, and there were 28 faculty members on the staff headed by Dr. B. S. Gowen, as principal, with Paul VanderEike, assistant principal. By this time Mr. VanderEike was often also listed as dean of the junior college program. Salaries for the staff ranged from $3,000 for the principal to a low of $900. The assistant principal was paid $1,800.

The commencement issue of The Oracle that year (1916) gives a summary of the high school program and includes a separate description of each of the departments of study. Actually by this time The Oracle, rather than being a combination newspaper, creative writing collection and yearbook, resembled a modern high school year book publication. The Blue and White, the school's newspaper, had begun operation in 1914, initially as an arm of The Oracle.

The junior college division is described in The Oracle as well on its way to becoming a proud part of the program of studies of the high school. Other departments are duly depicted:

Language - The offerings consisted of English and foreign languages. English was the most popular subject, although Spanish, French, German and Latin were offered. Two new courses in English were dramatics and oral English. Five teachers taught English, two French, two Spanish, two Latin and one German.

Mathematics - 335 students were enrolled in courses covering five years. They were listed as elementary algebra, plane geometry, advanced algebra, solid geometry, trigonometry and surveying. Three teachers held forth in this division.

<u>History</u> - Courses were ancient, modern and medieval, English, and United States. Three teachers were assigned.

<u>Science</u> - Here the description is more general, but there was the opportunity to specialize, and up-to-date courses were provided for every year of high school plus the two years of junior college. Three faculty members taught science.

<u>Domestic Science</u> - A four-year course was available with two teachers involved. Two new courses had just been added including dietetics and millinery.

<u>Manual Arts</u> - Students could learn to make wood articles and design furniture. Also taught was forging, including steel tempering and welding. There was a machine shop course in addition. The course offered such a level of expertise that students completing the entire curriculum in manual arts could "enter any shop as experienced apprentices." Three teachers were assigned .

<u>Music</u> - A new teacher had been at work during this year in the music department, and harmony and learning to sing by syllables were features of the course. The girls' glee club, boys' quartet, orchestra, and band rounded out the music offerings.

<u>Art</u> - Pencil drawing and clay modeling, charcoal, water colors, pen and ink cartooning, and illustrations were features of this department. There was even a course offered in what to teach in an art department.

<u>Farm</u> - Sixteen to twenty boys were currently enrolled at the farm, which was a separate institution with a full dormitory located at 25th and "M" Streets. The instructor was Professor George T. Berry "late of the University of California." Three courses were offered, with the expansion to four in the following year.

<u>Commercial</u> - The commercial program, which had its beginnings in 1899, included: shorthand, typing and practice in taking dictation from teachers so that students graduating would be "fitted for the business world." Two teachers taught courses in this department.

Student Activities. The 1916 commencement issue of The Oracle also contained a summary of important school activity programs engaged in by students. Particularly noted was the success, both journalistically and financially, of the student newspaper, Blue and White, which had been started some two years before. Another activity that gained attention of the student body was the Big "B" Club begun by Coach Griffith in the spring of 1909 for the promotion and encouragement of athletics. Interscholastic debating and public speaking were assisted by the Toastmasters' Club, and a new organization called the K. C. Society enrolled a combination of senior and junior college students. The latter was aimed at fostering scholarship, school spirit and activities.

This publication contained a full report on debating, which appeared to be one of the prestige school activities. This year the team had participated in the state championship meet, and the success was attributed to the coach, Mr. Elmer L. Shirrell. There were two debating societies - one for female and one for male students.

In commenting on dramatics, it was noted that the senior class play had been reinstituted after several years. Apparently it took some persuasion with the Board to get this particular activity reinstituted. The play that year was "The Touchdown," a comedy dealing with college life.

Athletics. By the 1915-1916 school year, Kern County High School had begun to assert itself as an athletic power in the Central Valley athletic league. Coach Griffith had arrived on the scene in the Fall of 1908, and almost immediately his influence was felt in all of athletics. The new coach was in charge of all interscholastic sports in which the school participated and had only one assistant. A man who was later to become principal of the school was one of his more notable assistants. His name was A. J. Ludden. Coach Griffith got started off right in the Fall of 1908, when his football team won the championship of the old Central California Academic Athletic League. The winning ways continued with the football team claiming the championship in at least four of the seasons during the eight years. The football team, in the fall of 1914, had so much success, that according to The Oracle that year, plans were discussed to enter the competition for the state championship; but because of finances this plan was delayed.

In spite of the publicity given to the success of football, however, the track squads were the most successful of all the athletic enterprises during that period of time. According to the accounts given in the various Oracles, the track squad emerged victorious from the annual field days in six of the eight years. The baseball teams won the league for four of these years; and the boys' basketball teams, which played in interscholastic competition for the first time during the 1910-1911 school year, won three championships. Reference has been made earlier to the success of girls' basketball. It was noted in the 1915 commencement issue of The Oracle, that for the first time in "the last four or five years," the girls' basketball team was not the champion of the league. When the interscholastic competition in girls' basketball was terminated in the 1915-1916 year, The Oracle recorded that this decision was received with great disappointment by the students in general and, particularly, by the girls.

Although tennis had been played sporadically in the early years of the operation of the school, it was not organized as a league sport until the 1911-1912 school year. There were no entries in tennis from Kern County High School until the next year, when a tournament was held at Visalia, and several boys were entered representing the school. Girls were not entered that year because of some "misunderstanding," according to the Oracle. They did take part in tennis on an interscholastic basis in the 1913-1914 school year, thus, re-entering the ranks of interscholastic competition after having been removed from the basketball court.

Another footnote to the athletic scene concerns football. Again, an editorial in the commencement 1916 Oracle states that "in 1915, after several years of rugby football, the

University of California decided to go back to the American game. The majority of the state high schools followed suit, among them being Kern County High." From other records it would appear that the school started playing rugby in 1910, because of the change at the university level; another example, no doubt, of the way in which the university has had a long and trenchant influence on the high school.

Before leaving this account of athletics, it would be amiss not to indicate the strong influence of the personality of Coach Griffith as reported in the pages of the school yearbook. After a somewhat unsuccessful season in football and track in 1912-1913, The Oracle adopted an apologetic tone, stating that it was not Mr. Griffith's fault that the team lost in these two sports. Unwittingly, the writer of this article was preparing the way for the years to come in which the school's football teams would win seven state championships.

Athletics, of course, received much publicity in the pages of The Bakersfield Californian during these years. A great deal of heat could be generated over an attempt on the part of one of the schools in the athletic league to eject the Bakersfield team from the league. This account, in the September 28, 1911, issue of the Californian, was reported as follows:

> "Saturday the annual meeting of the Central California High Athletic Association will be held in a session which promises to be one of the most torrid in the history of the organization owing to the effort being made by the Porterville representives to eject Bakersfield from the league. Bakersfield supporters, of course, will go to the meeting equipped to fight the issue to a standstill, and they will vigorously oppose all efforts made by Porterville or any of the other schools lined up with their program."

The account goes on to say that it is the scheme of "the orange pickers" to eject Bakersfield and bring in Fresno High School in its place. The reasons given were that Bakersfield School was larger and further away from the schools in the league. However, it was noted in the article that Fresno was equally as distant as Bakersfield from the other schools and had, in fact, even a larger enrollment.

> "The real trouble is, say those who have been closely following the trend of events in high school circles, that Bakersfield has been far too successful in the various athletics series to satisfy the Porterville team; and they believe if the athletes of this school can be gotten rid of by ejecting this school from the league, there will be a possibility of landing a few penants by the wearers of the orange and green."

The article mentioned that Professor Griffith and Robert Smith would represent Bakersfield at the meeting, and that the former was slated for the presidency of the league.

No report is available of the outcome of the meeting; however, Kern County High School continued in the athletic league for some years to come. The spirit engendered by the newspaper account of this meeting indicates the interest with which athletic affairs were followed throughout the community.

1908 - 1916 in Review

In this chapter, an attempt has been made to highlight the events which would seem to have modernized the curriculum and the activities of Kern County High School, with particular concern for taking care of students' individual needs. A cursory survey of the minutes of the Board of Trustees during this period of time will highlight and give dimensions to the happenings at the school.

Concern for the welfare and best interests of students were paramount in the action of the Board of Trustees. For example, the minutes of September 13, 1909, indicate this action: "Any student of Kern County High School who shall visit any house of ill faith or shall gamble or become intoxicated shall be excluded from said school."

Feelings of unrest continued to be shown in the relationships between the two student bodies, the academic and commercial. In 1911 the Board of Education denied a petition from the commercial students requesting that they be transferred to the new building. The denial was based on the rationale. . . "from the fact that experience had proved that having commercial departments among the academic departments, had not been a success."[24]

Relationships between teachers and the Board were highlighted in a joint meeting that occurred on September 8, 1911, when seventeen topics were discussed and authorized to be placed in a manual of rules and regulations for teachers. These topics, among others, included the address of student to teacher; uniformity of address in all rooms; nicknames of pupils and teachers; use of tobacco to and from and on school grounds; hayrides, joy rides and night proms not to be allowed; reports on moral conditions of the high school; and the prohibition of petitions. Another of the topics in this manual was the policy that the Board might call on any member of the faculty to consult about any matter pertaining to the welfare of the school.[25]

There was no dramatic instance of student rebellion, as in the case of the student walkout of 1902. However, one interesting reference in the Board minutes of March 6-7, 1912, was that five students were suspended because of placing their class flag on the flag staff in front of the new high school, and "subsequently greasing the flag pole." The Board took action to reinstate the students if the pole were cleaned, but noted that future occurrences such as this would result in an expulsion.

On another occasion the Board took action to reinstate a student from expulsion for smoking on the school grounds, and a letter of pledge was extracted from him stating in part, "This is to certify that I have voluntarily quit tobacco. . . and I will do all in my power to keep others from using it."[26]

Student self-expression is reflected in the December 5-12, 1914, minutes, when it was noted that school was closed from December 23, 1914, until January 4, 1915. However, a petition from the students requesting that the school be closed for two weeks was denied on these grounds:

1) School would have to be in session too late in the Spring. (2) School might be closed at any time on account of quarantine. (3) The teachers' salaries must be paid regardless as to vacation. (4) If the school remained in session after the other schools of the Valley, the Kern County High School Students would lose the best positions for the summer."

In another sign of the times, the February 1, 1915, minutes instructed Principal Gowen to have the janitor require the cleaning of the stables in the rear of the high school. The expense for the cleaning was to be collected from the students who had been using the stables. If students refused to pay up, they were to be "debarred from the use of the stables." In one more excerpt from the board minutes of this period showing the relationship between the Board and the school administration, this policy for the ensuing year was recorded:

"Mr. Dyer stated that he expected the principal to be the absolute head of the school without interference from members of this Board, and Mr. Chenoweth agreed with him. Mr. Pauly stated he wished it specifically understood that the principal was to do more work of supervision, and give closer attention to the management of the school. In the matter of the vice principal, it was ordered that he do less office work and give more attention to classes."

Although there is no statement of action in the board minutes, it can be inferred that these expressions of the two board members and the superintendent would be accepted as policy by the school administration.[27]

During this eight years the two major buildings, the original building in Elm Grove and the building across the street which housed the academic programs, were still the nucleus of the campus. However, a new manual arts building had been constructed north of the original building, and in Hudnut Park, at approximately 25th and "M" Streets, was located, of course, the new school farm. A dormitory housing some fifteen to twenty students was located at the farm. Student residents were transported back and forth from the farm to the school campus by motor vehicle – at this time variously described as a truck or bus which was rented by the school for this purpose, perhaps the beginnings of a transportation system for the District. The 1915 commencement issue of The Oracle proudly proclaimed that the new auditorium had been completed, and the first graduation ceremony was to be held in it. In addition, plans were underway for the building of a gymnasium.

The graduating class of 1916, with its 68 students, was the largest in the history of the school, as was the school enrollment, which stood at 580 at the end of that school year. Certainly, KCHS had come a long way from its beginnings in January 12, 1893, in the two rooms of the old Railroad Avenue School.

REFERENCES
CHAPTER II - THE EARLY BOOM YEARS 1909-1916

1. Robinson, W.W. *The Story of Kern County* (Bakersfield, CA: Title Insurance and Trust Company, 1961) p.41.

2. Miller, Thelma B. *History of Kern County* (Chicago: S.J. Clarke Publishing Co., 1929) p.359.

3. Robinson, p.40.

4. Rodgers, Glendon J. *Kern County is Our Home* (Bakersfield, CA: Merchants Printing and Lithographing Co.) 1956, p.42.

5. Robinson, pp.41-42.

6. Miller, p.384.

7. *Those Who Serve Kern County* (Bakersfield, CA: February 28, 1911) pp.52-53.

8. *Kern County, Land of Magic* (Bakersfield, CA: Kern County Board of Trade) 1955.

9. *The Oracle*, October, 1908.

10. Letter from A.G. Reim (Sacramento: State California Department of Education) September 12, 1958.

11. *Bakersfield and Kern County, a Half Century of Progress* (Bakersfield, CA: The Bakersfield Californian) 1912

12. Taped interviews.

13. *Minutes* (Kern County Board of Trustees, July 1, 1914.

14. Chism, Ray A. *A Preliminary History of Bakersfield College* (Bakersfield, CA: unpublished manuscript, 1981) p.3.

15. *The Oracle*, January, 1915, pp.33-34.

16. *Ibid.*, January 1916.

17. *Ibid.*, Commencement issue, 1916, p.49.

18. Kern County High School Circular Catalogue, September, 1915, pp.37-38.

19. *Californian*, March 10, 1916, p.12.

References - Chapter II (Continued)

20. Minutes, Kern County Board of Education, February 7, 1916. No other explanation of the reason for the change at this date is given in the minutes.

21. Boundaries of School Districts in Kern County (Bakersfield, CA: Office of the Kern County Superintendent of Schools, undated) unnumbered pages.

22. Brief Report on History of the Kern County Superintendent of Schools (Bakersfield, CA: Office of the Kern County Superintendent of Schools, undated) p. 2

23. Californian, April 16, 1910, p.

24. Minutes, Kern County Board of Education, January 14-23, 1911.

25. Ibid., September 8, 1911.

26. Ibid., March 20, 1912.

27. Ibid., May 3, 1915.

Built in 1907, the new high school building was at 14th and F Streets on the current site of the Bakersfield High School Cafeteria. This picture appeared in the 1913 **Oracle**. Until 1952 it served as the Administration Building for both the District (windows at right) and Bakersfield High School (windows at left).

Tennis was played competitively early in the history of athletics by both sexes. Shown here are the players pictured in the 1914 **Oracle**.
(L-R) Adolph Hubbard, Nellie Jenkins, Ruby Brite, Romona Hilliard, Leffler Miller.

Kern County Union High School Experimental Farm prior to 1916. The first school farm was located at 25th and "M" Streets.

Photo courtesy of the Kern County Museum.

Politics played a key role in the District's beginnings. This ad appeared in the 1914 **Oracle** at a time when the Kern County Superintendent of Schools was the legal head of the District. Lawrence E. Chenoweth won the election and became Superintendent in January, 1915. The following year the District became an independent District.

The Kern County Union High School band of 1917-1918. Theodore Hand was the student director, pictured second from the left. Howard Thompson is the tuba player.

Students in 1924 show how easy it was to get in and out of the new Mack 36 passenger bus. Driver Harry Drennan was concerned that the ease in exiting the vehicle might result in his loss of passengers - but that never happened. The vehicle is standing in front of C.N. Johnston, Body Works, where the bus body was constructed.

Photo courtesy of Kern High School District Transportation Department.

An early means of transportation was this 1916 GMC bus shown with driver Harry Drennan in 1920. The locale is the Kern River Oilfields on the Coloma lease. Mr. Drennan lived on this lease, one of the early bus routes. The bus was parked on a hill near his home which aided in getting the GMC started on cold mornings.

Photo courtesy of the Kern High School District Transportation Dept.

To the memory of our friend and leader
Arthur J. Ludden
this issue of The Oracle is affectionately
dedicated

Arthur J. Ludden, Principal of the Kern County Union High School from 1916 until his death in 1922. He was killed in an automobile accident on the infamous Ridge Route in January of that year. The picture is in the 1922 **Oracle** which was dedicated to his memory.

Kern County Union High School chemistry lab in the 1920's.

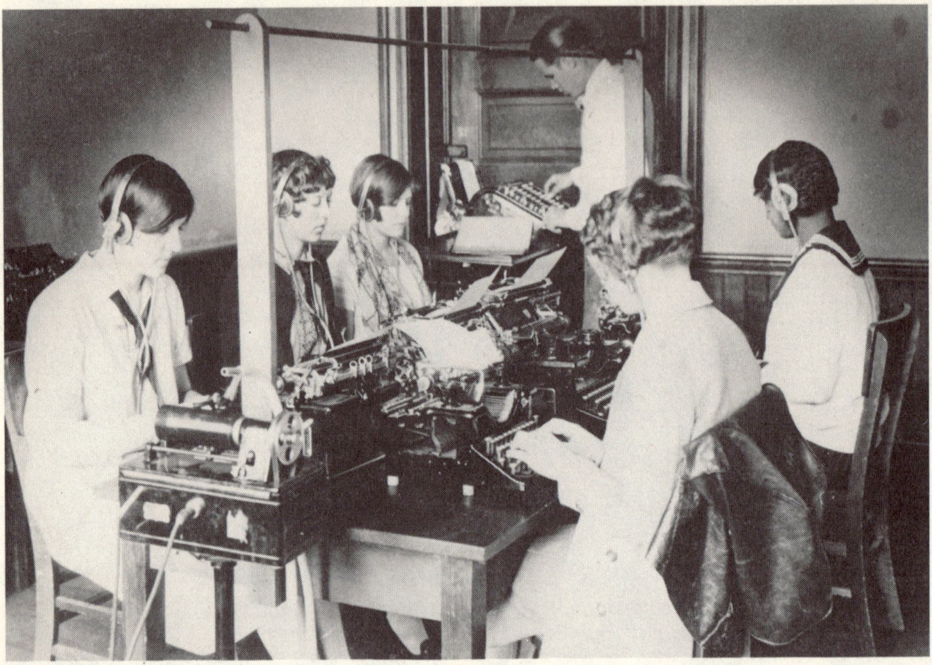

Commercial students use the latest office equipment circa 1927.

Robesky's Corner at the northwest corner of 14th and F Streets on the Kern County Union High School campus was a social center for students for more than twenty years after its establishment in 1921. It is shown here at the end of the twenties. The Robseky store itself is the brick building at right, while the snack bar behind the car was operated by other persons although owned by the Robesky family. Prior to 1928 the family lived in a house located directly to the left of the store. This picture was probably taken about 1930.

Three Superintendents of the District whose span of leadership totaled forty-six years. Herman H. Spindt, at right, was named Principal in 1922 after the death of A.J. Ludden (until 1932 the title of Superintendent was not used.) He was succeeded as Superintendent in 1938 by Thomas L. Nelson, center, who resigned in 1945 to be followed by Theron L. McCuen. The latter retired in 1968.

Photo courtesy of T. L. McCuen.

Judge T. N. Harvey, one of the most influential Board members, is shown here in his law office. Elected to the Board in 1927, he continued to be a member until his death in 1948. For nineteen of those years he served as Board president.

Photo courtesy of T. L. McCuen.

CHAPTER III

WORLD WAR I AND THE TWENTIES

The War and Kern County

The entrance of the United States into World War I, as would be expected, was to have far reaching effects on the business, social, and institutional life of Kern County. According to Kern County Historian, Thelma B. Miller:

> The first official militant reaction in Kern County to the declaration by the United States of war on Germany was the organization of home guard units and preparation to protect national resources and communication lines from any inimical influence. General William R. Shafter, Camp No. 31, United Spanish War Veterans, O. H. Lindgren, Commander, and W. R. Cook, Adjutant, took the lead, calling together a home guard regiment of 500 men.[1]

Almost immediately, Troop A, Kern County's own National Guard Cavalry Unit was organized with thirty men, and a local Red Cross chapter was formed. In Tehachapi, a volunteer home guard unit of forty-five members was organized to guard tunnels on the railroads between Caliente and Tehachapi. The Edison Power Company took action to protect its operational plants in the Kern River Canyon and announced that all visitors would be excluded from this area for the duration of the war. Recognizing the military value of their petroleum supplies, the oil companies hired private guards and special deputies to protect the oil storage tanks in the area. On a more positive note, members of the agriculture industry of the county recognized that their products were important to the war effort, and in the summer of 1918 the crop output in the county was increased 300 per cent to meet war needs. On April 13, 1917, only a week after war had been declared by the United States, the first of many patriotic demonstrations was held in the city. Among the well-known local

75

participants were the Kern County High School Principal, A. J. Ludden; Judge J. W. Mahon; Reverend George Ringo; F. E. Borton; and C. A. Barlow. Parade units of white-haired veterans of the civil war along with sixty members of the Bakersfield Germanic Lodge, Hermann's Sons, marched together, no doubt wanting to make sure that their loyalty to their adopted country was not in question:

> The crowd was in a solemn mood and there were many tearful faces as came home the full significance of the momentous national step of which this was the recognition.[2]

Within a few weeks, The Bakersfield Californian encouraged enlistment of a company of volunteers, and forty natives of Kern County left their homes for Fort McDonald in San Francisco to join the coast artillary. Later, in August, Troop A, the National Guard Cavalry, comprised of 101 men and thirty-two horses were bound for a camp in Arcadia, California, and eventually for Europe.

Those left behind in the County of Kern were anxious to show their patriotism and make their contributions to the war effort. Arthur F. Crites, prominent banker and graduate of the second class of the Kern County High School, was chairman of the first Liberty Loan Campaign. This campaign was oversubscribed by some 35 per cent and the result was $1,351,000.00 in funds, or $26.00 for every resident of Kern County, prescribed for the war effort. This was the beginning of several Liberty Loan Campaigns and their history in the county was that they were generally oversubscribed. Former County Superintendent of Schools and publisher of the Californian, Alfred Harrell, was chairman of another of the campaigns. Kern County Superintendent of Schools, L. E. Chenoweth, was active in a campaign called the "Four Minute Men Brigade." These were local orators who went about in the community and throughout the county encouraging the war effort among the residents. A unique contribution of the Kern Women's Christian Temperance Union to the war effort was the gift of a GMC ambulance which saw action on the battlefields in France.

The war finally ended after some eighteen months of fighting. The records show that 3,676 men from Kern County made their way to Europe and took part in the action. Of that group, there were 100 deaths, about a third killed in action, the others dying from various accidents or diseases.

An interesting footnote to World War I and its effects on Kern County occurred in 1923 when the cornerstone for the American Legion Post in Bakersfield was laid. This building was the new home of the Frank S. Reynolds American Legion Post and the first shovelful of dirt was turned by Herbert Hoover, a prominent Californian. According to historian Miller, at that time he seemed an unlikely choice for the Presidency of the United States.[3]

During the War Years

Even though there are evidences of some lasting effects on the schools as a result of World War I, the Board minutes curiously show little reflection of the hostilities. In fact, it is not until the May 4, 1918 meeting, that the minutes show a reference to the war. On this date a resolution was passed on the use of the auditorium during wartime. The resolution states that for the duration of the war, the auditorium was to be used solely for educational and patriotic purposes.[4] It arose as the result of some public protest that the local W.C.T.U. unit had been granted the use of the auditorium in opposition to some other organizations.

In contrast to the minutes, both the school yearbooks in 1917 and 1918 have numerous references to the intrusion of the war on school life. The <u>Oracle</u> of 1917 describes courses in "...drilling manuevers for boys in schools to prepare them for possible future necessities."[5] A sergeant from the U.S. Marine Corps conducted the drilling maneuvers, which were the actual beginnings of a formal physical education program in the high school. The next year the yearbook presents a rather detailed description of the physical education program in the school which grew out of the war effort. In fact, the instructor for the boys was called the Boys' Drill Master. Physical education programs for boys consisted primarily of parade maneuvers like army drills. The girls' instructor was called a Physical Trainer and she conducted the girls through various exercises that were described as "...throwing false dignity, high heels, and modish attire to the winds."[6]

Other echoes of the war in the school yearbook were the James Hill Memorial ceremony, in which a tribute was paid to the first graduate of the school to become a casualty of the war, and the memorial to Bernard Munzer in the 1918 <u>Oracle</u>. In that same yearbook, mention was made that the competitive athletic program was curtailed, and that, in fact, no state football championship was played that year because of the war. Several assembly programs, both in the spring of 1918 and in the fall, concerned the war. At one of them, there was a presentation of a service flag with 140 stars apparently indicating that many graduates of Kern County High School had been involved in the war effort. The girls' Patriotic League was formed, being a chapter of a national organization dedicated to the patriotic enterprise of supporting the war efforts, and at one assembly the program presented some of the realities of war. Principal A. J. Ludden and a new teacher, Grace Van Dyke Bird, talked at assemblies about the Army Y.M.C.A. and the campaign to raise funds for the war effort.

A personal testimony to the result of the war effort on the curriculum of the school is contained in an interview with Harry Drennan who entered Kern County High School in 1918. In his words,

> I remember another interesting program we had at the end of World War I. It was an organization called the California High School Cadets. The students could enroll in military drill in lieu of physical education. So I enrolled in military training and I think I learned quite a bit from it. We had quite a lot of fun and learned a lot of things. I think one of the biggest thrills I got out of it happened one morning when I walked down the front stairs of the old administration building on the corner of 14th and F Streets and a very well-groomed military man approached me. I saluted, he returned the salute, and little did I know it was Clarence Cullimore returning from duty the first day after being discharged from his service in World War I.[7]

The reader will remember that Mr. Cullimore had been on the staff prior to World War I as a teacher of drawing and an amateur playwright whose plays were enacted by the students. Harry Drennan, later to become a long-time employee of the high school district in the transportation department and as a teacher, also recalls, "...the most grueling experience we had... in the cadet corps." It involved a hike and a bivouac to the mouth of Kern River Canyon with a return hike back to Bakersfield the next morning. "....that convinced me I did not want to be a foot soldier."[7]

A tangible outgrowth of World War I was the realization by the Board that a physical education/athletic facility was needed by the school. In 1917 minutes of one Board meeting read as follows:

> Whereas, the Kern County Union High School is not provided with an adequate building for giving such instruction (i.e. physical education), know therefore it is hereby resolved by the Board of Trustees of the said Kern County Union High School that the public interest and necessity requires the construction of a gymnasium or athletic building.....[8]

The Board then stated its resolve to begin immediately building the gymnasium and proceeded to authorize purchase of land adjacent to the Administration Building.

Post War Education in the District

Fortunately we have a scholarly research study done by Kristianne Skjerve Evans (mother of E. Ben Evans, long time Supervisor of Library Services), in May 1918, which gives a complete and compact survey of education in Kern County including Kern County High School. Reference has been made earlier that, according to this account, Kern County High School was not the only institution of learning at this level in the county. In fact, by this time, five other high schools had been established. Mrs. Evans notes that the total high school enrollment of the county numbered 850 pupils with Kern County Union being the largest with 576. Thirty-two teachers were employed during the 1917-1918 school year to instruct the nearly 500 pupils and their salaries reached a grand total of $47,252.00.

79

The total expenditure for the high school that year stood just in excess of $66,000.00.[9] Other high schools according to size were: Conley at Taft, 99 pupils; Wasco, 65; Delano, 62; Maricopa, 34; and the Southern Kern County Union, 14.

The Curriculum in 1918

By the spring of 1918, Kern County High School had been organized twenty-five years, and it is important to note the extent to which the curriculum had been expanded from the two original courses of study, scientific and literary. Now, according to the Evans account, there were seven courses of study including home economics, agriculture, manual training, commercial, scientific, general, and college preparatory. Each of these programs provided the "basics" and, in addition, a sizable number of electives aimed at giving students a well-rounded educational experience. It should be observed that by this time the commercial course had been expanded to a four-year program leading to a diploma; although by special arrangement, students could also take the two-year program which would result in a "certificate". So-called core subjects such as English, mathematics, history, foreign language, and science, were scattered liberally throughout all seven of the courses with the exception of the commercial. Special attention is given in the Evans report to the boys' agricultural clubs which had been organized "under the auspices of the State Department of Agriculture in the the Farm Bureau."[10] The agriculture program had reached out to influence boys all over the county, with separate clubs and contests organized for elementary as well as high school boys. The highlight of the agricultural year was a visit to the farm program of the University of California at Davis offered to the boy who accomplished the best results in the agriculture program.

In the same study, reference is made to the junior college program and the attempts to set up courses corresponding to the lower division courses at the University of California. These courses are listed with the corresponding name of the course at University. Junior college courses were as follows: general botany, civil engineering, drawing, geography, mathematics, philosophy, political science, French and Spanish. In addition, courses were available in English, rhetoric and the short story, industrial and commercial geography, and history (a survey of nineteenth century history) all parallel courses to those at the University of California.

Physical Expansion of the Plant

The following quotation from the Kristianne Evans' research study has a familiar ring to the ear of educators, even today:

> It is characteristic of the phenomenal growth of school population in Kern County, that every time a new school building was planned, the public denounced those in charge, claiming that the buildings going up were too big, that they would never be filled, and that it was out of reason to go to such expense, and so on. Inside a few years, however, the quarters proved too small, new planning was done, new criticism offered for building too large, and the same rapid outgrowing, over and over again, until now, no prophecy is considered too big to believe.[11]

By 1918 the campus consisted of four major buildings, with a new gymnasium under construction. There was the original building constructed in 1895 in the area now called the Elm Grove. The major high school building across 'F' street to the west was finished in 1906, the mechanical arts building in 1911, and the auditorium in 1915. In addition, the school farm on "M" Street was in operation and consisted of some twenty-seven acres of land with several buildings including housing for students. According to Evans, the new gymnasium when completed would

> ...contain a huge dance floor, basketball courts, boys' and girls' gymnasium rooms, dressing rooms, showers, lockers, a swimming pool, a buffet kitchen, and a complete stock of physical exercise and training devices as well as several office rooms and store rooms.[12]

Late in 1919, the Board of Trustees embarked on a building program that was to carry over into the 1920's and served as a prelude of the expansion programs to the 1950's and later. In the November 13, 1919, minutes of the Board a resolution called for a $200,000.00 bond election to purchase

>...school lots for building two or more school buildings, for supplying such high school buildings with furniture, and necessary apparatus and for improving the grounds...[13]

This bond election was successful and the Trustees were encouraged to call for yet another bond election for the same amount, $200,000.00, in February of 1920. It also met with success and the building boom was underway. Immediately negotiations were undertaken by the Board to buy additional land to add to the campus in the area of 14th and "F" Streets, and plans got underway to construct domestic science and agriculture buildings which were to be completed in the early thirties. A careful search of the minutes of the Board shows no reference to tax elections held earlier in the history of the district. We, therefore, conclude that the bond election in 1919 was the beginning of a series of propositions put to the patrons of the Kern High School District asking for their financial support of the schools.

A Transportation System is Begun

In the previous chapter mention was made of an embryo transportation system, which began with the purchase of a truck to haul students back and forth from the school farm to the campus. This occurred in 1915. Two years later in the minutes of the Board, there is reference of attempts to secure vehicles for the transportation of students who lived in outlying areas to the school campus itself. Harold Pauly was the first Director of Transportation for the district. He came here in 1919 after a year's teaching in Visalia with the objective of organizing a transportation system for students in the outlying areas. He refers to the beginning of the transportation system as follows:

> To begin with, our transportation system started with a Buick truck that was used at the school farm that had let down side boards. ....and they ran that bus to the Kern River Oil Fields where a group of about ten students lived and were taken home after football practice. The bus system was the outgrowth of that particular run.[14]

This trial run was successful enough so that the Trustees were encouraged to extend the transportation system to Rosedale,

Arvin, Shafter, and Edison, and other nearby areas. Minutes of the Board of September 8, 1917, show that contracts for five buses were awarded, one to GMC for two vehicles seating thirty persons, and another to Studebaker, for three, seating twenty-five each.[15]

The District was definitely a pioneer in this transportation endeavor, and Mr. Pauly became well-known overnight. He recalls receiving letters from all over the country, and from foreign countries as far away as South America, making inquiry about the transportation system. The transportation staff in 1919 consisted of Mr. Pauly who, in addition to his transportation duties, was teaching two industrial arts classes, a mechanic, and several student bus drivers. The transportation director continued to teach classes until the 1930's. The Board records indicate a continual expansion of the transportation system. For example, in June, 1918, contracts were let for four cars as follows: one Moreland 25-horse power at $3,319.00; one Maxwell 25-horse power at $1,923.00; one Studebaker at $2,550.00; and one GMC at $3,600.00. Harry Drennan, who worked for the high school District as a bus driver after his graduation from Kern County High School in the early twenties, recalls one of the more exotic vehicles in the transportation fleet about that time. It was a bus that was purchased from the Tegeler Hotel and had been used by both the Tegeler and the Southern Hotels for transportation of guests to and from the railroad station. This particular vehicle was white and had seats made of genuine mulehide with plate glass mirrors throughout the interior of the bus. The students assigned to this particular vehicle felt themselves to be most privileged. The vehicle itself was so sturdy that it was later used for several years as a flatbed truck to haul supplies throughout the district.

Student Activities After WWI

In the fall of 1916 the Board of Trustees held a special meeting to establish some rather thorough guidelines for the conduct of student activities in the school.[16] The resolution adopted was quite specific in designating that all student activities should be under the control and supervision of a faculty committee, and this was to include any affair conducted in the name of the high school.

Activities were not to take place on any school night. A maximum of nine school dances were to be held during the school year. Each class was allowed to hold a picnic during the year, and both picnics and dances were to be "properly chaperoned." Student publications were limited to a bi-monthly newspaper and to a yearbook issued at the end of the year. Class organizations, student body and class meetings were designated. Each class was allowed the leeway to elect, in addition to its officers, a class advisor who was a member of the faculty. One of the chief duties of the class advisor was to arrange for a Literary Society meeting each Friday afternoon, each class was actually a "Literary Society." The number of student body plays was limited to three each school year and the admission for both student body plays and dances was limited to twenty-five cents per student. The general public was to be admitted to the plays at fifty cents per person, but the public was excluded from school dances. The sophomore class was allowed to give a reception for the incoming freshman class at the beginning of the school year. The specificity with which this is spelled out in the Board minutes indicates the importance with which adjunct activities were viewed by the Board and also the care they wished exercised in the operation of the activity program.

The <u>Oracles</u> during this particular era, 1916-1920, show that many activity programs were accelerated. Among these was debate, which, under the direction of Elmer Sherrill, with teams consistently winning championships and competitions throughout the state with representation at the state tournaments. The 1917 yearbook listed three plays, one a Greek tragedy, <u>Electra</u>, performed at the Greek Theatre in Beale Park. In addition, a vaudeville program called "A Football Circus" was described as twelve vaudeville acts arranged by Clarence Cullimore. This same yearbook indicated that dancing was a favorite pastime at the school and fourteen dancing activities were recorded. Apparently not all of these were official school dances, or this program of activities was certainly in violation of Board regulations. In 1918, The Oracle listed the following organizations as official school activities: a student body organization, a debating association, an athletic association, a book exchange, the band, orchestra, girls' glee club, a separate musical society, agricultural club, and Patriotic League for girls. Curiously, Bakersfield College was listed as an organization. One highlight of the activity season was a series of skits put on by the faculty. One entitled Catherine Parr, featured Grace Bird as Catherine, the wife of King Henry VIII, and Dwight Griffith as the King. Cast members of the two other skits included Principal Arthur J. Ludden, and staff members Mark Wilcox and Ysabel Forker among others. Grace Bird, who was a new member of the staff in 1917-1918, was destined to play a major role in the development of the junior college program in years to come. At this time she was teaching French in the junior college, and English and French classes at the high school.

Athletics

The big news in athletics during this period was the emergence of the football team as a power that was recognized statewide. The first of seven state championships was won by the football team in the fall of 1916, even though they got it, via the back door when San Diego forfeited to Bakersfield instead of playing the championship game. According to the sports writer in the 1917 Oracle, San Diego defaulted "...thinking how disgraceful it would be if they should be defeated by Bakersfield...."[17] This was a beginning of the dominant role which the Bakersfield football team played in the state championships until the fall of 1927 when the state program ended. The 1918 Oracle, in a commentary of the place of athletics in the school, pointed to the popularity of sports programs and the manner in which athletics had placed KCUSD on the inter-scholastic map:

> Were it not for accomplishments on grid-iron, diamond, track and court, we would be unknown to high schools beyond Kern County boundaries. As it is, we may safely say that Bakersfield, in reference to the school, is a familiar term in discussion of athletics in any part of California.[18]

It should be remembered that Dwight Griffith was still coach of all the major sports in the school including football, basketball, baseball, and track, assisted this period by Herman Spindt, who was later to become Principal and Superintendent of the District.

This same article in the Oracle bemoaned the fact that some of the excellent basketball potential of the school had been wasted because of the lack of proper court facilities and, of course, the basketball players, particularly, were waiting expectantly for the new gymnasium to be completed. Baseball had achieved some success. Notably, a championship of the Valley in 1917; Bakersfield track men were record-holders in the Valley and a few of them advanced to state competition. As a matter of fact, the state track meet was held for the first time in Bakersfield in 1920 with Los Angeles High School the meet winner. Theodore S. Hougham, who was a student in the school during those years, remembers trying out for the track team with little success, but his recollection is vivid of Dwight Griffith as the coach of all of the sports and of the track meets which were held those days in Beale Park.[19] Tennis in the school was primarily played by girls and had had a rather uneven history until this time. Mr. Hougham also recalls playing tennis on the Beale Park courts, not as a part of a team, but for recreation. In 1919-1920, tennis for girls was revived after being dormant for a number of years. But it was not yet considered a respectable sport for boys. Of historical interest is the fact that during the 1918-1919 school year it was necessary to curtail the athletics program as well as other competitive activities because of the epidemic of influenza. This particularly affected football, and it also cut into the participation in the debating program.

The Night School is Born

The minutes of the Board of Trustees for February 4, 1918 carry this item of action,

> That the Kern County High School establish a night school to teach such studies as Mr. Ludden thinks advisable.[20]

According to the yearbook, 175 students took advantage of this new program. The subjects which Mr. Ludden "thought advisable" were stenography, shop, Spanish, English, and mechanical drawing.[21] This new venture in education for the district was pronounced a success by the editors of the yearbook.

The Roaring Twenties

Tragedy Strikes:

School had just gotten underway after Christmas vacation in 1921-22 when an accident occurred on the infamous Ridge Route highway between Bakersfield and Los Angeles that sent shock waves throughout the campus as well as the community as a whole. Principal Arthur J. Ludden was on his way back to Bakersfield from visiting his wife who was hospitalized in Southern California when he was involved in an automobile accident that took his life. Mr. Ludden had been Principal since the resignation of B. S. Gowen in the spring of 1916, and he had been a member of the faculty since 1913. As a teacher, he had a mathematics assignment and he also had assisted Coach Griffith with the football team and in various other sports. After a memorial service was held in the auditorium, attended by students and various townspeople, the Board took action to name the new domestic science building Ludden Hall in his honor.

For many years after that, the Big "B" Athletic Society of Bakersfield High School held memorial services on the anniversary of his death, usually in Ludden Hall. On one such occasion in 1943, Mark F. Wilcox, who had been a member of the staff at the time of Mr. Ludden's death, was invited to speak, and his words paint a picture of this man and his contribution to the school district.

> Carlyle and Emerson have pointed out that in times of great need the right man always appears. As we look back over a half century of the development of the Kern County Union High School, we can now see that the right man needed to steer this school through that difficult period at the end of the first 25 years of the school's existence was A. J. Ludden. It was a

time when this Union High School had to prepare for a substantial growth that would either become a strong centralized institute or would fall apart by reason of its own ungainly bulk.[22]

Mr. Wilcox went on to speak about the first great building expansion which came during Mr. Ludden's regime, his interest and contributions to athletics, and his remarkable ability to "...name for you any boy or girl on campus..." Particular attention was called to the flu epidemic in 1919 when the school had been closed for two weeks and the Red Cross took over the new gymnasium turning it into a hospital. Mr. Ludden had been on the job day and night seeing to the provision of needed supplies, equipment, volunteer nurses and other assistance to the Red Cross in this hour of need.

Ruth Emerson Stutzman (then Ruth Heil) was also on the staff in 1922 as a teacher of art. Mrs. Stutzman remembers the Principal's kindness to her when she came to the campus in 1919. He took her personally to her room upstairs in the high school building and made sure she had the facilities and equipment needed to take over her art instruction duties. She also recalls that the Principal had a way of keeping perspective in the midst of unusual events such as the winning of a state football championship.

> Some of the teachers thought we should have a bonfire across the street....they went into the office on Monday morning after the game and said that there should be a bonfire for the championship the team won Saturday. Mr. Ludden stood behind the counter and said, "That was Saturday, this is Monday". He was able to distinguish between business and pleasure and set priorities that were recognized by those who worked with him.[23]

Harry Drennan was a student when Mr. Ludden was Principal and also was an employee of the District when the Principal was killed, for he had stayed on to work for the transportation department after his graduation in 1922. Mr. Drennan had the unusual distinction of never leaving Bakersfield High School after he entered as a freshman. After working for the district a few years in the transportation department, he became a teacher of automotive mechanics. Later, he would retire after a long career at Bakersfield High School and Bakersfield College as an instructor and department chairman. For a period of fifty years, from 1918 until he retired in 1968, he was continuously at the school as a student and employee, certainly a unique distinction. Looking back at Principal Ludden, he remembers that this man was highly respected by students, faculty members, and townspeople. The Principal had a direct way of taking action when a situation confronted him that required his attention. According to Mr. Drennan,

> When he asked you to do something it was a pretty good idea to do it. For example: One morning he and I were walking on the sidewalk at the corner of 14th and "F" Streets. One of the male students was standing on the corner smoking a cigar. He, in no uncertain terms, told the student to get rid of that cigar. The student told him where to go in no uncertain terms... and then the student picked himself up out of the middle of "F" Street.

An example of "direct counseling" was thus carried out to the ultimate degree.

Often, Mr. Drennan recalls, Principal Ludden would ask him to "fire up the Buick" and they would go down to the pool hall which was then on the corner of Wall Street and Chester Avenue. The Buick would be parked in the back and the Principal would enter the front door of the pool hall, soon flushing out a car-load of students who should have been in school. They would be transported back to the campus for proper disciplinary action.[24] In discussing the students in those days Mr. Drennan was reminded that many of the male students were in their early or mid-twenties, having come back from World War I, and so it was necessary for an administrator to use different methods in dealing with these mature young men than he might have used with teenagers. Apparently, according to those who knew Mr. Ludden, he was a unique schoolman, a sort of one-man administrative team who operated the school with all its facets, from the instructional program, the activities program, to the business program. It seems fitting then that after the earthquake of 1952, Ludden Hall should be one of the buildings to be restored and continue to bear the name of this remarkable person.

Two months after Ludden's death, a teacher of history, sociology, and the assistant football coach for the two state championship games in 1920 and 1921, Herman A. Spindt, was named Principal. The language of the Board minutes is significant in comparing the methods of selecting administrators in 1922 and now,

> Moved by Mr. Tyler, seconded by Mr. Fitzgerald, that nominations be opened and a Principal for the Kern County Union High School be elected for the balance of this year. Mr. H. A. Spindt was unanimously elected by the five members of the Board of Trustees, receiving all of the five votes cast.[25]

During the two months intervening since the death of Principal Ludden, Vice-Principal VanderEike had been authorized to sign anything needing the Principal's signature.

The Instructional Program in the Twenties

In turning to *The Oracle*, we find an overview of the instructional program, indicating that the program of studies at the school was moving towards what could be called in educational jargon developed at a later date, "the comprehensive high school." The 1922 yearbook carried a review of departments of the school which is curiously incomplete but which gives us a glimpse of the programs of study.

This is a description of the academic program:

> The Academic course offers the greatest variety of subjects. This course prepares a student for college. The languages taught are Latin, French and Spanish. Great interest is taken in all of these studies, and clubs have been formed in most of the classes.
> Students are taking great interest in the science courses, physics, chemistry, biology and general science being taught.
>
> Drafting, both architectural and mechanical, is taken by mostly boys and a few girls. This course is of great value to the boy intending to become an engineer.

> Ancient, medieval and modern, and United States history, civics and sociology are subjects offered in this course.
>
> Great interest is shown by the art students, a four-year course is offered. English, of course, is required in the first three years, but most of the students take the fourth year, too.[26]

The curious omission in this discussion of courses is that of the mathematics department, particularly in view of the fact that perhaps the most well-known teacher on the campus, Dwight Griffith, was the chairman of the mathematics department.

The discussion of the manual arts department might be considered sexist by the discerning person today, as was the reference to the drafting courses in the above discussion. The description stated that the manual arts department was "becoming one of the most popular for boys." Specific courses mentioned were machine shop, with attention given to small steam engines and lathe work, and auto shop where the boys learn "how the wheels go around", and in this department the school buses were kept in repair. Forging and welding were also taught, as was wood shop, with several girls actually enrolled in this course. In the wood shop courses, lathe work and cabinet making were included.

According to the yearbook, all the qualifications for good stenographers and bookkeepers were being met by instruction in the commercial department. Included were typing, shorthand, bookkeeping, penmanship, and business arithmetic. Reference was made to the business show held under the auspices of the commercial department where the skills of these students were on display.

In the music department, chorus, glee club, orchestra and band were featured.

> The glee clubs have sung for several social functions given in the city. That our orchestra is a good one is proven by the fact it has been requested to play for many of the entertainments given by various groups.

A final grouping of instructional departments in this particular discussion was that of physical education. It was, of course, divided into boys' and girls' departments. One particular summarizing statement in the section relating to boys' classes is interesting:

> Basketball, soccer, indoor baseball and swimming contests have removed the dislike for gym that was formerly manifested when physical education meant calisthentics and rigid discipline.

Interscholastic contests in these sports were held and there is an indication in the write-up that this was something different from the more rigid instruction which undoubtedly was the outgrowth of the military drills from which physical education instruction for boys originated. In the girls' department an even more advanced outlook seemed to be in evidence. "Good posture" was the slogan of the year and dancing classes were popular. Competition in football and hockey had been introduced by the staff and according to the yearbook, the girls thoroughly enjoyed these sports. Competition in track was particularly singled out as a highlight of the year.

> The girls showed the real Kern County spirit in the meet, which besides being inter-class was also inter-scholastic. Los Angeles High, Sacramento and Sherman Institute were the competitors. The juniors won the meet with 28 points.

Apparently this track meet was a combination of inter-class and inter-scholastic competition with the various classes of the school competing with each other as well as with teams from other institutions.[26]

Occasionally the researcher experiences a stroke of good fortune, giving an added insight into events of years ago. This occurred with the 1922 <u>Oracle</u> which is a part of the District's collection of school yearbooks. Glued into one of the front pages of this particular copy is an invitation to attend visitor's day at the Kern County Union High School on May 19 and 20, 1922, and the invitation contains a program of exhibits showing off the products of the schools. The exhibits were housed in the gymnasium, and a summary of the program is as follows:

Academic display of history work, agriculture department bees and poultry supplies, dairy equipment, tools and soil experiments; art exhibition, posters and applied art, pottery, basketry, metal and displays of first and second year art work; commercial department, business office equipped with multigraph, mimeograph, mimeoscope, calculating machines, adding machines, typewriters, filing system, dictaphone, check protector. Student stenographers will demonstrate equipment and be at the service of the public; domestic art and science, dresses and millinery and canned fruit; drafting department, architectural drawing: classic orders, house plans, public building plans, landscape plans, architectural sketching, rapid sketching by students enrolled in architecture, machine design, steam engine, gas motor detail, and assemble drawings, geometric drawing, show card and china painting, penmanship exhibit; mechanical arts, general machine shop work, exhibit of wood work made in shop, display of ornamental iron work; science department.

In addition to the exhibits, various programs were available, with the boys' physical education department giving exhibitions in tumbling, wrestling, boxing, and apparatus work, and with the girls presenting a festival 'Il Penseroso-- L'Allegro.' There was also a domestic arts fashion show, music recitals, band concert, and a music and play in the program listed simply as "a music and play."

Obviously, it was not practical to try to show the in-depth educational program, but this visitor's day offering certainly displays a breadth of program which might not be expected in a high school in 1922.

The school yearbook four years later contains another summary of the school departments, again curiously omitting mathematics. Emphasis on this write-up was to show ways in which instructors had been trying to make classes of instruction more interesting to students. For example, clubs had been formed in the foreign language department. Mechanical drawing classes had entered drawings in the state fair and had won prizes. Science students had gone on field trips to the oil fields and industrial plants, as had the civic classes to the county jail and the courthouse. The art classes had been active in competing in state and county fairs and art students had illustrated the yearbook, as well as making posters to advertise school functions. The band had participated in the parade at the Fresno "Raisin Day" and the glee club had staged a presentation of "Elijah."[27]

Programs of Special Interest

There seems to be a general agreement among the sources of information about this period in the history of the school that the primary reason for the strength of the program of studies, and its breadth and vitality was the competent cadre of teachers who had been attracted to the school. Some of those mentioned continuously should have attention. A program which certainly got its share of attention in this era was that of agriculture. Howard K. Dickson had come to the school just before the beginning of the twenties and was giving leadership to the development of an agriculture program through the Boys' Agriculture Club, which was a forerunner of the Future Farmers of America. State Senator Walter Stiern, a graduate of Kern County High School, remembers the growth of the agriculture program and particularly the concept of student projects. In Senator Stiern's words,

> The boys' Agriculture Club was very well known; and in project work, the agriculture teachers used to find good stock for the students to raise, especially good breeding stock, going out of state to get it when they had to. I remember them going into Oregon and Washington and bringing home Guernsey cattle. There were no cattle of that breed in Bakersfield. Guernsey cattle that developed around Bakersfield originated as a result of the work of that agriculture club.[28]

Senator Stiern recalls further that the agriculture staff at the school in those days mostly came from the University of California at Davis. Many of them, led by the Department Head, adopted a mode of dress to wear on campus that customarily had been worn by the seniors at Davis. The principal items were a Stetson hat, somewhat similar to the ones worn by the Mounties in Canada, with a hatband which said "University of California" on it. In addition, the particular dress included trousers worn like puttees stuffed down into leggings, a fashion probably influenced by World War I uniforms. Senator Stiern remembers that one staff member, from a college of another state, did not take to this particular style of dress, and was almost always "out of uniform." Thus, the Boys' Agriculture Club and the instructional program brought recognition to the school and influenced positively the agricultural operations of Kern County.

In another field of instruction, the programs of the school received a remarkable boost during the 1920's. This was the department of music. Although the school had had some rewarding musical programs prior to that time, there had been a lack of stability in the personnel resulting in programs being built up and then declining. The yearbook of 1918 describes the musical programs of the school as being popular, fostered, and expanded under the direction of a Elva Murray. There is even a Kern County Union High School band pictured in this yearbook, a brave little group of ten players. The text indicates that "the year opened with no leader for the untrained band, but Theodore Hand stepped into the breach and was very successful as director."[29] The latter was actually a student in the senior class at that time. An orchestra and girls' glee club are also pictured, both under the direction of Elva Murray, who later became Elva Dimon, wife of Asa Dimon, local head of the Bank of America.

In the early twenties, however, a man named Harold J. Burt came to the school who gave strength and stability to the musical programs. As a result, by the end of the twenties, the instrumental music program had grown to the extent that

> Kern County Union High School Band is one of the largest and best known high school bands in the State of California....the spirit of the band is shown by the generous way it contributed to many events of the year, in addition to their regular work of playing for all the football games as usual. Among these were Masonic educational week programs, Armistice Day Parade, the Lawrence Tibbett Parade...

According to the 1929 yearbook, the orchestra had also grown in numbers and stature and during that year took part in the operetta, "The Fire Princess", which involved the total music department. Both of these organizations are pictured in the 1929 yearbook with some forty members each.[30]

Gerald Smith remembers playing his trumpet under Harold Burt in both the band and the orchestra in the mid-twenties and recalls the pride which the students felt in these organizations. E. Ben Evans, a graduate of the class of 1927 who later spent a long professional career with the district, played flute and piccolo in the orchestra. Looking back on his years as a student he remembers:

> Harold Burt was in charge of the orchestra. He was an excellent person who could stimulate us to do things in music we never thought possible. Still, he was friendly and, in all, an excellent instructor.[31]

Later, Mr. Evans was to be a fellow instructor with his former orchestra director when he came to teach English at the school. There is evidence that the choral programs grew along with the instrumental part of the studies although his interest was primarily in the latter. Mr. Burt gave form and substance to this part of the instructional program throughout a long career of some 35 years.

In the kindred field of art, reference has already been made to an instructor who was influential throughout a long career in art instruction. Ruth Heil began the building of an art program in the twenties. Fresh from UCLA with some experience in teaching art in southern California, she brought a new method and modern approach, particularly in the areas of composition and design. She became interested in other art aspects of the school, particularly drama, and made a rather unexpected contribution to the stage in the auditorium.

At that time, the only curtain on the stage was the fire curtain, and a painter from San Francisco had been hired to decorate it with a scene from the Kern River. At the sides he had painted a simulated curtain with long cords. The total effect in the opinion of the drama teacher, Evelyn Smith, was gaudy and garish to the extreme. She finally prevailed upon her fellow art teacher to repaint the curtain. After receiving permission from Principal Ludden, Miss Heil got this project underway with the assistance of two students. She decided upon a design which seemed appropriate and placed numbers on buckets of paint. Rushing back and forth between her classes, and staying after school, she directed her assistants by calling out the number of each bucket and telling them approximately where to paint. This process was underway one day when an unexpected visitor came upon the scene. In the art teacher's words:

> One day when I was sitting there directing them by strokes, the door darkened, and it was Mr. Ludden. He came in and said, "Picture! The picture!" I said, "Well you gave us permission to do it." He said, "I thought you would just paint around the picture. They paid $500.00 to have that picture painted." I was so tired that I began to cry. He said, "Don't cry, don't cry. That's the worst thing to do." I said, "I'm so tired I can hardly lift a fork to feed myself." After thinking a moment, he replied, "I'll tell you what to do, you stay right down there and finish and I'll look after your classes." And that is what I did.[32]

The curtain was proclaimed a success. The crowning compliment came at a time when a visiting artist told the principal it was the best job he had ever seen done on an auditorium curtain, but he added he thought anyone would have to be crazy to take on such a job. Ruth Heil stayed on at the school for a period of time parallel to that of Harold Burt. Her leadership provided stability and continuance to the art program as did Mr. Burt's in music.

A former student who recalls with satisfaction the art instruction at the school is Harold Brewer, a great-grandson of Col. Thomas Baker. Mr. Brewer entered Kern County High School in 1925. He had classes from Ruth Heil (Emerson) and later from Eunice Ubele (Karpe) and became particularly interested in metal crafts and jewelry.[33]

He won a number of ribbons at the California State Fair competitions in Sacramento in the metal craft division; and at an exhibit in Los Angeles, he entered a silver ring:

> I had a letter from a Ralph Morris, curator of the San Diego Art Museum. He had seen this ring and wanted it, so he asked me to sell it to him which I did. He corresponded with me for several years urging me to attend college somewhere in Ohio where he had moved. I didn't have any money for college and besides I was working at Coffee's Clothing Store by now.[33]

He further recalls crafting an amethyst oval ring for Eunice Ubele which she returned to him many years later. His daughter now has this keepsake. Pewter was also a favorite media of this art student:

> I made this very plain bowl out of pewter and Grace Bird saw it and said she had to have it. She asked if I would sell it...I remember I sold it for $5.50-- making a profit of $5.00.

Both of his art teachers urged him to attend college to make art his career, but due to his financial situation, it was impossible. In May, 1929, the depression was just setting in and few of Mr. Brewer's classmates were able to go on to higher education.

> As a matter of fact, I was chairman of our fiftieth class reunion, and when the committee got together, it was suggested perhaps we should have someone make a brief greeting that would include the class members' background. Upon looking over the graduation list, we found an interesting fact: there was not a single attorney or doctor in our class. The realization came that we graduated just as the depression hit, and few in our class had any formal education after high school graduation.

Even if given the space, it would be impossible to go into detail regarding the contribution of a large number of other like instructors, but at least some can be mentioned here. In the field of English, the name of Mark F. Wilcox stands out as one who gave leadership and direction to the teaching of English and journalism, as he was for many years the advisor of the school newspaper, The Blue and White. In drama, it was Ethel Robinson who gave guidance to this program. Both in the high school and the developing junior college, the students in her dramatic productions testify to her influence and the pride they felt in the dramatic productions staged at this time and later. In the commercial field, O. W. Rister and L. B. Davey were stalwarts in shepherding this program from a two-year peripheral course to a full-fledged school curriculum. In the home economics program, situated in the new Ludden Hall, Lida Siemon was a steadying and ongoing influence. Clarence Cullimore has already been mentioned in a number of contexts, but he should not be overlooked as one who gave form to an important speciality in the curriculum, that of industrial and architectural drawing. In the kindred field of industrial arts, then usually called manual arts, a number of people provided impetus, including Walter Stiern, Kenneth W. Rich, and Clifford Scott. Besides his direction of the athletic/sports program, Dwight Griffith gave strong leadership to the mathematics program, his total career with the district spanning forty-six years. In science, George Sagen, Axel Petersen, and Robert Vivian are mentioned by students of that era as being teachers who influenced their lives. The latter left Kern Union High School District after a relatively short career and became Dean of the School of Engineering at the University of Southern California in Los Angeles. Mention should also be made of a young athlete who came on the scene during this era. In addition to making a name for himself locally and internationally in the field of track, and assisting in coaching several of the state championship football teams, he was an influential teacher and leader in the development of instruction. His name was J. B. (Cap) Haralson.

A Counseling Program is Organized

Until the late 1920's there was no organized counseling program in the school; although, of course, informal counseling had been a part of the institution ever since it was established in 1893. The first staff member to hold the title of counselor was Leo B. Hart, who had come to the school in 1925 as a psychology teacher and basketball coach for the Junior College Division. He recalls that after he had been at the school two years, he was called into the office by Principal Spindt and asked to take over the position of Head Counselor. Since there had been no such position up to that time, he was given a free hand to work out the program to best suit the needs of students.

One of his first projects was to establish a new system of registration. The arrangements up until that time were what might be called "mass registration," with students merely appearing at the school each year in September, the administration having no pre-registration information, particularly regarding incoming freshmen. The program of pre-enrollment for eighth graders to which all graduating elementary students were invited was instituted. They attended classes related to their major interests and were fed, the girls in Elm Grove and the boys in the agricultural area, by the home economics department. The visit also included information presented by student council members and students representing various activities, including dramatics, public speaking, athletics, etc. The second phase of the pre-registration program was a visitation to the feeder schools at which time a schedule of classes was set up for each of the incoming students. There was doubt on the part of some of the administration that the program would work, but finally Principal Spindt said, "We'll try it." The plan allowed teachers to have a list of prospective students on their desks before school started and made it possible for the person in charge of the bookroom to deliver books to the classes prior to the opening of school. A write-up of this successful program eventually appeared in the Secondary School Journal, which was the official publication of the Secondary School Administrator's Association in the state.

Mr. Hart had some practical experience in counseling. In addition to his teaching assignment, during his first year he was assigned as a monitor to the boys' dormitory and was involved in situations demanding informal advice to students. The new position carried the responsibility of taking referrals from teachers about students who were problems in the classroom. Furthermore, the counselor was responsible for the supervision of student organizations. The organizations at this time including a wide range of activities including: athletics, forensics, Future Farmers, publication, musical groups, dramatics and the various special interest activity groups. Also in this sphere of responsibility was the student council, various class councils, executive committee, and a program of assemblies. A primary source of income for the activity program was the pay assemblies; students paid a small admission fee to the programs. The class council system was completely reorganized at this time, emanating from the incoming eighth grade classes. The teachers of those students would be asked to select outstanding leaders to formulate the eighth grade student council. The councils thus established were responsible to elect student officers. There were representatives from each of the feeder schools in the district in the freshmen class council. The total school class council system was thus rejuvenated and, according to Mr. Hart, showed a high quality of leadership, resulting in diminished discipline problems in school.

Another innovation at this time was that of an auxilary curriculum developed through an advisory period into which all students were scheduled in the afternoon. In an effort to enliven and enrich the advisory program, students were asked to suggest subjects and kinds of learning they would like to have but which were not currently offered by the school. The result was that a wide variety of subjects was suggested. Teachers were also asked to name subject areas in which they had some expertise and which were not currently being taught. Eighty different subjects were mentioned by both students and teachers. As might be expected, some of the suggestions were beyond the knowledge and skills of the teaching staff. Local citizens such as architects, lawyers, cosmetologists, business men and others from the community were asked to volunteer their time to teach these informal classes during the advisory period. The resulting courses in such subjects as aviation, forestry, drafting, cosmetology, and national parks added to the breadth of the curriculum. It also added a tremendous administrative load for the counselor's office, with a staff of only one student assistant in addition to the Head Counselor. The outcome was that the program was discontinued after a year as a noble experiment.

In the age of the computer, it is difficult to remember the hours of labor required to make students' schedules and schedule classes, all of which had to be done in duplicate by hand. It is easy to understand why this program was regretfully abandoned, according to Mr. Hart:

> I counseled individually all of the students in the entire high school. They came in voluntarily, and I saw fifty to 100 each day.. There were 1,600 to 1,800 students when the program was put in, and there were 3,200 the last year I was there. There was no opportunity to keep detailed records which would have been helpful, but I did develop a very keen memory of all

the students. We made a practice, when the student wanted advice on his schedule, to save time we sent him to the walk-in safe in the hallway to get his own record from the file. This developed confidence and made students relaxed so they would talk about their problems with no hesitation....We had excellent relationships with students as we counseled them on academics, making adjustments in their schedules as seemed advisable. Each student at that time was carrying four subjects and physical education, and was credited one quarter unit per class per year, or one full unit per year for a full load.[34]

Although the counselor had no full-time secretarial help, Dorothy Donahoe, who was in charge of student records, did his secretarial work, and he was able to get some student help from time to time.

Athletics in the Twenties

It is difficult to describe athletics in the Twenties at the Kern County Union High School without giving so much emphasis to football that it would appear no other sports were enjoyed by students of the school. The football teams, beginning in 1920, reeled off a series of four straight state championships and then repeated in 1925 and finally in 1927, when the state championship football program was discontinued. This coupled with the first win in 1916 gave the Kern County Union High School teams seven wins out of the ten championships played. In 1924 the Drillers, as they had begun to be called in the early twenties, went to the finals and were defeated by Berkeley High School. The Bay area school had been their opponent in three other of the state championship contests. It is perhaps not too difficult to imagine the fervor which students and townspeople alike managed to generate for these state championship games. The finals in the fall of 1923 were played against Lick Wilmerding High School in San Francisco. Phillip M. Wagy, a graduate of the class of 1925, was among those who traveled in a special train to the game. His description of the trip is enlightening:

> We had a special train on the Santa Fe. Almost everybody in the town and in the school seemed to be on that train. We left here about 11:00 the previous night and about 9:00 in the morning we got to Oakland where we had to disembark and catch a ferry boat

across the bay. Upon landing at the old Ferry Building we formed a parade. I don't know how long it was, but my uncle, a man named Ogden who was then City Manager, was leading the parade on foot. We walked right up Market Street and stopped the traffic all the way up to the Whitcombe Hotel. It must have been a good mile, anyway.....The people in San Francisco, particularly those with their offices and stores on Market Street, didn't know what to make of this gang of hicks from Bakersfield blocking traffic.[35]

There were hundreds of townspeople and students who turned out. The final triumph was that the Driller team went on to take the state championship by a score of 27-13 over the San Francisco team. So effective were the coaching and teaching efforts of Dwight Griffith and his assistants that three members comprising the right side of the line of the Sanford Rose Bowl team of 1928 were former Bakersfield football players, Chris Freeman, Theo "Spud" Harder, and Don Robesky.

Even though the dominant athletic competition capturing the interest of the public was football, other sports were played at Kern County Union High School, too. In fact, the twenties seem to mark the emergence of strength throughout all athletic fields in general. The school's track team in the early twenties and into the thirties was marked by winners in Valley and County championships. In 1927, the school's track team went to the state meet, losing in combined totals by only one point. Likewise, in basketball and baseball, the school's teams were usually top competitors in county and valley championships. In fact, in 1929-30, the school won valley championships in basketball, baseball, and football. The Twenties also witnessed the advent of tennis as a sport to engage the interest of both sexes. It was the only sport in which girls competed with other school teams. An interesting insight into tennis is afforded by an interview with Phillip Wagy, who was mentioned earlier in another connotation. His older brother got him interested in tennis in the mid 1920's and they played together on the only courts available, located in Beale Park. After his brother tried to teach him how to play, they both decided they needed more scientific instruction and began reading books by William "Big Bill" Tilden and others:

To the best of my knowledge, he and I were the first Bakersfield people ever to try to learn to play tennis right. Everybody else would come out and try to win. We'd come out and try to learn. We would sacrifice winning by making ourselves do what we thought were the right things.[36]

He recalls playing tennis in the twenties with and against the outstanding net men in the Bakersfield area including Dave Urner, Clyde Hislop, Forrest Lynn, and his county champion doubles partner, James Wilt. The man he credits with fostering the "tennis boom" in Bakersfield in the Twenties was Lake Lovelace, whom he faced in two county championship finals in 1926 and 1928.

Although it is dangerous to present a roster of athletes in such an account as this, certainly a few names will evoke memories from those who were a part of this era. In football, outstanding performers were George Williamson, Monroe "Monk" Harmon, Cyril Giraud, John E. Loustalot, Paul Baldwin, Walter Caldwell, Phil "Spud" Harder, Robert "Dip" Cooley, Chris Freeman, and Willie Lewis. Later in that decade taking part in various state football championship games were Lawrence Johns, "Tex" Jones, Bernard "Frenchy" Uhalt, Robert Stockton, Edward "Bud" Cummings, Don Robesky, and Vivian Parra. In track the following names are frequently mentioned in the accounts of meets during this era: Walter Wickersham, Robert Stockton, Jim Tyack, Doug Knowles, and Spencer Selvey. Lawrence Johns was also a standout basketball player, and in baseball, "Frenchy" Uhalt went on to the major leagues.

Dwight Griffith continued to be the dominant figure in coaching sports at the school, managing to serve as head coach in football, basketball, baseball and track. Several other coaching figures though, also appeared. More responsibilities during this time were assumed by J. B. "Cap" Haralson as line coach in football and later for track. By the end of the twenties, Wallace "Jack" Frost, later to become head football coach at Bakersfield College, was increasingly recognized as an outstanding coach because of his work with the lightweight football teams called the Sand Dabs. After making a name for himself in football at the University of Southern California, John E. Loustalot, a quarterback for the state championship football team in the Twenties, returned to assist in coaching and also had responsibility in attendance supervision. Assisting Coach Griffith at this time was Ernest Dalbom and Jesse D. Stockton; the latter was later to become County Superintendent of Schools for Kern County.

Other Activities

Activity programs of all kinds flourished on the campus during the 1920's. The yearbook for the 1929-30 school year presents a vivid description of them. Foremost among the activities listed was the executive committee which apparently had taken on new life during this time. The student body president was Orville Armstrong who later established a reputation locally as an educator and regional historian. The musical activities consisted of girls' trio, boys' quartet, advanced girls' glee club, elementary girls' glee club, a boys' glee club, and the high school band and orchestra. Mentioned previously was the leadership of Harold Burt in the music program of the school at this time. Two pages in the yearbook were devoted to the agricultural club activities, including a note that the livestock judging team of the school won the state championship cup and thus was privileged to represent the state at Chicago in the world famous livestock show. Other activities included, of course, the publications, The Oracle and the Blue and White, the World Friendship Club, High-Y Club, California Scholastic Federation, Les Mousquetaires (the French Club), the Classical Club for Latin students, Big-B and Girls Athletic Association, the Pet-Tech Club (petroleum technology), and the Home Economics Club. Dramatics also gained in popularity at the school under the direction of Ethel Robinson. This year, 1929-30, the student body play was called "Merely Mary Hand," rating a two-page review in the yearbook.

Special attention should be paid to forensics which, towards the end of the Twenties, took on a burst of activity under the direction of Leland C. Tallman. In fact, the activity section of The Oracle in 1929-30 was dedicated to Mr. Tallman who had been at the school three years,[37] The 1928 yearbook cited the

105

formation of the San Joaquin Valley Forensics Association which was to give the school a larger and better debating schedule with other schools in the county and the valley.[38] The debating question during the 1927-28 school year has a curiously modern connotation: "Resolved: That the United States is justified in her present policy in Nicaragua." Dorothy Donahoe was a member of the successful debate squad during the 1927-28 school year. She stayed at the school as registrar for a number of years before being elected to the California State Assembly. No doubt her experience in debate provided a background to her state legislative career. Donahoe Hall on the California State College, Bakersfield campus is named after this Kern County High School graduate of 1928. The school's debaters were successful in the new league and, in fact, they won the state championship two years successively after its formation. In 1929-30, the school became a member of the Central California Public Speaking League and entered a contest in an extemporaneous speaking division, and the representative, Isabelle Hanawalt, ultimately won first place.[39]

An unofficial adjunct to the school's activities program during the 1920's was the Robesky Corner. In 1921, Thomas Albert Robesky established a family enterprise on 14th Street across from the campus which was for more than twenty years to become an intrinsic part of the school's operation. Al Robesky had previously been in the bakery business in Bakersfield; his idea was to build a store to prepare snacks for the students. It should be remembered that at this time there was no student cafeteria or other place for students to obtain food on campus. The store turned out to be much more than just a place to buy snacks. It actually was a social center for students. Eventually, they were able to buy homemade pies, maple sticks, and rolls from the Robesky Bakery as well as a full line of school supplies such as notebooks, tablets, pencils, and pens and ink. In the early Twenties, no student store existed on campus, and the school did not furnish these supplies. The Robeskys had three sons; Donald, who has already been mentioned as an outstanding athlete, Thomas, and Kenneth. All three of them were later to become educators with the District as well as two of their wives, Barbara and Margo.[40] The whole family worked in the store. Mother and father would get up at 4:00 a.m. to prepare the fresh bakery goods for the hungry students later in the day. Apparently Mr. Robesky believed in hard work and would not countenance students hanging around the store when they were supposed to be in class. Counselor Leo B. Hart recalls particularly that he was most conscientious in cooperating with the school.

In 1977, the school newspaper published an article written by Kenneth Robesky. This youngest member of the Robesky family was Principal of Bakersfield High School at the time of his death in the spring of 1977. The newspaper editor added the heading, "The Last Hurrah." The article mentions that the family lived in back of the store and he grew up with the campus as his playground. He made special note of the fact that Principal Spindt came into the store everyday "...at precisely 3:00 and had a coke...", making it most difficult for the young Robesky to think of cutting school. When Ken was a little tad in diapers, he spent a lot of time in the physical education department following Coach Griffith around, the latter apparently being the idol of most of the boys in town. Since the boy lived on campus, he had more opportunity than most to get to know the famous coach. One day, while following Coach Griffith in the stadium, Ken had an accident, not being able to get to the bathroom on time. When Coach Griffith discovered it, he "...put Ken immediately under the heat lamp---and returned him to his mommy in exactly the same way he acquired him."[41]

To give an added dimension to the school activities of the Twenties, we once again refer to the recollections of Harold Brewer. The school was quite large, even in 1925, and the freshman was concerned about making his way in this mammoth institution:

> I remember distinctly standing on the steps of the auditorium and I think I was literally shaking with fright. This fellow came up and started chatting with me, apparently to ease some of my tension. He introduced himself as Harry Smith, saying, "I'm president of the student body of Kern County Union High School". As a side light, Jack Smith, columnist for the <u>Los Angeles Times</u>, is his younger brother.[42]

After this encounter with a "big man on campus", the freshman felt much more at ease. As he got better acquainted, he found the social life of the school most enjoyable.

> For entertainment the students would go about once a month to a student dance....four or five couples went to all the dances together. After the dance, we would go to someone's home; for example, the Doctor Morris' home on the west end of 19th Street. The Morris' daughter, Isabelle, was often my date. Mrs. Morris would serve dinner to us and that would complete the evening. Once they came to our home on 17th Street near "B". My mother had just learned to bake enchiladas and served them to the group. In those days there were not so many Mexican restaurants as we have now.

There was dancing elsewhere in the city for high school students which was not school-sponsored. Mr. Brewer recalls private dances in a ballroom held above the Bakersfield Garage (across the street from the Fox Theater). Several girls including Frances Allen, Bernice Brandt, Viola Weir, and Virginia Voorhies had organized a club and held dances in the ballroom. He was often invited because of his interest in dancing. School dances were held in the gymnasium in those days.

As a footnote to student life during this era, one could say that interest in the automobile was universal. A few of the more fortunate students had access to autos, according to Mr. Brewer:

> In those days, the people of high school age who had automobiles were very rare. Those who had them included Angus Crites, Arthur Crites' son. He had a Lincoln roadster, a beautiful car. Martha and Martin Gundlach had a car, but were not allowed by their parents to pick up any of us who had to walk. Ethel Bailey (Guinn) had an old, beat-up Ford sedan. Donald Ross had a great big Chevrolet touring car which might have belonged to his parents, but he drove it to school. They all parked on 13th Street along the side of where the old auditorium used to be. People don't realize perhaps that this was a different era -- a time when automobiles were a novelty.

The Junior College in this Decade

Keeping pace with the growth of the district during the Twenties, the Junior College Division emerged as a full-blown "school within a school" during the decade. This growth was not only in terms of students, but also in terms of curriculum, activities, and athletics, all the characteristics that make up a college institution. This is well-chronicled by Grace Van Dyke Bird in an oral history recently completed at the University of California at Berkeley. In this account, Miss Bird tells of accepting, with many reservations, a position at Kern County Union High School in the Fall of 1917 upon the recommendation of a friend. Her reservations were due no doubt to the state-wide reputation Bakersfield had as a rough, western town. She was reassured, however, by talking with a scholarly friend who had given a lecture on classical Greece in Bakersfield. He, too, had some concerns about his reception. However, upon being a guest at dinner with the Alphonse Weill family, his appreciation for the area, and its level of culture represented by the Weill family and others he met, was greatly enhanced. According to Miss Bird:

> Well, I, too, found Bakersfield had contrasts; but, now there was a very high ratio of people of education and culture. It still had a frontier atmosphere with its major activities agriculture and petroleum, but it had an atmosphere of generosity, intelligence, and goodwill.[43]

Miss Bird was assigned to teach French to junior college classes, and French and English at the high school. Immediately, she fashioned a reputation as an effective teacher, one who cared for students and became actively involved with them in the educational process. As Phillip Wagy puts it:

> She taught me French when I was a freshman, and for about the first month, I didn't know whether I was coming or going, but she was very patient. Before I got through that class I got an "A". She was one of the best teachers I ever had at any time.[44]

In 1921, after serving the previous year as acting Dean of the Junior College Division in the absence of Paul VanderEike, Miss Bird was appointed full-time Dean of this division of instruction. There was no other woman in California who held such a responsible role in the junior college system, which was rapidly spreading throughout the state. For several years, she continued her teaching and for some time she also carried the title of Vice-Principal of the high school, with the responsibility for coordinating the instruction of the high school and the junior college.

By the end of this decade, enrollment in the junior college had grown from fifty students to approximately 400. The new Dean and other staff members attempted to keep academic standards high for the university transfer program, since a large majority of the students did go on to four-year institutions, some after only one year at the college. According to Ray Chism,

> The quality of instruction and standards of reading were well-supported by the university records of the transfer students. The reputation for excellent academic preparation was a source of quiet pride and a reason for the president of the University of California to be interested in this growing college.[45]

It was at this time that the Southern Extension of the University of California had been established at Los Angeles, later to be known as UCLA. President Robert Gordon Sproul, determined that quality education would exist in the new university extension, lived each year for one semester at Los Angeles. In passing through Bakersfield, because of these sojourns to the two campuses, he and his family often stopped over for a visit and lunch break with Grace Bird. These visits must have been a source of mutual enrichment for both the young junior college administrator and the University of California President.[46]

However, the college program was also concerned with the non-transfer students. Classes had been developed in accounting, business mathematics and office training as an extension of the high school's long standing commercial course. Two new curricula were developed during this time to meet community needs. One was in nursing, since there was a shortage of nurses throughout the community, and a second in electrical technology. The latter course was developed by Kenneth W. Rich who was later to become Principal of East Bakersfield High School.

A sizable portion of the 1930 edition of The Oracle is devoted to the Renegades and is dedicated to Dean Bird. The student newspaper, The Renegade Rip, had just been organized and according to the write-up in the yearbook, "...has done its bit to

110

unify the student body." Two prominent graduates of the college are given credit for the soubriquets "Renegade" and "Rip". Morris Chain, a long-time attorney in Bakersfield, is said to have coined the name "Renegades" in the middle Twenties in describing the rooting section as "...nothing but a bunch of renegades!"[47] E. Ben Evans, District administrator and a graduate of Bakersfield College, attached the name "Rip" to the student newspaper.[48] The student body was organized into the Associated Students and there was also the Associated Women Students, which aimed to provide a "...mutual understanding and interest among the women students."

Leland Tallman advised and coached the debate squad, which that year won the championship of Central California Junior College Association. Other activities included Omega Tau, the honor society; Delta Psi Omega, the dramatic honor fraternity; the French club; the Scribbler's Club; the Varsity Club for the Renegade athletes; Kappa Rho Sigma for the science students; YMCA On the Job; and the Rooters' Club.

In athletics, some strengths were beginning to emerge. The football team, coached by former Kern County Union High School football star, Theo "spud" Harder, was undefeated in the conference and won the Central California Junior College Association championship in the 1929-30 school year. Junior college athletes also participated in tennis, basketball and track, rounding out a fairly complete athletic schedule for a school of some 400 students. Completing the activities' program for the year, the college students produced two plays, "Mr. Pimm Passes By" and "The Queen's Husband", giving evidence to a vital dramatic program directed by Ethel Robinson. This was abetted and encouraged, no doubt, by Dean Bird who took part in the dramatics program of the school when she first came to the district. Forty graduates of the college are pictured in the 1930 yearbook.

Two New District Institutions

This decade was remarkable for the addition of two "branch campuses" which were located away from the city of Bakersfield

111

and the parent campus of Kern County Union High School. Both branches were established in rural communities fifteen or twenty miles away at the request of petitioners from the communities of McFarland and Shafter.

McFarland High School

McFarland High School has a somewhat longer history, according to the District Board minutes, than that of Shafter. As early as December, 1921, the Board was visited by a delegation from McFarland requesting establishment of a branch school. This delegation was headed by County Supervisor A. B. McFarland. The matter was taken under advisement by the Board, suggesting that "...the request was of such importance as would require a close study of the local and financial stages of the matter, and a committee would be appointed to investigate the proposition fully."[49] The branch was authorized by the Board in the minutes of the July 6, 1922, meeting. No further reference to the McFarland branch is contained in the minutes for some four years. However, according to a special edition of the McFarland Press, some high school classes were actually held, following the Board's direction, in the basement of the Brethern Church. These classes were conducted by a Mr. Hanawalt. However, according to this account, the effort survived only one school term, and students were later either transported by bus to Bakersfield or used their own transportation to go to Delano High School.[50] Undaunted, citizens from McFarland once more appeared before the Board in June of 1926 and requested that a branch high school be established.[51] Classes got underway that fall and were held on the upper floor of the grammar school with Edith Fitzgibbon and Miss Lindquist as teachers for thirteen freshmen students.[52] The 1927-28 Oracle lists four faculty members at the McFarland branch, Edith Fitzgibbon, Ann Harder, Paul R. Jackson and Ruth Smith.

Events moved rather quickly for McFarland High School after this. In the spring of 1928, the Board authorized a $300,000.00 bond election to acquire land, to erect buildings for the high school campuses in McFarland and Shafter, along with other school needs.[53] A page of the 1929 Oracle is devoted to the activities of McFarland High School with the total student body pictured in front of the new building. The account states:

> A real school spirit must be created within a group with no traditional standards to follow. Each one seemed to assume cheerfully his part of this responsibility. Consequently, we are closing the year with a strong student body organization, a working system of self-government and no small amount of pride and confidence in our school.[54]

It was noted that two plays had been produced under the direction of Edith Fitzgibbon, that both girls and boys had played a series of games in baseball and basketball with Shafter, and that the latter had taken part in a county track meet. Fifteen students were enrolled in the agricultural department, an indication of future growth in this instructional area. The music department had a girls' glee club and an orchestra, and they had given a combined recital. The new building with eight rooms including the principal's office was completed in November, 1928.

Shafter High School

The growing agricultural community of Shafter, some fifteen miles northwest of Bakersfield, also felt the need for an educational institution. One rationale for the new institution was that the commute to Bakersfield was long and uncomfortable for high school age students. Accordingly, in the fall of 1923, a delegation from the Shafter community appeared at a Kern County Union High School Board meeting with a petition for the establishment of a branch high school in Shafter. As in the case of the McFarland request, the Board set up a committee to investigate the matter.[55] No immediate results of the petition were forthcoming. According to an article in the Shafter Press published on the 50th anniversary of the establishment of Shafter High School, Principal Spindt and members of the Board of Trustees thought it would be too expensive to establish a separate school at Shafter. They also believed that the fifteen minute ride to and from Bakersfield was not an onerous burden for the few high school students to bear. However, a group of influential Shafter citizens were not content to let the idea die. Headed by W. B. Camp, Director of the Shafter Agricultural Experiment

Station, several determined citizens of the community including E. B. "Doc" Stringham, Herbert Midgley, and Clarence Campbell, set out to find candidates for the Board of Trustees who would be sympathetic to their point of view.

> First they approached Charles Melcher of McFarland, earlier developer of the Reiber grape and a member of local and state farm bureaus. It was a rainy day, Mr. Camp remembers, wet and slippery, as they drove into Melcher's ranch and entered the living room to sit by the fire. Mr. Melcher was sympathetic to the feeling that children in McFarland, as well as in Shafter, ought to be going to high school without having to travel so far. He finally agreed to run for the Board of Trustees if they could also persuade Judge T. N. Harvey of Bakersfield to run.[56]

This political ploy was a success and both Mr. Melcher and Judge Harvey were elected to the Board of Trustees in the spring of 1927.[57] In February of 1928, another petition was forthcoming from residents of the Richland School District in Shafter, and this petition would have more immediate results: a resolution by the Board for a $300,000.00 bond election scheduled for mid-April, 1928. With solid support by The Bakersfield Californian and the California Taxpayer's Association, the request was approved by taxpayers with a two-thirds majority. Funds were then available to begin the campuses at both McFarland and Shafter. In addition, there was financing to make improvements to the parent campus in Bakersfield.[58] One major problem remained for the Shafter school, and that was its location.

> The Shafter citizens decided they wanted the high school to be located north of the railroad tracks. That posed a problem for W. B. Camp. That land is where he planned to develop his ranch, but he knew he was obligated to sell the land if that is where the people wanted the school.[59]

A month later, the Board accepted an offer by S. A. and W. B. Camp for a parcel of land of some fifteen acres at the purchase price of $375.00 per acre. Thus the location of the school was decided.[58] Work began on the new campus almost immediately and the hope was that the school could open in the fall. Actually classes did open on September 17th, but not in the new high school building. Apparently, the Union Congregational Church and, perhaps, the Shafter Women's Club, and the American Legion buildings were the various sites in which the two classes of some fifty students, freshmen and sophomore, began their high school studies. It was not until later in the fall that the new building was ready for occupancy. In the 1929 Oracle, a page was devoted to Shafter High School as had been done for McFarland. A picture of the new building with the total student body and faculty is shown. According to the write-up, the student body had been organized with officers elected at the beginning of the year. Bill McClain was president.

> Splendid athletic grounds have been developed out of what used to be a cotton field. Competitive games were played between McFarland and Shafter girls in basketball and baseball. The boys also played basketball and baseball with McFarland, Bakersfield and Wasco, and were represented in track.
>
> A musical concert was given in April which was very successful. Fine work in dramatics was shown in the play "Seventeen" by Booth Tarkington, presented in the latter part of May.[61]

Vice-Principal Paul VanderEike wrote a congratulatory message to Shafter and McFarland High School student bodies in this same yearbook. His words may well have been representative of the feelings in both communities when he said,

> Your school may not be now all you expected, but you have a greater affection for it because it is your own in your home community. Although there is always room for improvement, I believe you are doing your best to prepare yourselves for the big job of making a life.

The affection for a school of their own continued to be manifested by citizens of both communities, as the two high schools grew in numbers and in the quality of educational programs. According to the June 3, 1929, minutes of the Board, both of these schools were made "regular four-year institutions". The first "outreach" institutions of the district have continued to expand in both numbers and quality of instruction throughout the years. While McFarland High School left the district in 1979 to become a member of the newly organized McFarland Unified School District, for some thirty-eight years it prospered and served the residents of that community. Shafter remains one of the District schools to this date, in spite of the several efforts at unification.

The District at the End of the Twenties

At the end of the 1920's, the Kern County Union High School District had enjoyed positive gains in almost all fields. Enrollment was nearing the 3,000 mark, which would be reached the following year (1930-31). The two branch campuses both had an enrollment of eighty-five students at the beginning of the 1929-30 school year, while the Junior College Division enrolled some 350 students. The parent campus in Bakersfield was a large institution with approximately 2,250. This campus was adding buildings at its location between 14th Street and California Avenue, now containing a dozen structures. These included the original building, now called the Commercial Building; the Administration Building with the Auditorium attached; two Gymnasiums; the Agriculture and Science buildings at the southern extremity of the campus; Ludden Hall for domestic science; Griffith Stadium, laid out personally by Coach Griffith and in use since 1923; the Library; and the two newest structures, a Manual Arts Building, which replaced the old one adjacent to the Commercial Building in Elm Grove, and the Junior College structure. In addition, the school operated dormitories for both boys and girls, for students who lived some distance from the campus. Of course, the major buildings at both Shafter and McFarland were in place by this time, with additions in planning stages. In the spring of 1929, Howard K. Dickson, the Agriculture Department Head, had presented an extensive plan for a school farm laboratory to be housed on an acreage some distance away from the campus. The result was an exemplary school-farm facility in place shortly after the beginning of the 1930's.

The budget adopted for the 1929-30 school year totalled $578,500.00, with an additional $35,000.00 to be expended for the purchase of land and instructional equipment.[62] Staff salaries ranged from $6,000.00, paid to Superintendent Spindt, to an $1,800.00, starting salary for beginning teachers.[63] In 1927, the Board adopted a salary schedule of eight steps beginning at

$1,800.00 and extending to $2,700.00. This is the first reference to a specific salary schedule to be found in the Board minutes. Certain options were reserved by the Board action

> The privilege of going outside the schedule for teachers with family responsibilities and for special salaries for heads of departments or special teachers.[64]

In addition, bonuses were allowed after a fourth year of service. An allowance of $50.00 per year was granted for two years provided the teacher attended summer sessions. Thus, the formula of salary schedules which extends to modern time was made with vertical steps for experience and lateral classifications for professional advancement through college work. Three years later some sophistication was added to the salary program with the adoption of a plan for professional improvement of teachers. This contained a provision that at least once each three years, a teacher must show evidence of professional growth in order to maintain the maximum salary or the regular rate of increases. The penalty was the reduction of $100.00 salary per year. Evidence of professional growth could be presented by the following:

1. Attendance at summer session carrying a total load of six units once each three years.

2. The carrying of extension work of an equivalent value.

3. The writing of outlines, syllabi, textbooks, or special articles dealing with the teacher's subject.

4. Extra curricular work within the high school student body of such a nature as to markedly increase the teacher's efficiency.

5. Travel or foreign places visited that will be of value in the teacher's work.

6. The reading or reporting on professional books or books dealing with the teacher's subject.

7. Individual committee or group study of special problems of the local district.

(This plan of professional improvement replaced the bonus system which had been in operation for several years.)[65]

It would be remiss to close this chapter without calling attention to the character of members of the Board of Trustees. Mention was made earlier in connection with the establishment of Shafter High School of the election in 1927 of Judge T. N. Harvey and Carl A. Melcher. In 1929, Judge Harvey was elected President of the Board to succeed Boyce R. Fitzgerald. Mr. Fitzgerald had been on the Board since 1918 and served as President since 1925, as well as during the 1920-21 school year. Another well-known Board member during the twenties was David E. Urner, Bakersfield businessman. Mr. Urner had been a mathematics teacher at the high school just before the beginning of the Twenties; and, in fact, had been assistant football coach for the first state championship team in 1916. Another prominent citizen on the Board for two years just at the end of the Twenties, was A. C. Dimon. Judge Harvey's tenure of office with the Board, beginning with his election in 1927, lasted until his death in 1948, and during that time he was President of the Board for nineteen years, certainly an enviable record of service to the school district and to the community.

Personalities who were associated with the district at the close of the Twenties are two men who were later to make an inestimable contribution in leadership to the district. They are the two men with the same unlikely first name who were friends at Stanford, Theron Taber and Theron L. McCuen. The former came to the District first in the 1928-29 school year as a teacher of mathematics and suggested to his friend from Stanford days, Theron McCuen, that he also apply for a position the following fall. The future Superintendent was assigned to the drawing department in the fall of 1929.

In closing the story of this era of the District, the words of Principal H. A. Spindt in the 1929-30 school yearbook are appropriate:

> The year 1929-30 has been marked by continued growth especially in the high school department. The

statistics of enrollment indicate that the increase in the freshman class is not nearly as great as the increase in the three upper years. This is especially borne out by the very great increase in a number of graduates this year. We have 330 this year in comparison to 257 last year. Increase in registration has been particularly marked in the rural districts of Kern County Union High School District, and, to take care of this great increase, Shafter and McFarland high schools have been made regular four-year schools, and three new buses have been purchased for Bakersfield. The establishment of vocational majors in the high school has seemingly caused a considerable trend toward vocational work on the part of our students. The Junior College has not increased appreciably in numbers this year but has increased in opportunities given to the students in the choice of studies...

. . . . . .

This message will not be complete unless I call to the attention of the Student Body the services rendered to the Kern County Union High School District and its various schools by the members of the Board of Trustees, whose pictures you find on the opposite page. They have given unselfishly of their time and energy in order that you might have the very best in educational equipment and instruction. Being a member of a school Board of Trustees is frequently a very thankless task. Might it not be our hope so to conduct ourselves both in school and after graduation that no member of the Board of Trustees may regret the efforts he has put forth on our behalf?

REFERENCES

CHAPTER III - WORLD WAR I AND THE TWENTIES

1. Miller, Thelma B., History of Kern County, California, Vol. I, (Boston: The S.S. Clarke Publishing Company, 1928), p. 511.

2. Ibid., p. 512.

3. Ibid., p. 532.

4. Minutes, Kern County Union High School District; May 4, 1918.

5. The Oracle, 1917.

6. Ibid., 1918.

7. Taped interview with Harry Drennan.

8. Minutes, Kern County Union High School District; May 23, 1917.

9. Evans, Kristianne Skjerve; An Educational Survey of Kern County, California; Part III, "The High Schools of Kern County", Unpublished, Unpaged document, 1918.

10. Ibid.

11. Ibid.

12. Ibid.

13. Minutes, Kern County Union High School District; November 13, 1919.

14. Taped interview with Harold Pauly.

15. Minutes, Kern County Union High School District; September 8, 1917.

16. Ibid.; September 18, 1916.

17. The Oracle; 1917.

18. Ibid., 1918.

19. Taped interview with Theodore S. Hougham.

20. Minutes, Kern County Union High School District; February 4, 1918.

21. The Oracle; 1918.

References - Chapter III (Continued)

22. Manuscript by Mark F. Wilcox in files of Bakersfield High School, 1943.

23. Taped interview with Ruth Emerson Stutzman.

24. Drennan interview.

25. Minutes, Kern County Union High School District; March 6, 1922.

26. The Oracle, 1922.

27. Ibid., 1926.

28. Taped interview with Senator Walter Stiern

29. The Oracle, 1917.

30. The Oracle, 1929.

31. Taped interview with E. Ben Evans.

32. Taped interview with Ruth Emerson Stutzman.

33. Taped interview with Harold Brewer.

34. Taped interview with Leo B. Hart.

35. Taped interview with Phillip M. Wagy.

36. Ibid.

37. The Oracle, 1930.

38. Ibid., 1928.

39. Ibid., 1929.

40. Taped interview with Margo, Donald, and Thomas Robesky.

41. The Blue and White, (Bakersfield High School student newspaper), June, 6, 1977, p. 1.

42. Brewer interview. A note from Jack Smith of the Los Angeles Times states that his brother, Harry, later became Student Body President at Whittier College.

43. Bird, p. 36

44. Wagy interview

45. Chism, Ray A. A Preliminary History of Bakersfield College, Unpublished manuscript (Bakersfield, California), 1981, p. 8.

References - Chapter III (Continued)

46. Ibid., p. 8.
47. Ibid., p. 8.
48. Evans' interview.
49. Minutes, Kern County Union High School District, December 5, 1921.
50. McFarland Press, (McFarland, California), Special Edition, November 17, 1968.
51. Minutes, Kern County Union High School District, June 6, 1926.
52. McFarland Press, November 18, 1968.
53. Minutes, Kern County Union High School District, March 5, 1928.
54. The Oracle, 1929.
55. Minutes, Kern County Union High School District, October 1, 1923.
56. Wheeler, Jeanette; "Shafter High School, Fifty Years of Teaching Local Students"; Shafter Press (Shafter, California), May 24, 1978.
57. Minutes, Kern County Union High School District, April 1, 1927.
58. Ibid., April 20, 1928.
59. Wheeler article.
60. Minutes, Kern County Union High School District, May 9, 1928.
61. The Oracle, 1929.
62. Minutes, Kern County Union High School District, June 3, 1929.
63. Ibid., May 1, 1929.
64. Ibid., May 9, 1927.
65. Ibid., May 3, 1930.
66. The Oracle, 1930.

James Bryant Conant, educator, scholar, writer, and well-known President of Harvard University visited the District in the Fifties. He is shown here with Kern County Union High School Board President, Harold E. Woodworth, left, and Superintendent Theron L. McCuen when he came to the District gathering information for his book **The American High School Today.** The book was published in 1959.

Dedication ceremonies for a new Bakersfield College campus in the Fall of 1956 fulfilled a dream of the "campus on the hill" for former College Director Grace V. Bird. Pictured here with Miss Bird are: Ralph Prator, College President; Robert Gordon Sproul, featured speaker and President of the University of California; Theron McCuen, Kern County Union High School District Superintendent and Kern County Union High School District Board President, Harold E. Woodworth. At this time, Bakersfield College was a member institution of the high school district.

Chester W. O'Neill is honored upon his retirement from the Kern County Union High School District Board in 1959. Shown with him are Edward Simonsen, Bakersfield College President, and Mrs. Mable O'Neill. Mr. O'Neill was first elected to the Board in 1940.

Superintendent's Advisory Council in the spring of 1962: Standing (L-R) Allen Cannon, Director of Instruction; Gerald W. Hedden, newly selected Principal of Foothill; Edward Simonsen, President, Bakersfield College; Kenneth Westcott, Principal, Burroughs High School; George Williamson, Principal, North High School; Grant W. Jensen, Principal of South High School; J.S. Wallace, Principal of Bakesfield High School; Thomas Henley, Principal of McFarland High School; Edwin De Mello, Principal of Arvin High School; E.C. (Bus) Mills, newly selected Principal of East Bakersfield High School; and Avery Allen, Administrative Assistant to the Superintendent.
Seated (L-R) Earl Murray, Principal, Kern Valley High School; John W. Eckhardt, Assistant Superintendent for Personnel and Instruction; Theron L. McCuen, Superintendent; Irving Lane, retiring Principal of East Bakersfield High School; and, Arthur Johnson, Principal of Shafter High School. Deputy Superintendent Theron Taber was not present for the picture.

Surrounded by a crowd of well wishers Coach Dwight M. Griffith is shown at the time he retired from coaching at ceremonies held in 1948. The famous coach is pictured with Governor Earl Warren, graduate of the Kern County Union High School class of 1908, who was the featured speaker at the occasion. The car is a new Buick automobile which was presented to Mr. Griffith as a gift by a group of Bakersfield citizens.
Courtesy of Kern High School District

The local advisory committee to the publication of the oral history about Grace V. Bird, former Bakersfield College Director, are shown conferring with the representative from the University of California, Berkeley, just before publication of the book in 1978. (L-R) Edward Simonsen, College District Chancellor; Robert Young, Bakersfield College professor; Thomas Merson, Bakersfield College Dean of Instruction; Margaret Levinson, retired Bakersfield College Dean of Instruction; Avery Allen, retired District Administrator; Ralda Sullivan, Regional Oral History office; Bancroft Library, University of California, Berkeley; and Edna Tabor, College Business Manager.

CHAPTER IV

THE THIRTIES AND WORLD WAR II

Facing the Depression

At the beginning of the 1930's, the Kern County Union High School District had emerged from the madcap Twenties seemingly with the expectation that the growth and progress which had been experienced during this decade would continue indefinitely. The size of the District was now approximately 3,000 students and outlying campuses at McFarland and Shafter were well established. In addition, the system had extended its instructional program to include the tuberculosis sanitarium at Keene during the 1930-31 school year. There were, however, some ominous signs on the horizon. The community of Bakersfield and the County of Kern were not to escape the depressing financial experiences of the decade which would devastate the country generally.

In his annual message to the student body in the 1931 school yearbook, Principal Spindt called attention to progress that had been made in building the campus and improving its general appearance with the optimistic prediction that "...we all look forward with great anticipation to the construction of our new auditorium." The astute school leader could not have known that events would occur that would delay the completion of this auditorium some eighteen years. He went on to comment about some of the District problems...."not the least of these is the financial one dealt with by the Board of Trustees. It takes a great deal of money to run a high school. We should all express our appreciation to the Board of Trustees...for the continuous services they have so freely and efficiently given us."[1]

While it would appear that Bakersfield and Kern County were not as sorely devastated by the dire economic conditions of the early Thirties which pervaded most of the country, the area certainly did not escape unscathed. In 1931 two representatives of the local contractors' association appeared before the Board and asked that consideration be given to building the auditorium "...in the near future - because of the low cost of materials at the present time and because of unemployment among the skilled trade workers of Bakersfield."[2] Soon, because of dropping assessed valuation per student in the district, Principal Spindt would be forced to recommend to the Board a reduction in salary schedules and a further look for ways to reduce the cost of operating the District.

Another effect upon the school system which reflected the times occurred later in the decade when, because of the "dust bowl" conditions in the midwest, large numbers of people were to migrate west and to Kern County. The result was booming enrollments, particularly in the junior college. This influx of migrants brought a national spotlight to the working and living conditions of these unfortunate people who came to Kern County, which was often unwelcome to many local residents. Best known, perhaps, of these expose's was the novel by John Steinbeck, The Grapes of Wrath, some of which was set in the Kern area. William T. Rintoul describes the banning of the novel from Kern County's libraries, quoting the resolution of the Kern County Board of Supervisors: "The Grapes of Wrath has offended our citizenry by falsely implying that many of our fine people are a low, ignorant, profane, and blasphemous type, living in a vicious, filthy manner."[3] Passed in August of 1939, the resolution further requested 20th Century Film Corporation not to complete the picture based upon the book. It was reported that Darryl F. Zanuck answered this request stating that the film company was obliged to continue or be sued by the author. The Supervisors' resolution included the schools in its ban; however, it is interesting to note that Grace Bird, in her oral biography, was particularly proud of the fact that the Steinbeck novel remained on the library shelves of the college.[4]

There can be no question, then, that these events of national prominence cast their long shadows over the operations of the Kern County Union High School District.

District Activities During This Decade

In spite of the financial hardships of the early Thirties, which affected the District to a serious extent, it was necessary to cope with the needs that grew out of the increases in enrollment and the geographical expansion to other campuses. One of the most consuming growth needs was that of the construction of a new auditorium. The building at the corner of California and 'F' Streets housed the Junior College Division. It later accommodated the music classes, and, finally, when the historic Commercial Building was abandoned, the commercial classes. The building was intended to be an adjunct to an auditorium to be erected in what is now Elm Grove. A letter from student body president, M. Glenn Bultman, was received in January, 1931, urging the Board to proceed with the new Auditorium.[5] The old Auditorium, which joined the Administration Building, was by this time sadly out-of-date, and was to be abandoned completely by the end of the decade.

Apparently the Board of Trustees recognized the need for a new auditorium and made some determined efforts to secure the funds for its construction during the mid Thirties. In fact, in early 1934, the Board passed a resolution calling for a bond election to the tune of $300,000.00 specifically for the construction of a new auditorium.[6] Apparently this was not an opportune time to ask taxpayers to increase their load even though the nation was emerging from the depression. Later that year another bond election was called and again it was rejected.[7] In the meantime, a new source of funds became available as a part of the Federal program to stimulate the economy, and on October 1, 1934, the Board approved a resolution to enter into an agreement with the Federal government for a loan and grant not to exceed $100,000.00 for financing the construction of an auditorium building.[8] The application for the PWA grant was completed by mid-1935, but it was to be another six years before work actually began on the building.

Curiously, further mention of the use of Federal moneys in building the Auditorium is absent from the minutes of the Board even though there are references to several PWA grants which actually materialized and were used during the 40's and until the beginning of World War II. After two more tries at a bond election, one was finally passed in December of 1935 with no reference to funds to be used for the building of the Auditorium.[9] Finally, in 1939, the old Auditorium was declared to be unsafe and the building was closed.[10]

At the opening of the 1939-40 school year, the Board took favorable action on the Principal's recommendation that the Auditorium seats be moved outdoors for the seating of students at assemblies, and "....that the tents be moved to a new location just north of the old Auditorium."[11] Early in 1940 the Board, apparently taking a dim view of students in tents for school activities, took positive action on plans for the new Auditorium. But, it was to be a tempestuous story of military intervention, lawsuits, and general frustration before the building was finally completed after the close of World War II.

In August of 1930, a building inspection had taken place at the Commercial Building, and the report to the Board indicated that, although it was structurally sound, it did constitute a fire hazard.[12] Mr. Spindt, in his message in the 1934 yearbook, states as follows:

> "A sentence of death has been pronounced on the venerable old commercial building built in 1895, and now declared unsafe for continued occupancy. Its place on our grounds will eventually be taken by the new auditorium, so badly needed from the viewpoint of safety. The commercial department will be moved to the new building between the music and junior college buildings."[13]

Thus, the historic structure was demolished to make way for an auditorium which was never to be built on that site. Actually, the eventual decision to build the structure on a site east of Elm Grove seems in retrospect to have been wise, for a parklike area was then created in the center of the campus which was eventually the home of some 5,000 students.

Staff Related Problems

During the Thirties there appeared in the minutes of the Board more items related to the welfare of staff members, particularly teachers, than was true earlier, except perhaps for such unusual incidents as have been recounted under the heading "The Peckham Incident" occurring in the early 1900's. In 1931, the Board took action on a policy relating to the status of married teachers. "...that married teachers shall not be given permanent rating. This shall not be construed to automatically discharge a probationary teacher after marriage."[14] It would appear that this policy might pose difficulties in its future application, and it is evident in the actual operation of the District that it was not strictly followed.

Salaries of staff members received a great deal of attention during this year. In 1932, the Principal presented a comparative study of salaries in twenty of the leading cities of California. The comparison showed, "...that the average schedule in these twenty cities was above the salary paid in the Kern County High School District."[15] Although the study was discouraging, the District was unable to raise salaries. In fact, the salary schedule for 1932-33 contained reductions over the previous year. Beginning salaries for teachers were to be $1,740.00 in comparison with the previous year's $1,800.00. All staff members re-hired were to receive no reduction on the first $1,200.00 of their salaries, but all moneys over that were to be reduced ten per cent. The Principal, who was now called "Superintendent" for the first time in the minutes of the Board, also took a pay cut with a salary of $5,520.00 reduced from $6,000.00.[16] The following year the Board mandated the Superintendent to order a salary schedule that was reduced fifteen per cent over that of the previous year. However, when the final action was taken, the fifteen per cent was ameliorated somewhat, both for teachers and non-teaching staff. In recognition of the fact that teachers had contributed liberally of their salaries to student aid and community enterprises, it was agreed that no teacher's salary should be reduced more than fourteen per cent over the previous year. Again, Superintendent Spindt led the way in recommending a reduction of his own salary to $5,100.00.[17]

The following year, along with the rest of the country, the Kern County Union High School District was feeling some release from repressive times and teachers were given a flat increase of $100.00 for the 1934-35 school year. It is noteworthy that salaries of teachers were to be paid on a twelve month basis "...subject to a personal agreement to return any part of the salary paid in advance in case a teacher did not return for service in September." Beginning teachers would still be paid on a ten month basis, however.[18] The action was taken by the Board after the teachers were polled in an election and the vote favored a twelve month plan. This is one of the first instances in which the Board took cognizance of the organized expression of teacher opinion.

Significantly, the following spring the Board received a letter from one Wiley K. Peterson, a successful teacher of forensics, asking for an increase in salary because "of my hours of extra work". His request was supported by the Superintendent, and the Board directed the latter to present a list of "...suggestions for increases based on either superior teaching or extra-curricular activities."[19] Accordingly at the next Board meeting, the Superintendent presented a list of twelve staff members who qualified for "merit increases". These staff members received salary bonuses of $50.00 to $100.00. This list included the names of Grace Van Dyke Bird, Harold J. Burt, Wallace D. Frost, Wiley K. Peterson, Donald A. Robesky, George Williamson, Robert H. Young, Gerald Smith, Cornelius Siemens, Orpha Mae Barnes, Mary Jacobs, and Emily Wentner.[20] Courageous action, perhaps, on the part of the Superintendent and the Board of Trustees in the controversial arena of merit pay, still an unresolved educational issue.

At the beginning of the 1936-37 school year, the salary schedule was again adjusted upward. Beginning teachers were to receive $1,600.00 and increases were scheduled from $50.00 to

$100.00, depending upon the place on the schedule, with those in the lower salary brackets to receive the greatest increases. That sexism remained in the schedule is indicated by the following statement: "The maximum schedule for women teachers was fixed at $2,350.00, with possible maximum for men teachers with special responsibilities, $2,500.00."[21] The Principal's salary was now back at the $6,000.00 level, where it had been in 1933 before the salary cutting program. To complete the circle of salary movement in the Thirties, in the spring of 1939 for the ensuing year, a new salary schedule was adopted, complete with fourteen steps, beginning with $1,800.00 and ending with a maximum of $3,000.00 for the fifteenth year. The schedule allowed up to six years of experience in other secondary school systems at one-half the actual experience time. It also permitted the addition of $20-$50.00 for "extra duties above the average teacher load on the recommendation of the Superintendent". Department heads would receive $50-$200.00 above the schedule. Salaries for administrators "...and other positions not on the regular teachers' schedule will be determined by the Superintendent". The final provison was for salaries "...in any position to exceed the regular schedule on recommendation of the Superintendent". This latter stipulation was to be used "...when supply and demand or the conditions make it advisable". Furthermore, the schedule included ten days sick leave accumulative to thirty days, with additional sick leave time to be charged to the teacher on the difference between his or her salary, and that of the substitute. There was also an inservice provision for four units of college work or the equivalent to be completed once every five years. The summer school bonuses which had been granted on the previous informal salary arrangements were to be phased out; they had allowed $50.00 per year for a three year period.

The 1939-40 schedule was the real beginning of the modern salary schedule for the Kern County Union High School District. It should be noted, however, provisions were not so automatic as those in the modern salary schedule. The Superintendent was responsible for recommending the amounts appropriate for extra duties, department heads, and for others not on the regular schedule.[22] The Superintendent himself was given a four-year contract with salaries progressing from the $6,000.00 figure for the first year, to $6,600.00 for the final year. A final note regarding personnel relations in that decade occurs in the minutes of the Board under the subject "Policy on Tenure" during the 1939-40 school year. The statement is as follows:

> "The matter of policy of tenure was discussed. The consensus of opinion seemed to be that we should be very careful in recommending only the best of teachers for permanent tenure."[23]

School Programs and Activities

Instruction

The records of school activities of some fifty years ago contain rather scant reference to the program of instruction which was carried out in the various classes of the school system. Minutes of the Board of Trustees are almost devoid of qualitative information on what was going on in the classroom. Luckily, we do have the recollections of some of the participants of that era including both former students and teachers, and it would appear that the District, including certainly the Board of Trustees, was concerned with the principal business of education, that of learning in the classroom. Occasionally, instructional matters did come to the attention of the Board. For example, in the mid-1930's, Principal Spindt reported that certain students were not meeting the requirements in the commercial course, particularly those subjects which had to do with shorthand. His suggestion for the amelioration of this problem was that a merchandising course be worked out with businesses in town for students who were not able to learn shorthand. Further, he recommended that "since a large proportion of our graduates will eventually work in one phase or another of the oil industry, that more attention should be paid to the oil industry in their courses". These suggestions were approved by the Board.[24] Commenting indirectly on the quality of the instructional program was a report a few years later to the Board by Superintendent Spindt regarding enrollment increases. He observed that these increases had been constant through the thirties with the exception of one year, 1933-34, and that the track record of the district was contrary to that "countrywide tendency for school enrollment to decrease in proportion to the total population". This he attributed to the tendency for high school and junior college students to stay in school longer in the District than elsewhere in the country.

M. Glenn Bultman, mentioned earlier as the student body president of the class of 1931, recalls that the instruction he received, both in the high school and the junior college, prepared him well for his college and legal training. Mr. Bultman was to become a well-known Bakersfield attorney and long-time school board member with both the high school and junior college Districts. He recalls particularly the demanding regimen of the mathematics classes taught by "Goldie" Griffith and the colorful manner in which Jesse Stockton made history come alive. William T. Baldwin, graduate of the Kern County Union High School class of 1933, and also a student body president, cites particular attention to outstanding instruction in the social studies class of Eleanor Frater and the mathematics classes of Eileen Boling. Mr. Baldwin, who in adult life became a Board member, also was in the debate program conducted by Wiley K. Peterson, whose forensics teams were highly successful in the Thirties. Jack Hilton, graduate of the class of 1934 and long-time staff member with the District, remembers with appreciation the musical education he had as a member of the Driller Band under the direction of Harold Burt:

> "I just have nothing but tremendous respect for Harold Burt....I came to know him not only as a fine teacher, but as a respected friend. He did a number of things for me as a student that helped me greatly, and I know it just wasn't for me alone. Harold was a man who went out of his way to help any student whenever he could to achieve musically as well as develop themselves as persons. Later, as a teacher, I had an opportunity to work with Harold Burt. He was not only an outstanding musician, but he was a great teacher and friend of the students."

Mr. Hilton recalls also the prestige that the musical organizations, particularly the band, enjoyed on the Bakersfield campus, throughout the community, and statewide as a result particularly of appearances in the Rose Bowl parade.

Donald Hart graduated in the class of 1933, and was later to become a respected businessman in the city, and for several years the Mayor of Bakersfield. He recalls another program of studies at the school that became highly recognized. This was the dramatic program under the direction of Ethel Robinson. According to Mr. Hart:

> "I took speech and a dramatics class or two from Robbie, thinking perhaps I was a thespian. Involvement in the school play taught one poise and articulation. It taught you expression and, if anything, as she used to say, it gave you 'a command appearance.'"

Gerald Smith, a staff member during the Thirties, was a participant as an instructor in the dramatic programs, assisting Miss Robinson with stage construction and technical aspects of the program. He remembers particularly the problems to be surmounted when the old auditorium could no longer be used. Then the director rehearsed plays in classrooms, and they took shows to various auditoriums throughout the area including Standard School, the new auditorium building at East Bakersfield High School, and even to Wasco High School. It was necessary to build the sets in three foot pieces so that they could be hoisted out of the narrow confines of the old auditorium facilities.

The mechanical arts program is also well remembered by Mr. Smith, since he came here as a new instructor in 1930 fresh from four years at Santa Barbara State College, as it was then called. Having had classes in the mechanical arts department in high school, he had been impressed in retrospect by the excellent instruction and quality of the equipment at high school. He realized that there was more equipment there, and often better instruction, than he received in college. So, he was happy to join the mechanical arts staff at Kern County Union High School. "In 1930, I came back and started teaching in the fall. I had quite a varied shop program, being the youngest on the faculty. My first year I had auto shop, machine shop, welding, stage craft, and a drawing class." Five preparations a day kept the new teacher quite busy. Classes were small enough so that the teacher got to really know the students....."I had the good fortune of working with my old teacher, Noble Stutzman, who was not only a long-time friend, but an expert welder. He helped me with a lot of things I had questions about, such as equipment, budget, and the like." Later Mr. Smith's teaching program settled down to be primarily welding and electricity classes. In the latter, he again worked with a man he considered to be a skillful teacher, Forrest Lynn. "Students in these classes were particularly mature and sharp", according to Mr. Smith.[25]

Another instructional program that received much attention in the District was agriculture under the leadership of Howard K. Dickson. By the beginning of the 1930's the school's farm laboratory in southwest Bakersfield was firmly in place. According to the 1931 Oracle:

> "From the students' point of view the school's farm laboratory is a great place. We have all the things that go to make up the kind of a farm you read about. It has a fine pair of black horses which we use in regular farmwork. It has herds of registered Holstein and Guernsey cattle. It has about six cows of each breed. The boys in the farm- practice class learn to milk them, and the rest of us get practice in judging their good and bad points."

The yearbook goes on to describe the school farm site telling about cattle, hog and sheep pens, the scale, the dairy barn, and the beef cattle. Some 600 white leghorn hens were in the poultry pens where instructor Ben Sutton and students looked after them. Crops were grown on the laboratory farm including hay for the livestock, a vineyard, an orchard, and a vegetable garden where freshman students raised carrots, beets, turnips, and sweet potatoes.[26] By 1933, the agriculture department students had organized a Bakersfield chapter of Future Farmers of America and during the year, a member of the Kern County Union High School chapter was state president of the organization. He was Frank Wattron, who was later to be a member of the staff at Bakersfield College as a teacher and an administrator, as well as a Bakersfield resident playwright.[27]

Mention should be made again of the counseling program which was begun in the mid-20's by Leo B. Hart. Two graduates of that era, Don Hart (no relation) and Jack Hilton, remember well the personal attention which Mr. Hart gave to students, in spite of the fact that he was the only counselor for a very large school. Don Hart comments that when students were searching for "their destiny," as was the case of most high school students, they needed someone to turn to and the counselor was always available. Jack Hilton remembers that Mr. Hart kept track of students long after they left the school and is remembered by the graduating class of 1934 in that they always ask him to attend their class reunions. Leo B. Hart's remarkable memory for recalling names is attested to by both of these graduates. He was able to call most former students by their given names some fifty years later.

State Senator Walter Stiern, a graduate of the class of 1932, in talking about the curriculum has this recollection:

> "In the days that I was at the high school, you went to school preparing to go the academic route, which meant you intended to go on to college. Otherwise, you decided on the industrial or commercial course. Those in the academic studies as freshmen usually took English, Latin, algebra, and general science. If you went into industrial arts, you loaded up with shop-related subjects, and if you planned to enter some craft, the school had a large commercial department which trained lots of students especially young women, for commercial jobs. The teachers worked very hard and had great followings; they were interesting personalities. I remember them very, very well."

Among the colorful personalities on campus according to Senator Stiern, was Hattie Hoenshell, a chemistry teacher and a member of a pioneer Bakersfield family...."a tiny woman, she usually wore a smock and kept her hair in a tight knot on the back of her head. She always reminded me of Madame Curie as she worked around her laboratories."

During the Thirties there were three Petersens on campus; Basil, the junior college basketball coach, who taught chemistry and physics; Wiley, the coach of the forensics teams; and Axel, teacher of biology. Senator Stiern remembers they were often jokingly referred to by the students, "Basil, Axel and Weasel."

Many other instructors are also recalled with fondness by the Senator, including Laura Soper, Virginia Stearns, in English; Olive Chubb, Dwight Griffith, M. A. Buckley, Margaret Myers, mathematics; George Sagen, science; Cecile Mae Coulthard and Edith Ross, teachers of Latin; Hazel Churchman, biology; Ernest Dalbom, "Cap" Haralson, Wallace (Jack) Frost, physical education; Harold Burt, the bandmaster; and, Ethel Robinson, drama. In the mechanical arts department some of the well-remembered instructors, according to the Senator, were Gerald Smith, Forrest Lynn, Noble Stutzman, Clifford Scott, Dean Smith, Erwin Vandam, and the Senator's own father, Walter Stiern.

Senator Stiern has this further recollection regarding two of his teachers:

> At the time I was in school, a love story was going on, and I followed it through the years. There was a young man teaching mechanical drawing who had graduated from Stanford University. His name was Theron McCuen and he was new at the school. I was taking third-year history in another building from a lady whose name was Hazel Kelley, a graduate of the College of the Pacific, now called University of the Pacific. Both of these people were new on the Bakersfield campus. I do not know if they had met before they came, but at least being on the same faculty and campus nurtured the friendship that turned into a story of love and marriage.
>
> I had Hazel Kelley as a teacher of U. S. History and Constitution and Theron McCuen for my advisory period. In those days we had advisory periods related to our interests. One of mine was stamp collecting, and although Theron didn't know much about the subject, he was willing to learn with his students.
>
> You can understand how I have enjoyed watching the later development of both these persons. Both were very capable teachers and Theron became Superintendent of the system, well-liked by everyone, completing a most successful career. In retirement Theron became an educational consultant and well-known photographer.

Even discounting the afterglow of memories, the solid evidence emerging indicates that there was much positive growth in instructional programs of the District. This was true at the Kern

County Union High School campus in Bakersfield, as well as at the developing campuses in Shafter and McFarland, and at the newest school in East Bakersfield.

Athletics and Other Activities

With the state football championship's program at an end, Kern County Union High School no longer received the widespread publicity for its athletic programs, particularly football, that it had enjoyed in the Twenties. However, football maintained its popularity locally and the sport was successful at the Valley level in the Thirties. During this time, a spectacular record was achieved by the B-level football players, known as the Sand Dabs, under the leadership of Coach Wallace "Jack" Frost, and later coached by George Williamson. The Sand Dabs in 1934 could boast having gone five years without a defeat, and at the end of the 1938 season, they could look back five years to a record of four valley championships. During the Thirties, track came into its own under the leadership of J. B. "Cap" Haralson, and the teams won six Valley championships. It was not until later that decade that basketball came to be a dominant sport at the school and showed strength in the Valley. In 1937, the first Valley championship was garnered by the Driller basketball team, followed by four more Valley championships prior to the World War II years when all sports were cut back.

Tennis, a sport that had been relegated to the background for some time, began to be recognized under the coaching leadership of Forrest Lynn. It was, of course, the one athletic enterprise in which the girls participated with the boys in interscholastic competition. A strong tennis team was fielded in 1941, coached by Lawrence Hall, featuring Andy Davidson and Louise Snow. Other participants in this sport in 1941 were Charles Owens, Downing McKee, Charles Lynch, along with Bonnie Rogers.

There were, of course, other competitive athletic sports programs including baseball, swimming, both for boys and girls (although apparently the girls did not participate interscholastically at this time, but practiced their skills and presented an annual aquacade). Golf was also gaining in popularity under the coaching of George Williamson and, in the early forties with Norman Harris, the teams were able to boast respectable seasons in interscholastic competition. Girls are pictured in The Oracle as early as 1941 as a part of the golf program, but they apparently did not enter into the interscholastic competition, playing matches only among themselves. Other sports, such as boxing and tumbling, received attention from time to time, especially when a coach took a particular interest in this sport. In fact, participants in the boxing program coached by Jack Frost, referred jokingly to "Frost's Hour of Harm", after a well-known radio program of the time. The latter had been an outstanding boxer in interscholastic competition. Girls continued to participate in a wide number of sporting activities in intra-mural competition under the aegis of the Girls' Athletic Association.

The athletic scene continued to be dominated by the magnetic personality of Dwight "Goldie" Griffith. Jack Hilton, who played under Coach Griffith and later coached with him, remembers the universal respect he was accorded. When the time came for the venerable coach to give up the head coaching reins in 1946, he did so graciously. Mr. Hilton assisted the new head coach, Homer Beatty, a former player under Coach Griffith; his recollection is that the veteran coach backed the new coaching regime completely, giving advice only when called upon.

Both Don Hart and Jack Hilton recall the influence of Wallace "Jack" Frost upon the athletic program of Kern County High School and later the junior college. He was not only outstanding in his own athletic skills and his ability to teach students to play the game, but he was a true gentleman who seldom raised his voice in giving instructions. In the words of Mr. Hart, "He didn't need to be a coach to be an important person in the community." The contribution of "Cap" Haralson to the sports program, particularly in track, has already been mentioned. He was line coach for the Driller football team for a number of years and is remembered as one who always had time for individual players. Later he received outstanding recognition in a national A.A.U. track program throughout the nation, bringing national track meets to Bakersfield.

It is often surprising to newcomers to Bakersfield to see the regard and reverence given to athletics, particularly football. Looking back through the years, former Mayor Donald Hart has this reflection on what athletics, particularly football, symbolized:

> For many years the game has been the primary release for oilfield men, cowboys, and ranchers who live in the area. With its violence and agressiveness, football was swept to the top of Valley sports and each week during the season forged these people for a few brief hours into a new community. "All brothers together," as J. B. Priestly wrote, for not only had they escaped the lesser life of work, wages, rent, sick pay, nagging wives, ailing children, and demanding bosses, but they escaped with most of their friends and neighbors, and half the town cheering together cheering for the Drillers. And, when the chips were down (and a lot of wages bet), time and again the Drillers would deliver the ultimate win and with that win send them all into another altogether more splendid sphere of life.
>
> It was the mood of the people that made the Drillers great. The Drillers moved through the schedule like a juggernaut -- sometimes smoothly, sometimes turbulently, expressing the hopes and desires and the moods of the citizens more and more with each game until the Drillers and the City of Bakersfield were one -- known throughout the nation for greatness as a team, townspeople and players together.[28]

Before leaving this section, it should be pointed out that previous references have been made to other activities programs emerging from such classes as music, dramatics, and agriculture. In the 1934-35 year, the forensic competitors of the school were bringing the national spotlight to Bakersfield. Quoting from <u>The Oracle</u> of that year,

> By virtue of two state championship titles, Dorothy Hanawalt, Jess Jones, and David Goldberg, accompanied by their coach, Mr. W. K. Peterson, through the effort and interest of local supporters, journeyed 2,500 miles to Kent, Ohio, to compete in the national speech tournament.
> The debate team with Hanawalt and Jones made it to the finals in the competition only to be defeated there by the eventual

national champions from South Dakota. Jess Jones reached the quarterfinals in orations. But, again, the outstanding forensic event for the school up to that time was realized when David Goldberg achieved a national championship in extemporaneous speaking. "Mr. Goldberg captured six out of a possible seven first places by discussing the topic 'Our Next President' in the championship contest."[29] The champions were greeted at the train by Counselor Leo B. Hart, student leaders, and the Kern County Union High School Band under the direction of Harold J. Burt. Later, Alfred Harrell, publisher of The Californian, Principal Spindt, and Mr. Walter Osborne of the high school Board, gave congratulations before 2,500 students in the school stadium.

Forensics continued to be a strong program at the school in the years that followed into World War II. After Mr. Peterson left the school, Leonard McKaig continued to provide strong coaching leadership.

Two New Campuses are Established

East Bakersfield

By the mid 1930's, the problem of growth and the attendant necessity to make building plans was faced by the Board. In the fall of 1935, Principal Spindt made an extensive statistical report along with some general recommendations for the future. Average daily attendance for the 1934-35 school year had reached an all-time high of 3,407 students, with the prediction of at least 3,600 for the 1935-36 year. Architect Charles H. Biggar had been busy studying the situation and giving information to the administrative staff. Mr. Spindt's recommendation for additions to the main campus were as follows: (1) the establishment of the music department in the northeast corner of the block to be occupied by the Auditorium; (2) a second story on the agriculture building to provide classroom space; (3) construction of additions to the girls' physical education department; (4) construction of a new wing in the Library Building; and, (5) construction of new shops north of 14th and west of "F" Streets, which would allow abandonment of the shop buildings in the area to be occupied by the new Auditorium (Elm Grove). The last paragraph of his report was the official beginning, at least as far as the Board minutes are concerned, of the new campus on the east side of town.

> "These changes would provide comfortably for a school of 4,000 students. It is questionable if the Bakersfield plant should be expected to take more than this. Since the prospect this next year is that we will have about 3,600 students, the time is probably not far distant when we must begin thinking about what is to be done with subsequent increases. If we are to build 9th and 10th grade schools in Oildale or East Bakersfield, studies should be made of available sites, and, if a favorable opportunity should arise, we should be ready to purchase sites. There is, of course, the alternate plan to build a separate junior college plant -- a plan somewhat more expensive than to build 9th and 10th grade schools."[30]

In addition to indicating the need for at least one new campus in the Bakersfield area, the report also shows indecision about the direction the organization of the school system should go. Apparently, some members of the staff were intrigued with the concept of the 6-4-4 organizational plan of elementary, high school and junior college systems, which had been recently introduced in the state, particularly in Pasadena. The problem here, of course, was that there were, in Bakersfield, two separate school districts, a K-8 elementary/junior high system and a six-year high school/junior college organization. If the 6-4-4 plan were eventually to be adopted, and if the school districts would merge, it would be wise to build a two-year junior college campus so the shift could be more easily made to the four-year junior college (grades eleven through fourteen). Actually, even after the campus in East Bakersfield was open, a delegation appeared from the community to request that the school be made a four-year high school (grades nine through twelve). It was some time later that that decision was actually made.[31] This concept influenced the planning of the buildings and is felt to this day, particularly in the case of the gymnasium which has been woefully inadequate throughout the years for a high school athletic program.

Funding had been one of the problems faced by the District through the Thirties and was apparently the cause of some delay in moving the building program along, particularly in the face of the bond election defeats. However, in January of 1936, a $200,000.00 bond was passed which gave the "green light" to the East Bakersfield project along with other additions to the main campus and to Shafter and McFarland. Shortly after the successful bond election, representatives from the East Bakersfield Progressive Club appeared before the Board and recommended that the location of the new campus be in the Olcese tract.[32]

Another source of funds eyed by the Board was the Federal government through Public Works Administration. The previous year application had been made for federal moneys to build a new auditorium. The Principal reported at the time of the recommendation from the East Bakersfield group that no PWA funds were available for building at that time. However, apparently enough encouragement was received on funding to go ahead with the project so that, in two months time (May 4, 1936), the Board approved the purchase of a site at Quincy and Mt. Vernon Avenues for "East Bakersfield Junior High School for the sum of $6,552.00."[33]

Another significant step taken at this same Board meeting was the filling of the recently established position of Business Manager, designed to assist the District in financing the building program and the other burgeoning business operations. The man selected was Theron L. McCuen, who had been on the staff as a drawing teacher since 1929. Mr. McCuen was later to become Superintendent and serve one of the longer periods of tenure of superintendents within the state. Later, in 1936, architect Biggar presented the general plans for the new East Bakersfield buildings, which were approved by the Board and he was ordered to proceed with the working drawings. Almost exactly a year later, the bid of the contracting firm of L. H. Hansen and Son was accepted by the Board at the basic cost figure of slightly in excess of $300,000.00. As the work proceeded on the basic buildings in April, 1938, the architect again presented plans for the shop building and ten additional classrooms, which were approved and sent to the state division of architecture. A few days later at a special Board meeting, action was taken to accept $164,250.00 from the Federal government for financing the construction of the new school.[34]

The listing of staff members presented in June for the 1938-39 school year carried the names of 22 certificated staff to be assigned to the new school. Heading the list was Kenneth W. Rich as Principal. Others were Ruth Bogardus, librarian; H. A. Anderson, Aubry Lee Berry, Alice Briglio, Lois Curry, Francis Embry, Genevive Kratka, Alma Gloeckner, Jack Hill, Karl Jensen, I. E. Lane, Phil Martin, Lorna Mullen, Mary Owens, Jack Rowe, Walter Shore, Donald E. Shoup, Edward C. Simonsen, Lois M. Smith, Donna Thorpe, and Marjorie Wright, all teachers. The newly designated Principal, Kenneth W. Rich, had been with the District as head of the Manual Arts Department of Kern County Union High School. He was able to bring with him a number of local experienced teachers as well as promising newcomers.

Before the school opened in the fall of 1938, the name of East Bakersfield High School had been officially chosen, thereby showing deference to the community spirit prevalent in the East Bakersfield area, dating back to its early existence as a separate identity from Bakersfield itself. But, it is much more interesting to hear from some of the people involved in the 1938 undertaking plan than to quote from the records of the Board of Trustees. Ruth Bogardus (Allen) was the librarian for the new campus, and in her words,

> "We were an enthusastic band of young teachers plus one librarian who had arrived that fall in 1938 to open a new high school under the guidance of Mr. Rich, Principal. Because this was the first school to be established within the city to relieve the overcrowded Kern County Union High School, we felt a special excitement as time neared. We gladly struggled with dust, dirt, and mud around the new administration building until walks were added and lawns planted. In addition to the main building, which included a combination study hall and library wing, only the girls' gym had been completed. Until the larger boys gym was constructed, the girls were sent outside to play volleyball for their exercise, while the boys unsurped the inside equipment.

Until an auditorium could be built, the east wing of the administration building served a variety of purposes. At one end, a small library was arranged, the middle space was filled with desks for study hall use, and the front end of the room filled with chairs served as a study hall."

The former librarian goes on to describe the organization of the student body, including sophomores who had transferred from Kern County Union High School and freshmen students arriving from junior high schools. Because of the excitement in the new enterprises, both students and teachers were willing to overlook the lack of facilities including a cafeteria. "Some were able to get home for lunch, while others brought theirs in brown bags or patronized Hoppy's Snack Stand across the street. This favorite gathering place featured school supplies and interim 'meals for $.10 and up'." In describing the developing school spirit, the former librarian used a phrase that became associated with the East Bakersfield High School campus and has persisted to this day, "....we felt like one large family."[35]

One prospective student for the new school was not at all enthusiastic about the ideas of joining the East Bakersfield High School "family". The previous year he had been a freshman student at Kern County Union High School, where his father and other members of his family had graduated, and even before he entered the school, he had looked forward to the educational experiences so often discussed at home. In his freshman year he had become involved in the prominent speech and forensics program at the school under the direction of Leonard McKaig. As a result of these strong feelings, he persuaded his mother to talk to the school officials about a possible intra-district transfer to allow him to stay in Kern County Union High School. No exceptions were being made, however, and this disappointed young man, Jean Philippe, appeared on the new campus at the opening of the school in September of 1938. Currently, the Principal of East Bakersfield High School, Jean Philippe has spent a long professional career as a teacher and administrator at the school, having graduated with East's first class in 1941.

Soon after school started he was feeling differently,

> "It wasn't a month after I started that it dawned on me how lucky I was to be a part of something new. There were about 500 students with some 20-25 teachers and there was really a tremendous family feeling all of the time. People occasionally kid us now about this, but we still foster that family feeling at East Bakersfield High School."[36]

Part of the reason for the easy transition to the new school, according to Mr. Philippe, was the fact that Principal Rich had been able to bring with him from Kern County Union High School a number of outstanding teachers and had gathered a complimentary staff of enthusastic newcomers. Irving Lane came over as a Dean of Students and assistant to the principal, without title at that time. The speech program started off well under the direction of Frances Embrey who had also been a part of the Kern County Union High School staff and a member of an old Bakersfield area family. Sophomore Philippe was able to get into a competitive speech program from the beginning. He also went out for football, played golf, and was active in student body affairs. In athletics, East Bakersfield High School won the small schools' golf championship early in its history, one of the first athletic successes of the school. However, as Mr. Philippe remembers it, basketball from the very start was the sport in which East Bakersfield High School excelled even though the "pavillion", as the undersized gymnasium was called, was never really adequate. But, most of all, Mr. Philippe remembers the enthusiasm of the parents, as well as the support that generally came from the community as a whole. In fact, the Bakersfield Californian gave much space to the new school and Jim Day, sports editor and later city editor for the newspaper, is generally given credit for originating the term "Blades" as the name for the school's varsity teams.

Under the guidance of a new staff member fresh from the College of the Pacific, Edward Simonsen, student body government was a strong influence in the school within the first year. The reluctant transferee from Kern County Union High School, Jean Philippe, represented the students of his school as student body president and speaker at the first graduating exercise in 1941.

A footnote to that first graduation ceremony concerns another speaker who appeared with student body president Philippe. Her name is Billie Crawford, and she was also an outstanding student leader, having been editor of both the school's yearbook and newspaper during her student career, president of the prestigious California Scholastic Federation, and active in other school affairs. According to publicity released later about this student,...."paraphrasing the commencement theme of the class of '41, 'Pioneering at East Bakersfield High School,' Billie Crawford (Davis) truly epitomized the pioneering spirit and helped to provide a foundation for the traditions and standards and spirit on which fourteen classes succeeding her have built."[37] Billie Crawford (Davis) was later to become well-known as a religious educator and speaker on inspirational subjects to students in schools throughout the country at a time in the mid-50's when the schools were criticized for weaknesses. In the public press and other news media, she became a spokesperson for the school. The article which appeared in The Saturday Evening Post entitled, "I Was a Hobo Kid," was the start of this publicity, and it told of her home background as a member of a nomadic hobo family which had no roots and moved from place to place; but, most of all, it stressed the fact that the public schools she attended, among them East Bakersfield High School, had given her stability and purpose in life. She always said in her speeches that she knew the schools were not perfect....."at the same time I believe in our public schools because history has forced me to believe, and I offer my story for what it is worth at face value--as concrete, objective evidence of the success of public education in America."[38]

Edward Simonsen always assumed that, after finishing College of the Pacific at Stockton, he would return to his home in the Bay area, to pursue a professional career. However, he was offered a position at the new high school in Bakersfield and, because of the opportunity to get in on the ground floor of a new institution which seemed to hold much promise, he was happy to sign on. He still believes that one of his chief qualifications for the job was his versatility. With a major in music and minors in history and physical education, he had adaptability. His first assignment in 1938, demanded as many as six different preparations in an eight or nine period day. He taught classes in history, physical education and had the instrumental music program. Alma Gloeckler was assigned the choral program.

According to Mr. Simonsen, the initial instrumental music organizations were at least enthusiastic, but

> "...soon we began to develop a good program even during the first year. In fact, it went so well in the first two years that we were able to add another music teacher for the third year of school. This was a young man whom I had known from the bay area, a University of California graduate named Larry McArdell. The band, orchestra, and later the swing band, all became strong organizations."[39]

Along with his teaching program of physical education, history and music, Mr. Simonsen was appointed student body advisor, and in this area, he recalls the spirit of the students as they developed programs from the ground up. He particularly remembers early student body presidents Scott Bradford and Karl Schafer and, during his third year at the school, Jean Philippe.

> The thing that made our job so much easier than it might have been was that the parents were so active. The PTA did a fantastic job and helped us in many ways. That group of parents meant much to the school, and I understand that the same spirit has persisted to this day. People are proud of E.B.

Mr. Simonsen also recalls that the classified staff gave excellent support to the efforts of teachers and parents. He particularly remembers the expertise of May Schmidt and Evelyn Ferguson in the Principal's office, and he received unexpected assistance in training the marching band from one of the classified staff members, custodian Lloyd Fath. This man had been a bandsman in the U.S. Army for a number of years and was an accomplished musician. He helped in training the marching bands, serving as drill master. He is pictured in the early photographs as one of the band members. Above all the impression that comes across once again is the "feeling of community" that persisted on the east side of Union Avenue.

Arriving at East Bakersfield High School in the fall of '39 was a young history teacher, Orville Armstrong, who was later to become Vice-Principal of the school. His recollections, too, include interesting ancedotes from those first years.

> On a Saturday afternoon, a business education teacher, Ruth Boyans, drove her car into a fire plug and broke it off sending thousands of gallons of water into the basement of the main building, where all of the lumber for the industrial arts department was stored. Her face was as red as the fire trucks which came to shut off the water. The next month I backed into another fire plug located at the rear of the main building and broke it off. It was on a Sunday afternoon, just as Vic Manley, another teacher, was walking by. He ran to the school's water tower, climbed over the high fence, and shut off the value. The water, thousands of gallons, came down the hill, rounded the main building, flowed into Quincy Street, down Mt. Vernon Avenue, and into a large irrigation ditch six blocks away. The industrial arts department considered themselves lucky. My face, too, colored up when I had to tell the whole story to Ken Rich, the principal.

Mr. Armstrong recalls that Phil Martin, head of the English department, wrote the words for the school's alma mater, and Kenneth Rich, whose hobby was photography, took movies of the school's construction period and scenes of happenings of the first two or three years.

> "The auditorium, built by PWA, was not completed during the first year. During the second year, 1939, there was no furniture. All the students and faculty sat on the cement floor when assemblies were held there. In the early days the library was located at one end of the study hall....a very unsatisfactory arrangement for both. Later an 'optional' study hall was developed which was housed in a much smaller room, and the library was expanded to the full length of the room where the study hall had been--a much more satisfactory arrangement. With the optional study hall, students who did not want to study could go to a fenced area where there were tables and benches under trees where they could socialize with their friends. Students decided each day where they were going to spend their free time period -- in the study hall or outside."

One of the popular students and a song leader in those early years was a coed named Mary Kay Jaynes (Shell). In her adult life she became Mayor of the City of Bakersfield, and is currently a Kern County Supervisor. Mr. Armstrong well remembers "Pop" Drennan, the first head custodian. He was popular with students and faculty and he had the same pride in the campus as if he were the Principal. This man's name was Charles I. Drennan, who was at East Bakersfield High School from 1938 until his retirement in 1953. The senior class of that year insisted that he "graduate" along with the class and he was presented a diploma by H. E. Woodworth, Board President. Mr. Drennan's son, Harry, who is mentioned elsewhere in this volume, was a long-time staff member of the District. Such were the beginnings of the new school east of Union Avenue.

A Campus in the Kern River Valley

In the latter part of the 1930's, the area in the Kern River Valley, some fifty miles east of Bakersfield, became populated primarily with ranch families. This area was one of the early mining areas of the county, but by the Thirties, the mining industry had declined and ranching was the foremost occupation. Actually, in 1938, the Kern County Union High School Board authorized an instructional program to be established in the Kern Valley area. Permission was granted at the request of the Kern County Probation Department for a teacher at Camp Owen, then known as the Kern County Probation Forest Camp. This, of course, did not serve the educational needs of the residents of the area. Up until this time high school students from the Kern Valley region lived in the dormitories provided on the high school campus in Bakersfield, weekend transportation being provided by the school district. In accordance with a permissive state law, parents were paid a fee in lieu of daily transportation and, while this did not cover the cost of board and room, it did provide some monetary assistance.

After expressions of concern regarding the necessity for students to be away from home to attend school, particularly sensitive for the younger ones, some positive steps were taken towards the establishment of an educational campus in the Kern River Valley. In the fall of 1940, Thomas L. Nelson, who succeeded H. A. Spindt as District Superintendent, made a report to the high school Board regarding a meeting with parents in the Kernville area. His opinion was that at least 75 per cent of the parents he met with wanted a local campus.[41]

The next month the Board heard a report on a proposal by the County Superintendent of Schools office to establish a four-year school with the district to be separated out from the high school district boundaries. This report may have galvanized the District into action, because not quite a month later, on December 9, 1940, to be exact, the Superintendent again reported to the Board on the Kernville situation and, "...the agitation in various other parts of the high school district for the establishment of schools". Action was then taken to establish a ninth grade in the Kernville area during the next school year, "...to be followed by a tenth grade in 1942-43, provided the ninth grade proves to be satisfactory to the residents and patrons of the area and to the school".[42] Another provision was attached to this action: it was "...subject to the elementary districts involved remaining in the Kern County High School District,..." A significant footnote to this action is that, at the same Board meeting, on a recommendation of a letter from the educational advisor to the C.C.C. Camp at Isabella, the District employed two teachers for that camp. No doubt about it, educational activity was picking up momentum in the Kern River Valley.

In the spring of 1941, after a study of the area by the Superintendent and other staff members, the Board of Trustees authorized the purchase of ten acres of land east of Kernville from I. L. Wofford. The price was $100.00 per acre and the Board acted subject to the approval of the County Planning Commission and the State Department of Education.[43] These further steps were taken in good time and on July 14, 1941, a contract for the construction of the Kernville school building was let to C. C. Foley for a contract price just in excess of $10,000.00.[44]

The school opened on September 8, 1941, and the October enrollment report showed a total of twenty-three students, ten ninth graders and thirteen tenth graders. It was necessary to find temporary housing for the classes for the first semester, since the building itself was not to be completed until February of 1942.[45] World War II took its toll on the staff of the Kernville High School and in the spring of 1943, Manville Pettys, the school's first Principal, went into the military service. Lawrence Wiemers was the Principal/teacher for the next year and a half, until June of 1944. It was during this period of time that Helen Ramsey joined the Kernville faculty. Thus, by the beginning of World War II, another campus had been added to the Kern County Union High School District, located in the picturesque Kern River Valley and serving a population quite different from that of Bakersfield and the Shafter and McFarland areas.

Thomas B. Merson followed Lawrence Wiemers as Principal of Kernville High School. He was in this position for three years (1944-47). Mr. Merson had been on the staff of Bakersfield College prior to 1944 and returned there in 1947. He later became Director of Instruction for the college. His recollections of those early years at Kernville High School provide an insight which gives dimension to that small mountain school and the community itself.

> The area served by Kernville High School was essentially the mountainous Kern River Valley. The nearest high schools were a small school at the sawmill in Johnsondale in Tulare County and the school beyond Walkers Pass at the Navel Ordinance Test Station at Ridgecrest.
>
> Students lived mostly within a radius of approximately twenty miles of Kernville, and they were collected each morning by the Kernville High School bus which was driven by the Principal. Parents of students living beyond the bus route brought their students to regular pick-up points. The distance of the total collection drive (as I remember it) was about forty miles. This bus service was greatly appreciated by the community and, of course, was essential to the operation of the school.
>
> The area in which the high school was located was a typical mountain school community cluster. The population centers were all very small, in most instances they were only a grocery store and gas pump, although several supported small elementary schools. Residents of the South Fork Valley were

mostly ranchers. There were many large cattle ranches, and the cattle in the summer were herded long distances into the high mountains surrounding the valley.

Local community pride was clearly evident and each community felt it was superior to the others. The high school, possibly through the bus service, did a lot to reduce isolation and to enhance feelings of general unity.

The staff was comprised of a total of three individuals during this period: the Principal-teacher, a second teacher and the janitor. The second teacher was chosen for his/her ability to teach subjects that the Principal was least qualified to handle. Three different persons occupied this role during Mr. Merson's stay. The first was Helen Ramsey James, who had taught earlier at the school, but had retired. However, she agreed to stay on until a new teacher could be found. She was relieved a few weeks after the 1944-45 term began by Phyllis Anderson, who was completing her teacher preparation in the San Francisco area. A year later she returned to the Bay Area and was succeeded by Mrs. Bertha Downing.

The student body, ranging from twenty to thirty in number at this time was about equally divided between ninth and tenth graders. Mr. Merson's recollections continue:

"Because of the small number of students, the curriculum was limited to the essential freshman and sophomore subjects. It was further limited by the abilities and background of the two teachers as well as by the educational background of the students. The curriculum emphasized English, mathematics, science, social science, and physical education. Other basic subjects such as business and foreign language were taught when possible.

Mathematics can serve as an example of the constraints on course offerings. It was evident from test scores that freshman mathematics should be a general course and algebra should be a sophomore course. This proved very effective because students were able to raise their mathematics achievement scores three-four years by one year of basic mathematics instruction. English followed a similar pattern. A second illustration of constraint was that there was limited science equipment and no laboratory facilities. Adaptations, of course, were made. In the main, these limitations were compensated for when the students transferred for their junior/senior years to one of the Bakersfield high schools."

Mr. Merson recalls that extra-curricular activities were limited by the transportation factor involving practically all of the student body.

"The basic extra-curricular event was organized around an inherited problem -- poor attendance. The Principal had been forewarned of the previous poor attendance record, and so an attendance contest between freshman and sophomore classes was organized. At the end of each month, the losing class would provide a party for the winning class. Party events would vary according to student preference. This program received unusual support. Attendance regularly exceeded ninety percent, and students themselves became the attendance monitors. Moreover, both students and faculty enjoyed these social events and the families were happy to provide refreshments.

Interscholastic athletics as such were non-existent; touch football contests with Kernville Elementary School were sometimes held, and on rare occasions baseball games with Johnsondale schools were arranged.

Periodically school plays were rehearsed and presented to the community in the Kernville movie theater and/or Camp Owen. One very touching Christmas presentation at Camp Owen elicited a spontaneous response from individuals in the Camp Owen audience in the form of testimonials essentially saying -- "I wish I hadn't done it"."

It should be noted here that part of the Principal's responsibility was the supervision of the educational program at Camp Owen, the Kern County Probation Forest Camp. The instruction there was handled by a single teacher at this time, and Mr. Merson notes that the provision of meaningful educational program was "indeed a challenge".

In evaluating the program at Kernville in those early years, former Principal Merson observes that the school satisfied parents who wanted to keep their youngsters at home, and that the testing program and follow-up accounts of students attending classes showed that, on the whole, they made satisfactory progress educationally. Another measure of the school's success was a substantial increase in the number of students who entered and graduated from college.

Other Expansion Plans

North of the River

As early as 1935, Principal Spindt, in a report to the Board on enrollment increases, recommended that the Board look at possible plant sites in Oildale as well as in East Bakersfield. This recommendation ultimately resulted in the establishment of the East campus, but the plan for the North of the River location remained dormant for some time, four years to be exact. In the summer of 1939, the subject of a north campus once again surfaced and President of the Board Judge Harvey indicated that he would investigate the possibility of securing land near the Teak Dairy.[47] Re-introduction of this topic resulted in action in the fall of 1939. Three different sites were selected before one was found that satisfied the criteria of the Board, the County Planning Commission, and the State Department of Education. Finally, on December 18, 1939, the third site was approved and 23-3/4 acres of land at $340.00 per acre were purchased bounded by Douglas Street, McRay Street, and Charlana Drive.[48] Prompt action was not to be taken on the building at this location, however, for World War II intervened. In April of 1942 the land on this site was leased to the U. S. Army who had offered either to buy or lease it. The decision of the Board was not to sell. The wisdom of this decision was not to be realized until after World War II.

Arvin and West Bakersfield Sites

In spite of the oncoming hostilities that were to engulf the nation, the Board of Trustees was unshakable in its belief that, eventually, further expansion would be needed. Therefore, in June of 1941, still another site was purchased after proper approvals had been secured. In this case, it was in the fertile agricultural area of the community of Arvin, some fifteen miles southeast of Bakersfield. Forty acres of land were purchased from Mr. A. N. George at $350.00 per acre, to eventually become the site of Arvin High School. Again, the consumation of this school campus would await the outcome of the war.[49]

Approximately a year later, the Arvin site was leased to agriculturalist Hugh Jewett. He was given a five-year lease at $1,600.00 a year with the stipulation, curiously, that the land not be used to raise sugar beets.[50] The stage, then, was being set for the rapid expansion of the high school district during the post war era of the 1950's.

Still another possibility was being seriously considered by the Board prior to World War II. In 1940 a possible west Bakersfield site was discussed in at least one Board meeting, and periodically during the war, sites were analyzed which would eventually lead to the establishment of West High School.[51]

The "Outlying Campuses"

By the end of the decade the two "outlying campuses," Shafter and McFarland were seasoned high schools, each having developed programs of studies and activities uniquely suited to the communities in which they were located.

Shafter

Shafter High School, situated in the larger of the two communities which were geographical extensions of the Kern County Union High School District, quickly occupied the community spotlight as a center of interest and local pride. A series of articles published in the <u>Shafter Press</u> at the time of the 50th anniversary of the opening of Shafter in 1978 reflect those early years. The articles were written by Jeanette Wheeler, a veteran teacher at the school and journalist for the local newspaper.[52]

The first article tells of the activities of the first graduating class of the school in 1931. These students had begun as sophomores when the school opened with most of them having attended their first year of high school at the Kern County Union High School campus in Bakersfield.[51] This was the year of the publication of the first yearbook named The Laurion. The yearbook was dedicated to Mrs. Hazel M. Robertson, the first Principal of the school. By the 1930-31 school year, Elmer J. Peery had become Principal, and Mrs. Robertson was still on the staff, along with James V. Wilson, Frasquita Sullivan, Glen Nay, Martha Ione Barnett, Myrtle Gloeckler, Roy Dreisbach, and Helen Habicht. Vice Principal Paul VanderEike of the Kern County Union High School staff was assigned the responsibility of seeing to the day-to-day needs of both Shafter and McFarland.

Twenty-one seniors graduated in the first class of 1931. There was a music department with a girls' glee club consisting of eleven members and an orchestra with twenty-four players. The student body was organized with a full set of officers for each semester. In addition to the yearbook publication, there was a newspaper staff, although at this time there was no school newspaper as such. The school had an arrangement with the local newspaper, The Shafter Progress, to publish student articles. The agricultural program and Future Farmers of America were already growing elements of the school. The latter was destined by the middle Thirties to be the largest F.F.A. Chapter in the country, with a nationwide reputation.

By the 1930-31 school year, dramatics was already popular in the school, with a student body play, "Agatha's Aunt", and a senior class play, "The Arrival of Kitty", produced during that year. A successful debate program was underway which was to reap local and statewide honors before the end of the Thirties. Football, basketball, and baseball were the interscholastic sports and the team name used in those days was the "Cardinals". A program in girls' intramural athletics had also been organized. In the next year, 1931-32, the sports program added tennis and track.

By the end of the Thirties, growth in the school was substantial: a new auditorium was added to the building program and additional acres had been purchased for the school farm laboratory. In fact, in the 1940 Laurion, the school farm laboratory was proudly proclaimed as, "...the outstanding and most ideal example of school farm laboratories in the state and perhaps in the United States".[53] Its primary features were its proximity to the campus, the diversity of programs in field crops, animal husbandry and poultry, with housing for 250 chickens.

By 1940, the football team, now called the "Generals" after General William Rufus Shafter, for whom the town was named, had won its second Sierra League Championship, and the baseball team had won its first championship. Forty-two graduates made their appearance on the commencement program.

Two industrial resources of the Thirties contributed to the growth of Shafter. One was agriculture, with the development (at the agricultural experiment station near Shafter) of the strain of cotton particularly suited to the San Joaquin Valley, and the other was oil, with the bringing in of the Rio Bravo oil fields. Not to be overlooked was the development of a variety of potatoes, which came to be known as the "Shafter Potato", giving impetus to agriculture in the Shafter area.

In reviewing the high school activities in the community, one unique feature was related to the music in the school. Shafter was a strong church community influenced by the Mennonites with German and Russian cultural heritage. For a number of years it was customary to produce religious cantatas as a part of the music program of the school. Later these gave way to musicals, but religious music influenced the music in the school, according to Jeannette Wheeler.[54]

McFarland

As in the case of Shafter, McFarland High School held its first official graduation ceremony in the spring of 1931. Eighteen seniors received their diplomas. Growth and positive changes had been evident at the school located in an agricultural community some twenty miles northeast of Bakersfield. Two large classroom wings had been added to the main building. For the 1930-31 year, nine faculty members were listed in the minutes of the Board: Dorothy Albaugh, Evelyn Reynolds, Huntley Webb, Ann Harder, John H. Porterfield, Edith Fitzgibbon, Joanna Morgan, Ruth Pauline Smith, Shirley Troner (the school's first official coach), and U. C. Allen.[55] Mr. Allen was the school's initial agriculture instructor, who immediately began to develop a vigorous course of study. He stayed with McFarland High School until his retirement in 1947. On the athletic fields, football first made its appearance in the fall of 1930. Jack Webster, president of the junior class that year, had submitted the name "Cougar" as the winning entry in a contest to choose the mascot name of the school's teams. The first football game was played in November at Tehachapi High School, and, according to one of the players, the field had just been disked: "Dust was so thick even the referee couldn't see what we were doing." Players furnished all of their own equipment and many players were shod in tennis shoes.[56] The total football season for the Cougars that year was two games against Tehachapi. It was an undefeated season, with both games won by 6-0 and 33-0 scores.

By the next school year, the students were publishing a yearbook named the Recuerdos. E. P. Janes had become Principal and twenty-four seniors are pictured in the graduating class. Activities featured in the yearbook include the honor society, forensic club, biology, home economics, a High-Y organization, the FFA, the annual staff, and the new school newspaper named "Cougar Cry". A chorus and orchestra comprised the school music program and the Block 'M' Society was established for athletes. The football team continued its winning ways in the fall of 1931 and won the Sierra League Championship. Basketball had been set up, and A, B, and C squads in track and tennis were offered. The Girls' Athletic Association had a program of intramural sports.[57]

By the mid-1930's, a formidable debate squad had been developed at McFarland under the coaching of Charles F. Flanagin, and in 1936 the Recuerdos boasted that the debate squad won the Sierra League Championship for the third successive year.[58] By that time, Leslie W. Hedge had become Principal (He was later destined to serve a lengthy tour of duty as the Bakersfield High School chief administrator). Football continued to be successful and tennis was now being played on the new court. The yearbook contained the notation that the new facility "improved the quality of the game". The dramatics program was active in the mid-Thirties, and in 1936 the senior class play was "The Charm School". The music program, in addition to the orchestra and girls' glee club, included a brass quintet. A dance club had been established in the physical education department. By 1939, baseball and tennis were strong, players in both sports winning the Sierra League Championship during the 1938-39 school year. At the end of the 1930's, the school again had a new Principal, a man who had been an English teacher during the early part of the Thirties. His name was J. H. Porterfield. The school continued to grow into the World War II years. The agricultural department was particularly active and in 1940-41, the Future Farmers entered livestock in the County fair at Bakersfield as well as the State fair. However, the big money maker for the Future Farmers continued to be bee hives.[59] There is ample evidence that McFarland High School developed instructional courses and activities which served well the high school students in this hardy agricultural community at the northern boundary of Kern County.

The Junior College in the Thirties

The depression economics of the Thirties brought about some major changes in junior colleges generally in California, and particularly in Bakersfield. According to Director Grace Van Dyke Bird, until the depression 80 per cent of the students in the junior college program came from Kern County. This changed to a 60 - 40 per cent mix in the mid-Thirties.[60] By the 1935-36 school year, enrollment in the college program had reached 900 with a faculty of 65.[61]

After graduation from Kern County Union High School, M. Glenn Bultmann enrolled in the junior college program during this time. His recollection is that the college was still struggling for its identity. Although located in an out-of-the-way corner of the campus, the school was on the move under the positive leadership of Grace Bird. Theo "Spud" Harder had moved from the high school to the junior college football program and had developed some strong teams. Basil Peterson, one of the three Petersons in the high school/junior college, was the basketball coach, and Mr. Bultman's recollection is that the basketball five were Valley champs two years in a row during the middle Thirties. More importantly, however, transfer students to the University of California had built up an excellent scholastic reputation. Mr. Bultman recalls that his pre-law course prepared him well for law school. In addition, the former Kern County Union High School student body president competed in forensics where his speciality was extemporaneous speaking; he also took part in student government, and during his second year served as student body president.

With some difficulty, the Junior College Division managed to build up student spirit and to separate itself from the high school. Sports programs, drama, and forensic activities all were a part of this separated movement. All in all, Mr. Bultman believes that he had solid preparation for the University of California and its some 25,000 students. Actually, his scholastic record at the University was somewhat better, to his surprise, than it had been at Bakersfield Junior College.[62]

Grace Bird recalls that she and her staff, notably assisted by Margaret Levinson, worked hard at developing courses of study. In fact, it was during this era that the concept of "community oriented curriculum" emerged, with strong emphasis on agriculture, farm management, animal and plant science, a police officers' training program, and a technical petroleum course. A move also began towards changing the designation of "junior college" to a less negative connotation statewide. The denotation "community college", however, was not to be common parlance until a later era. There was also an effort to coin a common term for the chief administrator of the college and by popular usage the change began to move from "dean" or "director" to "president".[63]

Moving into the Forties, the mood of the junior college personnel of the District was optimistic, with increases in enrollment and the ability to finance programs fitting the needs of the community. It was almost as if the growing momentum had been built up so that the institution could brace itself for the difficult times of World War II, which brought changes in programs and an abrupt decline in enrollment and changing programs.

Other District Programs

Mention needs to be made in closing out the pre-World War II era of two other programs which had been growing during the Thirties. One was that of the adult school. At the beginning of the 1939-40 school year, adult school classes had been established at East Bakersfield High School and a man, who was to give leadership to the adult school for a number of years, was named Principal of the District Adult School; he was Guy Garrard.[64] In the eleven-year period from 1927-28 to 1938-39, the adult school enrollment had almost exactly doubled from an attendance of 114 to 237. In addition to the East Bakersfield program, evening school classes had also been conducted at McFarland and Shafter since 1930. The numbers in these programs, however, were small.[65]

The District Moves Ahead Into World War II Times

An event of significance to the district in 1938 was the resignation of the long-time Superintendent, H. A. Spindt. His resignation was accepted reluctantly by the Board, recognizing that he had been offered a prestigous position with the University of California as Manager of the Bureau of Placement and Vocational Guidance. A resolution adopted by the Trustees in April of 1938 indicated the depth of feelings generated by the loss of Mr. Spindt. The resolution is quoted in part,

> "Whereas, the said H. A. Spindt has for the past twenty years been in service to the district either as a member of the teaching staff or as such Superintendent; and

"Whereas, the last sixteen years of his said service has been devoted to the duties of office of Superintendent of the district,

"Now, therefore, the Board of Trustees of the Kern County High School District desires to place upon the records of the district as testimonial to the effect that H. A. Spindt during his long years of service to the district has been faithful to his duties, unselfish in the expenditure of his time and energy, efficient in his administration, an inspiration to the teaching staff, the other employees of the district and to the thousands of members of the student body who have been in attendance in the high school and junior college of the district during his service...."[66]

Later in 1938, Thomas L. Nelson was elected by the Board as Spindt's successor. During the next year other personnel changes occurred, involving persons with long attachment to the District. Leo B. Hart resigned in January, 1939, after having been elected Kern County Superintendent of Schools. Mr. Hart had been with the District nearly 15 years, and for a considerable portion of that time, occupied the position of the first and only counselor in the high school. During the same month, Attendance Supervisor John E. Loustalot resigned because of his election as Sheriff of Kern County. At the same Board meeting that these two resignations were accepted, a teacher at East Bakersfield High School, Aubrey Berry, resigned to accept an administrative position with the University of California. Mr. Berry was later to become well-known to many student teachers at U.C.L.A. and the University of California, where he occupied the position of placement director, eventually supervising the placement system of the entire university complex. H. W. (Pat) Kelly was designated to take Mr. Loustalot's place as Attendance Supervisor for Kern County Union High School. Another notable personnel change effective in the fall of 1939 was the appointment of Leslie W. Hedge as Principal of Kern County Union High School. Mr. Hedge had been counselor and Dean of Boys at the school, and at one time had served as Principal of McFarland High School. Robert J. Wright was named to the Dean of Boys/Counseling position, and Theron Taber was appointed Dean of Men at Bakersfield Junior College, succeeding Mr. Wright.[68]

The Auditorium

Since final approval of the new auditorium plans in February of 1941, progress was slow in the construction of this long-desired addition to the campus. At the February 27, 1941 meeting, a decision was made by the Board, which was to be of lasting benefit to the campus at 14th and 'F' Streets, as well as to the new auditorium itself when it was finally completed. That decision was to purchase land just east of the Elm Grove area across 'G' Street and locate the new building outside of the area now known as Elm Grove.[69] Plans for the construction of this facility, which had stretched over some ten years of time had attracted much attention throughout the community. Discussions had taken place with community groups relative to the seating, the stage facilities and, in fact, regarding most of the important aspects of the building. Finally, it was decided that the building would be constructed to seat some 1,800 persons, 1,000 less than the request from one of the community groups.[70] The revolutionary orchestra lift would be installed afterwards at the cost of nearly $10,000.00.[71] Thus, progress was well underway on the construction of the auditorium. Until late fall of 1941, it appeared that the building would be completed in spite of the worsening international conditions that threatened construction of any kind.

In November, the Board received a report from the Office of Production Management of the Federal government concerning the possibility of getting a priority number which would allow the building to be completed without interference from the government. However, "in spite of all efforts such a general number seems to be out of the question and the Office of Production Management has even suggested further construction be deferred."[72] Then, for the next few months, the situation worsened. In April of 1942 contractors Opperman and Ashby asked to be released from the contract to finish the building.[73] The Superintendent and the Board apparently believed at this time that the contractors were not pursuing the matter with all the resources at their command, and the next month a letter was sent indicating that, in their opinion, the delay was unreasonable. A legal process, termed "friendly action", ensued and a local firm of attorneys was retained to handle the contractor's request that his contract be terminated. In late 1942, the auditorium contractors were notified to proceed with the work or, "...we will proceed to do the work ourselves and charge the cost to the contractors."[75] In early 1943, with the request to get priorities from the Federal government apparently no longer viable, all attempts at further construction were halted. The Board made arrangements to do protective work, thereby keeping the framework of the building intact until such time as materials would once again be available.

A tragic footnote to all this occurred shortly after construction on the building was officially halted. The incident was witnessed by the Attendance Supervisor, H. W. (Pat) Kelly. One of the problems connected with the framework of the building, which stood for several years unattended, was to keep youngsters from playing on it and hurting themselves. Mr. Kelly had been on his rounds supervising various areas on campus, when he arrived at the auditorium framework in time to see a youngster, who had been climbing on the structure, lose his balance and fall into the pit below. The young man was killed. In spite of the best efforts of the District and the contractor to keep the public from the building, the uncompleted structure remained a hazard.[75] The building framework for the new auditorium was to lie dormant for approximately three years during the war, with construction resumed in late fall of 1945.

The End of an Era

Before closing out the Thirties, mention should be made more specifically of the influence of Federal funds through the Public Works Progress Administration on the building program of the District. Beginning in the mid-Thirties and up until the end of the decade, a number of PWA grants were received to assist in the building program, including allocations for the East Bakersfield auditorium, for auditoriums and gymnasiums at Shafter and McFarland, and for additions to locker rooms at Shafter, among others. This occurred in the time before aid to education was accepted as a responsibility of the government in Washington.

The District continued to be fortunate in the election to the Board of persons of responsibility and dedication who thought first of the benefits of education to students. Foremost among these was Judge T. N. Harvey, who served as President of the Board from 1929 until his death in 1948. The testimonies of administrators who worked with him and other persons connected with the District indicate that he was a positive force, moving the Board forward. Another person who served alongside Judge Harvey during this period of time was A.D.M. Osborne, whose service period covered a span of some eighteen years. Towards the end of the 1930's, H. E. Woodworth came onto the Board, and he was another of those lay citizens coming from a successful agricultural background, who gave of his leadership abilities over a long period of time. He was to succeed Judge Harvey as President upon the latter's death in 1948. In 1940, C. W. O'Neill became a Board member, and he was to begin a long period of service through the Forties and Fifties during the post-war growth era of the District.

World War II and the District

The war clouds on the horizon for the nation affected the Kern County Union High School District by the spring of 1941. First to feel the influence were personnel in the District, with leaves of absences being the order of the day for many male employees of military age. By October, 1942, the number of certificated employees who had left for the service or other wartime related activities had swelled to almost one-third of the teaching staff.[76] Even though the administration and the Board battled for completion of the auditorium for some time afterwards, by the mid-year 1941, it became clear that building programs were going to come to a standstill. In fact, in June of 1941, the Board adopted an emergency policy, "...all building construction and capital outlays, except such as appear absolutely necessary, be deferred until the present emergency is over."[77] The day after Pearl Harbor, the Board took action on another resolution pledging that all District facilities would be reserved for the use of the national government because of the war with Japan.[78]

In January of 1942, the Board became involved with a civilian pilot training program started at Meadows Field and later also at Lone Pine in conjunction with the Los Angeles School District, and mechanic learner courses were approved for the Junior College Division in cooperation with the United State Army Air Corps and the U. S. Civil Service Commission. An interesting resolution was passed at the same Board meeting approving these two programs. It stated that, because of the shortage of clerical help, married women could be so employed for the duration of the hostilities.[79]

With the opening of the fall term in 1942, the Board was presented with the problem of delaying the start of school, as requested by agriculturalists in the area, so that students might assist with the harvesting of crops during the war effort. The District opted to use the usual starting date, September 8th, and take care of work demands by "...a liberal policy of granting work permits."[80] Later in the fall, the County Agricultural Committee and the County U.S.D.A. War Board asked that the school be closed for three weeks to speed up the cotton harvest. Again, a position was taken which appeared to be in the best interest of students: the Superintendent was instructed to do everything possible to cooperate and still preserve the educational program for the students. Schools were closed for a shorter period of time than requested during November, and this action was applauded by a PTA delegation from the community.[81] Harvest holidays were permitted at various times during the war effort when the demand was acute and when the educational program of the students would not suffer.

The school district was also able to make financial contributions to the war effort. In the fall of 1943, $500,000.00 of District money was invested in war bonds. In the spring of that year, a policy was established to allow seniors entering military service to receive a diploma under emergency conditions. They must have completed twelve units of work, be at least seventeen years, ten months of age at the time of leaving school, have completed the first quarter of the senior year and state subject requirements, have stayed in school until one week of being called to active duty, and have served in the armed forces from the time of induction until commencement day of their class.[82]

As a matter of fact, students became closely involved in the war effort, including those who were not eligible for military service. Cadet programs were established throughout the schools for young men of pre-military age. These programs became an important part of physical education instruction. Students in the FFA raised victory gardens. All students were available to pick cotton and perform other agricultural chores during the harvest holidays. A common activity for female coeds was the preparation of Red Cross bandages, and military balls became the highlight of the social seasons.

Because of the lack of transportation facilities, it was necessary to curtail athletic programs. Intramural sports became the way of life for most schools. In September of 1943, a District football plan was adopted with intramurals at Bakersfield, East Bakersfield, Shafter, and McFarland, complemented by round robins in Bakersfield. There was an all-star game involving all schools at the end of the year. Some of the schools, most notably Bakersfield (KCHS), dropped the names of their regular athletic teams and used temporary nomenclature to designate the various teams during the wartime season.

The Junior College Division experienced perhaps the most severe repercussions from the war of any of the District's programs. Enrollment dropped from a high of 1,900 at the beginning of the war to a low of approximately 200 students during the height of the hostilities. It was, of course, necessary to reduce staff drastically, although in many cases, this occurred automatically because of military leaves of absence. In fact, according to Ray Chism, it was necessary to terminate only two

Junior College staff members because of the abrupt shift in enrollment, and no formal reduction-in-force plan was needed.[83]

College Director Bird kept up a massive correspondence with college students and staff members in the service. One of the recipients of these "letters from home" was Edward Simonsen, who, although not officially connected with Bakersfield College prior to the war except for having been enrolled in an aeronautics course while teaching at East Bakersfield High School, remembers with gratitude the news from home that came in the Grace Bird letters. On a regular basis, he received them in the far away places and strange environments where he was stationed in the United States Marine Corps.

In spite of all of the wartime hardships that curtailed the building programs, the school programs did not die and students continued to get a good education. Jeanette Wheeler came to Shafter High School as a teacher of journalism and advisor to the yearbook in September of 1944. Her recollection is as follows:

> It was in the depths of the war and there were not many men available for they were all in the service. In fact, less than one-third of the faculty at Shafter High School were men. The high school had not had a journalism and yearbook advisor the year before, since the teacher had left in the middle of the year because of unavailability of housing. I was told that the previous year, the students had gone to school in the morning, and in the afternoons had picked cotton during the fall months to keep the harvest moving. However, the year I came there were German prisoners of war in a migrant camp nearby who picked the cotton and the students were relieved of that duty. Another thing they were happy about is that they had gotten their football program back because for the previous year or two, they had played rugby. Now they had a new coach, Lowell Todd, and they beat Wasco for the first time in three years."[84]

During the spring of 1943, H. W. "Pat" Kelly, the Attendance Supervisor for the District, moved to Shafter to succeed Principal E. P. Janes. Even though it was in the middle of the war, Mr. Kelly remembers that the school program at Shafter was moving ahead, and he particularly appreciated the move to an attractive environment for his own growing family. "We got excellent cooperation from the community as well as the staff, and I was particularly pleased that there were so many top academic students in the programs at Shafter High School."[85] Although it was a low point for athletics generally during the time he moved to Shafter, Mr. Kelly's own interest in athletics, stemming from participation in sports at Stanford University and some coaching duties in the Bay Area before coming to Kern County, led him to take an active interest in rebuilding the athletic program at the school after the war.

The grimness of the wartime years did not prevent the District from celebrating its 50th anniversary with a pageant in January of 1942. Allen Cannon, then a teacher at Kern County Union High School, was designated by Superintendent Nelson to act as director of the pageant. The fiftieth anniversary extravaganza presented scenes from Kern County history covered by the fifty years of the District's history. Closely involved in this project was a new teacher with a specialty in dance at Kern County Union High School. Her name was Margo Crane (Robesky). Her recollection is that the pageant lasted some three hours and featured in one scene, "The Dance of the Oilwells," with Jean Chambers, Betty Whidden (Moehnke), and Miss Crane. Superintendent Nelson was particularly interested in dance as an activity for the high school and was often an interested spectator at rehearsals.[86]

The 1944-45 school year saw the beginning of the return of normalcy to the campuses of the District. Football seasons for the schools in the fall of 1944 were generally extended, although the athletic programs really were not back at full strength until the following year. In the spring semester of 1944, the Board adopted a policy to allow credit for military service, anticipating the return of large numbers of high school students whose educational programs had been interrupted by military service. Superintendent Nelson tendered his resignation in the spring of 1945, and his successor was to be a man who had been a staff member since 1929, having taught drafting and having been the first business manager for the District. He was Assistant Superintendent for

Business, Theron L. McCuen. Mr. McCuen, beginning with the 1945-46 school year, embarked upon a twenty-three year career as Superintendent of the Kern County Union High School District.

A New Campus is Born Out of Military Activity

In the summer of 1944, the high school district engaged in correspondence with the Indian Wells Valley School District, some 115 miles east of Bakersfield in the Mojave Desert. The Indian Wells Valley School District served an attendance area that was the site of the establishment of a military base to be known as the U. S. Naval Ordnance Test Station at China Lake. California Institute of Technology had begun rocket testing in the desert as early as 1939. The Navy soon became involved and took over the program, with construction beginning on the base in 1943. The base grew quickly into a major installation and needed skilled civilian employees as well as military service personnel. It was obvious that a plan was needed to provide a complete elementary and high school program for the sons and daughters of those working on the base and of service personnel stationed there.

After a series of maneuvers to find the best way of providing secondary level education, special legislation was passed in 1945 to allow the Kern County Union High School District to operate a high school program on the base. On September 10, 1945, Burroughs High School officially opened, named after Captain Sherman E. Burroughs, the first commanding officer of the China Lake Base. Principal of the school was F. R. Wegner, who was also the Superintendent of the newly organized China Lake Joint Elementary School District. Earl Murray was to be Vice-Principal of the high school, and simultaneously he was to be Assistant Superintendent of the China Lake District.[87] Thus, out of the military activities related to World War II, another campus was added to the District.

Ellis Tiffany describes the opening of the Burroughs High School:
> Despite the fact that the huts still in use on the first day of school as temporary classrooms received an overflow influx of elementary pupils, 161 high

school students also reported to the compound for enrollment. This latter contingent was met by twelve faculty members, only four of whom had been processed for employment by the time the Kern County Board met that evening. These four were: Mrs. Katherine Brown, instructor in social science; Lloyd Wollen, shop teacher; and, Mrs. Alice Woolf, art instructor. Another Board action, taken in conjunction with the above, authorized its president to sign an agreement with the China Lake district for "the joint operation of the schools on the Naval Ordnance Test Station."

Thus, September 10, 1945 saw the terms set up for the official launching of Burroughs High School as a separate educational entity, though it was destined to pass through the first fifteen years of its existence on the same campus with an elementary institution.

Wegner's term of office as Principal of Burroughs High School ended with the close of the 1945-46 school year. The Kern County Board (Kern County Union High School District) at its meeting of May 13, 1946 elected Murray as his replacement on the same half-time basis as it had used with Wegner. Succeeding Murray as Vice-Principal was Kenneth W. Westcott, whom the Board had employed on the previous January 28 as the school's science teacher.[88]

An evening high school was established at the beginning of the 1948-49 term in conjunction with an apprenticeship program. Lloyd Wollen, mechanical arts teacher at the school, was the first Principal of the evening high school.[89]

The school yearbook, El Burro, noted, "The history of Burroughs High School is in a large measure the history of the Naval Ordnance Test Station."[90]

The beginning athletic program included basketball, A and B levels softball, tennis, and volleyball. Drama, chorus and band were also available to students. Kenneth W. Westcott, later to become Principal of the school, was the marching band instructor."[91]

The sports program was expanded in the second year of operation to include football, track and Girls' Athletic Association, with varied sports. El Burro also contains descriptions of such activities as a student council, student newspaper, photo club, and office practice. In music an addition was the "Swingteensters", obviously a student swing band.[92]

REFERENCES

CHAPTER IV - THE THIRTIES AND WORLD WAR II

1. The Oracle, 1931, "Principal's Message"

2. Minutes, Kern County Union High School District, (Bakersfield, California) March 2, 1931.

3. Rintoul, William T. "The Banning of the Grapes of Wrath", California Crossroads (Bakersfield, California) January, 1963, pp. 4-6.

4. Bird, Grace V. Leader in Junior College Education at Bakersfield and the University of California, Vol. I, University of California (Berkeley, California), 1978. p. 32.

5. Minutes, Kern County Union High School District, January 5, 1931.

6. Ibid., January 22, 1934.

7. Ibid., August 6, 1934 and September 19, 1934.

8. Ibid., October 1, 1934.

9. Ibid., January 24, 1936.

10. Ibid., March 27, 1939.

11. Ibid., Septbmer 11, 1939.

12. Ibid., August 29, 1930.

13. The Oracle, 1934.

14. Minutes, Kern County Union High School District, March 2, 1931.

15. Ibid., January 4, 1932.

16. Ibid., May 2, 1932.

17. Ibid., May 19, 1933.

18. Ibid., May 7, 1934.

19. Ibid., June 3, 1935.

20. Ibid., June 17, 1935.

21. Ibid., June 1, 1936.

22. Ibid., May 8, 1939.

23. Ibid., April 8, 1940.

References - Chapter IV (Continued)

24. Ibid., December 2, 1935.

25. Taped interviews with Gerald Smith, Donald Hart, Jack Hilton, and State Senator Walter Stiern, p. 9-12.

26. The Oracle, 1931.

27. The Oracle, 1934.

28. Hart, Donald, unpublished written memorandum.

29. The Oracle, 1935.

30. Minutes, Kern County Union High School District, September 4, 1935.

31. Ibid., May 1, 1939.

32. Ibid., March 4, 1936.

33. Ibid., May 4, 1936.

34. Ibid., April 29, 1938.

35. Allen, Ruth (Bogardus), unpublished written memorandum.

36. Taped interview with Jean Philippe.

37. News story on Crawford: contents given the author by a friend of hers, exact reference not available.

38. Davis, Billie, "I Was a Hobo Kid", The Saturday Evening Post, December 13, 1952, pp. 25, 107-109.

39. Taped interview with Edward Simonsen.

40. Armstrong, Orville, unpublished memorandum.

41. Minutes, Kern County Union High School District, October 6, 1940.

42. Ibid., December 9, 1940.

43. Ibid., March 10, 1941.

44. Ibid., July 14, 1941.

45. Ibid., February 7, 1942.

46. Merson, Thomas B., unpublished written memorandum.

References - Chapter IV (Continued)

47. *Minutes*, Kern County Union High School District, June 28, 1939.

48. *Ibid.*, December 18, 1939.

49. *Ibid.*, June 23, 1941.

50. *Ibid.*, August 24, 1942.

51. *Ibid.*, January 12, 1940 and January 10, 1944.

52. Wheeler, Jeanette, Material in this section taken from a series of articles in *Shafter Press*, (Shafter, California), on graduating classes of Shafter High School, May 24, 1978 through January 31, 1979.

53. *Laurion*, 1940, p. 35.

54. Taped interview with Jeanette Wheeler.

55. *Minutes*, Kern County Union High School District, May 3, 1930.

56. *McFarland Press*, November 17, 1968, special edition.

57. *Recuerdos*, 1932.

58. *Ibid.*, 1936.

59. *McFarland Press*, November 17, 1968.

60. Bird Biography, p. 50.

61. Chism, Ray A., *A Preliminary History of Bakersfield College*, unpublished manuscript (Bakersfield, California), 1981, p. 10.

62. Bultman interview.

63. Bird, pp. 58-63.

64. *Minutes*, Kern County Union High School District, July 10, 1939.

65. *Ibid.*, October 6, 1938.

66. *Minutes*, Kern County Union High School District, April 26, 1938.

67. *Ibid.*, January 9, 1939.

68. *Ibid.*, July 19, 1939.

69. *Ibid.*, February 27, 1941.

70. *Ibid.*, March 11, 1940.

References - Chapter IV (Continued)

71. Ibid., August 12, 1941.
72. Ibid., November 24, 1941.
73. Ibid., April 27, 1942.
74. Ibid., November 23, 1942.
75. Taped interview with H. W. Kelly.
76. Minutes, Kern County Union High School District, October 26, 1942.
77. Ibid., June 23, 1941.
78. Ibid., December 8, 1941.
79. Ibid., January 26, 1942.
80. Ibid., August 24, 1942.
81. Ibid., November 9, 1942.
82. Ibid., May 24, 1943.
83. Chism, p. 13.
84. Taped interview with Jeanette Wheeler.
85. Kelly interview.
86. Taped interview with Allen Cannon.
87. Tiffany, Ellis L. Public Education and the United States Naval Ordinance Test Station of China Lake: A Brief History, an unpublished manuscript (China Lake, California), 1966, p. 40.
88. Ibid, pp. 41-42.
89. Ibid., pp. 42-43.
90. El Burro, 1946, Yearbook of Burroughs High School, p. 14.
91. Ibid., p. 18.
92. Ibid., 1947.

CHAPTER V

THE END OF WORLD WAR II AND THE FIFTIES

The Return of the World War II Servicemen

World War II finally came to an end in September of 1945, with the signing of the surrender of the Japanese aboard the Missouri. In the 1945 issue of the Bulletin, the newly organized Kern County Union High School District internal publication, Orville Armstrong, Homer Beatty, Paul Freed, Jack Hilton, Lawrence McArdell, Jack Rowe, and Theron Taber were welcomed home.[1] Earlier that year, the minutes of the Board had made reference to the fact that the high schools could now return to normal athletic procedures with the proviso that public carriers would be used until the federal restrictions were removed on the use of school vehicles for athletics.[2] With a new Superintendent on board, Theron McCuen, and the new Assistant Superintendent just home from the service, Theron Taber, the District was ready for the re-awakening of new life into the many school programs which had been in hibernation during World War II. Former Superintendent Theron McCuen has this recollection of the situation which presented itself in the District.

> Our chief problem immediately after the war was that of growth. I recall that when I became Superintendent, the average daily attendance in the high school and junior college district was 5,000. That was in 1945. When I retired in 1968 as Superintendent of both the high school and junior college districts, the ADA was in the neighborhood of 28,000. It must be remembered that, in 1945, we had only four high schools: Bakersfield, East Bakersfield, Shafter, and McFarland, plus the college. Therefore, in assuming the office of Superintendent, I found it was necessary to look down the road a ways - you can't live for the moment or even for the next year - you have to plan ahead. In my investigation of the factors that assist one in determining growth, it clearly showed that we had problems ahead if we did not take steps immediately to build some new schools.[3]

The giant step taken to alleviate the oncoming problem was the proposal to the Board that a bond issue of six million dollars be presented to the voters.

Another measure taken in the summer of 1946 was the hiring of a new administrative staff member who was to have a major responsibility immediately for the improvement of instruction in the District, and who was later to carry a most influential leadership role for a period of some thirty years, including just prior to his retirement, that of Superintendent. John W. Eckhardt was named Coordinator of Instructional Programs, which position had been set up by Superintendent Nelson just prior to his leaving the District. The resignation of the first person to serve in this role, Don Harrison, led to the appointment of Mr. Eckhardt.

Before his tour of duty in the Navy during World War II, the new Coordinator of Instruction had been a member of the Kern County Office of Superintendent of Schools. He recalls that his duties with the County office had often led him into an adversary position with the District since he was in charge of assisting the outlying schools to formulate plans for separation from the Kern County Union High School District. Another of his duties was that of coordinating a program of articulation for eighth grade students into the high school system, and there was some conflict with the District related to these duties also. However, in spite of these "friendly adversarial" stances into which Mr. Eckhardt had been placed with Mr. McCuen and other administrators from the District, they had developed mutual respect for each other in their professional responsibilities.

The program of coordination of instruction from the District level had not been a successful one largely because the schools were highly individualistic and did not care for the idea of "District meddling" in their instructional affairs. Mr. Eckhardt recalls some of the first efforts that he made to breathe some new life into the program of instruction.

> "I had to originate some ideas and one of them was to get several committees of teachers together to analyze areas of instruction that would include the four high schools. The first one that we started with was home economics. We got the home economics teachers together to evaluate the program and see

what good practices could take place in schools in a similar manner. Another thing that was needed and Mr. McCuen asked me to get it started, was to conduct some workshops for teachers who had not been in any kind of in-service training for a considerable period of time."[4]

The workshop program was established with an outside consultant secured to assist. In addition, some District guidance activities were inaugurated, including a District-wide articulation program in which the new Coordinator of Instruction had been involved at the County Superintendent of Schools Office. Further, a District testing program was established. These activities gave the new District administrator a busy first three years in his new assignment.

DISTRICT CONCERNS

Bond Election of 1947

Having surveyed the current status of the District in the spring of 1947, Superintendent McCuen proposed to the Board that a bond election for six million dollars be placed on the ballot. The Board approved and the election was scheduled for May 7th. Mr. McCuen recalls that the last bond election which the District had placed on the ballot was for $400,000 and this one at the six million dollar figure was greeted with some consternation by staff members. Among these was Hazel Jordan, a member of the history department at Kern County Union High School. In the Superintendent's words: "One of our very fine teachers asked me one day as she passed me in the hall, 'Theron, do you really think we can pass that?' I said, 'I don't know but we've got to try because we must do it.'" The March issue of the <u>Bulletin</u> carried this editorial by the Superintendent:

> With plans underway for a six million dollar bond election, it is imperative that each teacher understand the needs of the District in terms of the number of students to be educated, as well as the plan to meet these needs. At the present time, the schools of the District are overcrowded to the extent of 1400

students. Over forty emergency or substandard classroom facilities are in use. In October, 1933, there were 3,517 regular day students in the high schools and junior college. Last October this figure reached 7,101, and it is estimated to reach 11,850 by October, 1956.

Following a study of various plans of financing the building program needed to house these students, the Board of Trustees has concluded that a bond election is the most satisfactory plan. A bond election is to be called early in May. Each teacher will be acquainted with a program and plan of campaign through small-group faculty meetings. Every teacher can be of inestimable help in carrying the election to a successful conclusion.

Much ground work has been laid and reactions from the public have been most heartening.[5]

A FACTS sheet was developed which gave a breakdown of the way in which the proposed six million dollars was to be spent. Included were allocations for a four-year Bakersfield junior college and a District administration building, an increase in the size of the East Bakersfield plant, an agriculture and farm mechanical unit for McFarland, new facilities for Shafter, and an allocation for sites to satisfy additional needs. The three largest allocations were $1,500,000 for the Arvin plant; $1,000,000 for the proposed Oildale high school and $2,200,000 for a West Bakersfield high school plant.[6] A sophisticated organization was established to assure the success of the election with a bond committee comprised of school personnel, a series of Superintendent's bulletins issued regularly to give progress reports, and a public relations program which assured the support of the community leadership, especially the Bakersfield Chamber of Commerce. In fact, according to an issue of the Bakersfield Californian, dated April 29, 1947, headlines stated that "...28 prominent Kern organizations endorse the $6,000,000 issue."[7]

The careful planning paid off, for when the election day was concluded the voter count indicated that the bond had been approved by a vote of six and one-half to one. According to Superintendent McCuen, funds from the sale of bonds were invested in government securities immediately so that no money was allowed to stand idle. And, for a considerable period of time, the interest paid on those bonds was a fraction of one percent.

Apparently the building program moved ahead smoothly and without delay, supported by a cooperative Board of Trustees and carried out by local architects and contractors. In fact, Mr. McCuen recalls that two of these architects had been students in his drafting classes at Kern County Union High School. He believes that his background in engineering drawing was a great help in working with the architects as the program moved apace.

A Public Information Program

The District's Public Information Program, which played such a large role in the bond election of 1947, actually dates back to 1940. At that time, with some encouragement from <u>Bakersfield Californian</u> publisher, Alfred Harrell, Superintendent Thomas Nelson established a District Public Information Program. He hired a person who had had a public relations background at the University of Southern California in the Coordination Office and Speakers' Bureau. Avery Allen was the man selected for that position which was half-time public relations and half-time teaching. Mr. Allen took the job because it was his goal to combine his background in journalism and writing with that of promoting education. And, the new position in the Kern High School District seemed to be the ideal opportunity for the realization of this goal. The additional activity needed to inform the public of the issues involved in the bond brought about a change in the duties of the Supervisor of Public Information. In his own words:

> In the spring of 1947, the District went for a bond election for funds to build Arvin and to do other things needed in the District. It was a wonderful day for me when I was informed, just after the election was announced, that my job was full-time in the District Office. Actually, while the job had been established as half-time public relations and half-time teaching, it had developed into a full-time public relations and half-time teaching. So it was nice to have it a little more clearly defined.[8]

The Public Information Program had been organized with individual representatives at each school whose responsibility it was, on a part-time basis, of course, to write news articles that would be of interest to the public, and they found their way through Mr. Allen's office at the District to the media outlets, including, newspapers and radios, and, later on, television. Mr. Allen wrote news stories of general interest from the District, and, for some twenty years, covered the news from the Board meetings. However, the hard work paid off and the program got attention from the State Superintendent of Public Instruction and from other districts, one from as far away as the Phoenix Union High School District in Arizona. As a result, the District was asked to send ideas and a format of the organization there and to other districts. Again, quoting Mr. Allen:

> Our program was built on integrity. We attempted to keep it on a professional basis -- particularly in our relation with the media. But, it was our goal to represent the events in the member schools, the actions of the Board of Trustees, and the operations of the District office factually, and to do it with integrity. I think in the long run this was a most successful road to success.

Later when television became an important medium of information, a staff member from Kern County Union High School, Allen Cannon, spent time developing television programs around school activities. A news photographer was added and the District in-house <u>Bulletin</u> was established. The relationship of the public information position in the District was important in the opinion of Mr. Allen. The fact that he was responsible directly to the District Superintendent led later to his title being changed to that of Administrative Assistant to the Superintendent. This direct responsibility to the Superintendent was an asset in the development of the program.

A footnote should be added here which relates to another staff member of the District, who was quoted in an earlier chapter. Ruth Bogardus, the first librarian at East Bakersfield High School, contributed some of her recollections on the opening of that school. Her father was Professor Emory S. Bogardus,

Chairman of the School of Sociology at the University of Southern California. While he was in attendance at USC, Avery Allen took classes from Professor Bogardus and became acquainted with him personally. Because of this connection, the two young people met at the first faculty meeting attended by Mr. Allen in the fall of 1940. Two years later, they were married. Thus, not only did this young man find the job that he had coveted in Bakersfield, but he was also fortunate to find a companion for life.

Completion of the Auditorium

Readers will recall that the music/auditorium building, later to be named Harvey Auditorium, was under construction prior to World War II. Progress on the building was brought to a standstill because of federal restrictions on wartime construction of nonmilitary related buildings. Construction on this building had actually been approved in 1941. When the government finally cleared the continued construction of the building in the fall of 1945, an unusual procedure was used to make sure that there was public support for this action. On November 8, 1945, an open meeting of the electors of the District was held to decide on compromise offers from contractors to complete the building. The meeting was attended by 118 electors and the problem was outlined by Judge T. N. Harvey, President of the Board. The resolution to complete the construction was passed by a vote of 112 of those present, with six abstentions.[9] At the next meeting, the Board passed a resolution to enter into a contract with Ashby and Opperman to continue work on the auditorium building.[10] Three years later, on November 8, 1948, the completed building was dedicated and named in honor of Thomas Norman Harvey, who served on the Board of Trustees from May, 1927, until his death in October of 1948. This building, with its main auditorium seating 1,200 and its two smaller auditoriums, the little theatre and the audio visual classroom, together with its dramatics and radio broadcasting facilities was to be an important adjunct to the District's facilities. In addition, it was to serve the community as an auditorium for cultural and civic events.

Gerald Smith, who had been placed in charge of operation of the auditorium, recalls opening night that fall with a production of "La Boheme" by the San Francisco Opera Company. The auditorium had just barely been completed in time for opening night, and, in fact, Mr. Smith and Roger Lewis, who was a student assistant, found a number of problems before the opera company got to town: the footlights had the colors mixed, the electrician foreman complained because of union problems since the opera company had its own crew of approximately 300 members, the dimmers would not work properly and portable dimmers had to be brought by the opera company. After the company arrived in five railroad cars and brought on the sets, parts of the light fixtures, called rondells, kept falling down. In fact, it was not possible to correct this problem before the performance and one of the performers was hit on the head by a falling light fixture. He was a real pro and kept on with his role according to Gerald Smith. Finally a piece of glass from one of the lights actually fell into the violin of one of the musicians, and he had to stop his part of the musical performance to dislodge it. However, in spite of all of these problems, "La Boheme" was a great success and was hailed by those in attendance as the beginning of a new cultural era in Bakersfield brought about by the completion of Harvey Auditorium.[11]

The Schools in the Post-War Era

Bakersfield College

Of all the campuses in the District, it would be expected that Bakersfield College would feel the effects of the war more dramatically than the did the high schools. The primary reason, of course, was that so many of its students were in the service of their country. In fact, during the World War II years enrollment dropped into the 200's with graduating classes of no more than 30 to 50 students per year.[12] However, with the close of the wartime activities, enrollment at the college took a dramatic upsurge so that by the fall of 1946, there were actually 1,200 students on the campus.[13] One of those who returned to the campus after the war was Edward Simonsen, later to become a future Chancellor of the college system. Prior to going into the service, he had been a faculty member at East Bakersfield High School. Immediately after his release from the Marines, he went back to the University of California campus at Berkeley to study in the junior college field since he had received encouraging communications from both Grace Bird and Theron McCuen that there might be a place for him on the campus in Bakersfield. It was believed that, because of the new faces on campus, a large number of them former servicemen, it would be beneficial to have a person with military experience to serve as Dean of Students. Thus, in September of 1946, Edward Simonsen returned to Bakersfield, this time to the college campus as the new Dean of Students.

It must be remembered that Bakersfield College in those days was located on the same campus as Bakersfield High School and this in itself posed problems because of the mix of mature servicemen and high school age students, some as young as fourteen or fifteen years of age. High on the list of problems that the new Dean was supposed to resolve was that of the smoking restrictions placed on the junior college students, so that "when the smoking lamp was lit," they would not be mixed with the high school students. College students were expected to use the parkway area on California Avenue for smoking, keeping themselves separated from the high school students for this activity.

Dean Simonsen was also to mix and mingle with college students in the student lounge areas of the campus and encourage them not to waste their time playing cards and other frivolous activities, but to give themselves over to the solid pursuits of education. He soon found, however, that these mature students were already motivated, having realized that those who were to succeed in the peaceful civilian life, were those with a good education. Particularly this was true in the engineering and science fields and Bakersfield College was well on its way to developing strong programs in these fields under the leadership of such outstanding instructors as Ed Hemmerling, George S. Sagen, and Paul Baldwin, among others.[14]

In reflecting back over the period of ten years between 1946 and 1956, at the conclusion of which the college was ensconced on the new campus "on the hill", Mr. Simonsen recalls the generally positive relationship that existed between the college and the high school at a time when more than 6,000 students were on the campus with a maturity range of students from early teens to adult ex-servicemen, aged prematurely by life on the battlefields of World War II. Grace Bird had built a spirit of excellence into the institution, the watchword being "quality" as it related to personnel. According to Mr. Simonsen, she had the affinity for attracting personnel who were to provide strong, positive leadership in the various educational fields which the college provided.

In the fall of 1949, Miss Bird submitted her resignation to the Board of Trustees and asked that she be relieved of duties as of March 1, 1950. She resigned to accept a position of Associate Director of the Office of Relations with Schools at the University of California in Berkeley.[15] Immediately the Board began to search for a replacement and appointed Assistant Superintendent Theron Taber as Interim Director of the college for the remainder of the year. The District <u>Bulletin</u> has this to say regarding Miss Bird:

>News of the resignation of Bakersfield College's distinguished Director, Miss Grace V. Bird, to accept a new position with the University of California, came with a suddenness that left teachers and students breathless...
>
>The regret felt by all over Miss Bird's leaving is only tempered by the realization that her thirty-two years of professional service and outstanding achievement in the District are being recognized by such an eminent institution as the State University, where her professional life will find its capstone.[16]

In March of 1950, the Board of Trustees announced the selection of Ralph Prator as the new head of Bakersfield College. Prior to his election, the title of "Director" had been changed to that of "President." The new President came from an administrative position with the University of Colorado, where he had graduated with his bachelor's and master's degrees; however, he had taken his doctorate at the University of California and had experience teaching in elementary, high school, and junior college levels in California, New Mexico, and Colorado.[17]

President Prator turned his attention to making some changes in the structure of the college and it soon became evident to those who worked with him, including John Collins, teacher-counselor at that time and a future President of the College, that he had been given his "marching orders" from the Board of Trustees to make the college into a more comprehensive, collegiate-type institution. Thomas Merson, the new Dean of Instruction, and Norman Harris, Dean of the new Vocational Technical Education Division, were key leaders in this transition along with the other faculty members mentioned earlier. Already plans were being formulated for the move to the new campus, and Dean of Students Simonsen was given additional duties to work with the faculty on developing educational specifications for the new campus and organizing the staff for the move.[18]

Bakersfield High School

The "mother" school of the District, named Bakersfield High School in 1945, while sharing the high school enrollment in the metropolitan Bakersfield area with East Bakersfield High School, had become a large high school. In fact, the enrollment in September of 1946 was just two students short of the 4,000 mark. The Principal was an experienced District administrator, Leslie W. Hedge, assisted by a staff of veteran teachers, counselors and co-administrators with a sprinkling of newcomers who were just beginning to make an appearance after World War II. Athletics was back in full swing with full schedules in all of the sports. The 1947 Oracle was dedicated to Coach Griffith, who had just been succeeded in the fall by a new head coach, a graduate of Bakersfield High School, named Homer Beatty. While there is not space in this section of our account to deal with individual student honors to any degree, we cannot pass over this era in the history of Bakersfield High School athletics without making reference to a Driller football player who was later to be well-known throughout the country and the world as a broadcaster and commentator on athletic events. Frank Gifford was a graduate of the class of 1948. He later went to the University of Southern California to make a name for himself in football. After graduation he played professionally with the New York Giants professional football team before going into television.

East Bakersfield High School

The second oldest high school in metropolitan Bakersfield, East Bakersfield High School, had an enrollment of 1,243 students in September, 1946. The high school yearbook, the Sierran, that year was dedicated to Principal Kenneth Rich, who had been the school's head since its beginning in 1938. Irving Lane was now Vice-Principal and Dean of the school. The District Bulletin of 1947 noted that, "Teachers in East Bakersfield High School have formed an East Bakersfield High School Teacher's Club and will soon receive recognition from the California Teacher's Association as an affiliated classroom teachers unit."[19]

Shafter High School

In the bustling agriculture community of Shafter, the high school by the fall of 1946 had attained an enrollment of 413. The previous year a new Principal had been assigned to the school after the departure of H. W. "Pat" Kelly, who had been at the helm during the war years. The new man was featured in the March, 1947, issue of the District Bulletin and was introduced as follows:

> Jack M. Hill, Principal of Shafter High School, is a man of many interests and abilities and a native Californian. Jack entered the University of California and was outstanding in athletics. Following a trip to

Japan with the University of California's baseball team, and a short session of major league baseball, Jack went into business. A few years later he decided to enter teaching and enrolled at Fresno State College.

Principal Hill had come from Bakersfield High School, where he was the attendance officer, and prior to that, had been assigned for five years at East Bakersfield High School having been Boys' Vice Principal. The high school yearbook, the <u>Laurion</u> made particular reference to the football team as being "...among the best in the history of Shafter High School". It also noted that it was "a record year" for the Future Farmers and 69 seniors were pictured. Among them was Fred Starrh, who in his adult life became an agriculturist in the Shafter area, and in the 1980's a member of the Board of Trustees of the Kern Union High School District.[20]

The Kern River Valley School

Nestled in the scenic Kern River Valley some forty miles from Bakersfield up the tortuous Kern Canyon Road, was Kernville High School, as it was called in 1946. Mention has already been made in the previous chapter of the origin of the school, with some personal remembrances by the Principal, Thomas B. Merson. In the 1946-47 school year, Principal Merson was still on duty, assisted by Bertha Downing, rounding out the complete certificated staff. Actually the pupil-teacher ratio was quite low, there being a total of twenty students enrolled in September of 1946. In March of that year, it was noted in the District in-house publication:

> "Close cooperation between parents and the school is an actuality in Kernville High School, where meetings of the parent-teacher association are devoted to frank discussions of such items as the interpretation of standardized test, weaknesses and strong points of the school program, and the future development of the school.[21]

The following year, E. C. Mills became Principal of the school and presided over the moving of the high school to a new site. The move was necessary because the Army Corps of Engineers had plans to build a dam near the location of the high school, and, in fact, the original site of the school is now under the waters of Lake Isabella. After negotiations with both the Army Corps of Engineers and Kernville Union Elementary School District, a location to be used by both school plants was selected on the Erskine Creek Road. This site was selected primarily so the two school facilities could be located near each other to coordinate transportation; thus buses would pick up both elementary and high school students and not duplicate identical routes. The October, 1952 issue of the District Bulletin contained this item:

> Among notable changes in the upper Kern Valley which have taken place because of the Isabella Dam project was the moving of Kernville High School to a new site several miles distant. The new campus is adjacent to a new site which is to be developed for the Kernville Union Elementary School. At a recent meeting of the Board of Trustees, the name of Kernville High School was changed to Kern Valley High School, a name appropriate to the new setting.[22]

A High School on a Naval Base

More than 100 miles east of Bakersfield in the middle of the Mojave Desert, the newest of the District schools, Burroughs High School, had an enrollment of just over 200 students in the fall of 1946. This was the second year of the school's existence. Principal Earl Murray was also the Superintendent of the China Lake Elementary School District. In addition to the regular high school program, an evening school session for adults had been opened with an enrollment which outnumbered that of the regular school -- some 300 adult students. The District Bulletin indicated that the school was organized around a home room plan with an extensive and unique activities program being encouraged. At this time the high school was located on the Naval Ordnance Test Station at Inyokern; soon a move to a new location was to occur.[23]

The Adult Evening School

The Adult Evening School had also survived World War II. In the fall of 1946, the Bakersfield Evening School offered a varied schedule of classes in such locations as Standard School, Lincoln School, Bakersfield Women's Club, North of the River Women's Club, and at the Belridge Oil District. Separate evening school branches also existed at East Bakersfield High School and Burroughs High School. A popular public educational series, the Open Forum, in the fall of 1946 featured the theme, "Are We Winning the Peace?". The programs featured such speakers as Winifred Walker on "Western Europe - Post War"; William Winter, "Democracy for Export or Soviet Challenge in Asia"; Merryle Stanley Rukeyser, "What's Ahead for the United States?"; Ellis L. Spackman, "Occupation, Success or Failure?"; Erica Mann, "Report from Europe"; and Hubert Herring, "What About Democracy in Latin America?".[24]

A New School Opens and Another On the Drawing Boards

It will be remembered that shortly before the outbreak of World War II, the District had purchased a school site southeast of Bakersfield in the rural community of Arvin. Since construction could not be considered during hostilities, the site had been leased to a farmer, who put it to good use growing crops needed during the war years. Now plans were moved ahead to construct Arvin High School. Accordingly, in the fall of 1946, forty acres adjacent to the site the District owned were purchased to be used for a school farm. And, in the next month, preliminary plans for the school were shown to the Board by architect, Ernest McCoy.[25] Two years later the Board authorized a call for bids for the school, and in June, 1948, the Principal was selected. Clyde Dawald, then Principal of McFarland High School, was named to this position.[26]

By February of 1949, a number of veteran teachers in the District had been chosen by Mr. Dawald to move out to the new school, which was scheduled to open the next fall. Among these were Arthur Johnson, Dean of Students; Hester Reina, English; Oliver Paris, mathematics; Earlene Waters, counseling and English; Edwin DeMello, counseling and teaching; and Holger Hansen, to head the Agriculture Department. It was expected that a staff of between thirty and forty teachers would be required for the

600-700 students anticipated when the school opened.[27] Actually the opening day enrollment was a little below the estimated figure, but before the year was well underway, the 600 estimate had been reached. An interesting sidelight to the construction of Arvin High School was a report by Superintendent McCuen to the Board in January, 1949, that a model of the Arvin High School construction was to be displayed at the "School House of Tomorrow" exhibit at the American Association of School Administrators conference in San Francisco that year.[28]

North of the River

The war had also intervened in the development of another school site purchased in 1939 north of Kern River on Douglas and McCray Streets, bounded by Charlana Drive. With prospects of an onrushing enrollment at hand, it seemed practical to develop this site further. Actually arrangements were made with the Standard Oil Company to purchase forty-five acres of land near the site which the District already owned to develop the new school. This site was situated north of Douglas Street, and according to Theron McCuen, the original land area of twenty-three acres was sold for enough money to purchase this more-desirable and larger site.[29] Shortly after the location was secured, the Board of Trustees took action to name the school after the founding father of the Kern County Union High School District, Alfred Harrell.

This move was not greeted enthusiastically by some of the residents of the area who wanted a name which would give geographical significance to the new school. In the fall of 1950, the Board received a letter from Mrs. Berniece Harrell Chipman, daughter of Alfred Harrell, who requested that the school accede to the wishes of the north of the river residents and not use the publisher's name for the new school. Her letter indicated that the publisher's family saw the merit in the wishes of the people in the area to select a geographical name, and, therefore, asked that a change be made. Forthwith, the Board named the new school "North of the River High School".[30] At the next meeting of the

Board of Trustees, the preliminary drawings for the new school were approved and North of the River High School was on its way.[31]

The West Campus

Again, since before World War II, discussions had taken place regarding the need for a campus in the west part of Bakersfield, an area that was predicted to grow even before a decision many years later to place a state college in that area. Discussion continued from time to time after the war. As a matter of fact, in the bond issue of 1947, an allocation was set aside for the purpose of securing a west high school site.[32] At one time, the Fourth and 'P' Street location was thought to be an appropriate setting for another school in the metropolitan area. However, this plan was discarded and a decision was made to use the property there for athletic purposes, primarily by Bakersfield High School since that campus was really too crowded to accommodate the burgeoning athletic programs.[33] Therefore, the new school in west Bakersfield was simply put aside for the time being because of the need to accommodate more pressing obligations.

Planning for New Growth

In the spring of 1950, Superintendent McCuen felt that it was time to outline for the Board of Trustees, the staff, and community, the needs indicated primarily by enrollment trends for the future of the Kern High School and Junior College Districts. Therefore, he, together with the staff, put together a report entitled "Next Steps in the Development of the Kern County Union High School District." In a preface to the body of the report, the building projects completed or under construction since the end of World War II were summarized. Included were: 1) the construction of Arvin High School; 2) additions to the East Bakersfield High School plant; 3) additions to Bakersfield High School and College, including completion of the auditorium; 4) the additions of the agriculture, shop and classroom buildings to McFarland High School; and, 5) the cafeteria and classroom buildings and other additions to Shafter High School. It was noted that other buildings/additions were on the drawing boards.

Taking into account the available data, a projection was made some twelve years ahead to October, 1962. The total figure of the projection was shocking for it was expected that by October, 1961, the total enrollment for the District would be almost 21,000 students in the high schools and junior college.

At least three implications were apparent from this report: 1) The building program underway since World War II would need to continue and be greatly expanded; 2) A large number of staff members would need to be added. (It was estimated that the professional staff would need to be increased from 400 980); and, 3) A program of financing would be needed. The report went into detail regarding the junior college situation, reviewing the history of these institutions, both in California and elsewhere in the nation, with considerable attention given to the organization of the junior college system. In prior discussions regarding organization, much attention had been focused on the four-year junior college system, which had been developed in a few locations throughout the State, most notably in Pasadena. After reviewing the implications of the four-year junior college arrangement, the Superintendent recommended that, in the Kern District, the college remain a two-year institution. The primary factor influencing this recommendation was that the organization of the elementary schools in the area was either in eight-year units or six and two-year units, which would not fit with the four-year college plan. To quote the report:

> Under the particular conditions existing in the Kern County Union High School District, it is believed that the clear-cut, logical approach to the organizational pattern calls for a separate two-year junior college. Such an institution would fit clearly into the pattern of District schools, would attract students from all high schools, and would operate in the atmosphere of a community college. As a member school of the District, close cooperation would exist in matters of curriculum, guidance, and even sharing of staff if necessary. It is recommended that a two-year junior college plan be established in the very near future.[34]

It should be noted that the reference made hereto "... in the atmosphere of the community college," projected ahead the terminology used to describe this institution in California today. The other important recommendation was that the junior college have a separate plant from that shared with Bakersfield High School.

In addition, the report recommended an expansion schedule, starting with the 1952-53 school year and opening of North of the River High School with the ninth and tenth grades; the 1953-54 moving of Bakersfield College to a separate campus; also in 1953-54, the addition of the eleventh grade to North of the River; then to 1954-55 when North of the River would add grade twelve. It was further suggested that plant additions be made to the existing campuses, and that a new District office unit be built. The total estimated cost of these projects was just over nine million dollars. In a review of the financial situation the Superintendent pointed out that some six million dollars would be available from bond funds and current allocations on July 1, 1950. To meet the difference between this sum and the total required for the suggested program of expansion, it was recommended that a special tax be voted for a five-year period, effective with the 1951-52 school year. It was suggested that a thirty cent increase of the tax rate of $1.10 over the five year period would provide these needed funds.

Before action could be taken on these plans; however, a natural event of such magnitude intervened that would change the course of the building program and its financing for the immediate future.

The Earthquake Hits

We refer, of course, to the earthquake of 1952. In the summer of that year, a series of earthquakes struck the southern San Joaquin valley with a ferocity that dealt body blows first to the Tehachapi area and then to metropolitan Bakersfield. At the Board meeting on August 7, the Superintendent was authorized to prepare a detailed report on buildings in the District damaged by the quake; the County Counsel gave the opinion that the customary competitive bidding procedure could be dispensed with in an emergency such as this, and repairs could begin immediately. Such structures as the old auditorium building and the apartment buildings on the Bakersfield High School campus were damaged beyond repair; bids were accepted at the August 15th meeting for the demolition of these buildings.[35] As more damage became evident in the schools, it was decided by the Board to set a later school opening calendar for those schools severely damaged. This included Bakersfield High School, Bakersfield College, East Bakersfield High School, and Kern Valley High School. The other schools were able to begin at the earlier date of September 8th. On September 22nd, an assessment of the damages was provided by the Superintendent, and six temporary classrooms were authorized for the Bakersfield High School/Bakersfield College campus. In addition, a number of citizens were invited to a meeting to be held in October to counsel the Board on the building needs and the procedures to be used to provide funding for satisfying those needs. Temporary quarters for the District administrative staff were secured at a building on Bernard Street, and offices for the junior college administrative staff were leased at the Hayward Lumber Company on the corner of 14th and 'H' Streets.

Early in October the Citizens Advisory Committee meeting was held and it was a consensus that a bond election should be held as soon as possible in an attempt to raise funds for the building needs. January 28 was the date set for the election and $17 million dollars was established as the dollar amount needed. By a vote of 16,178 to 2,031, the bond election was passed. In the February, 1953, issue of the <u>Bulletin</u>, Superintendent McCuen had this to say,

> The people of the District gave a clear-cut endorsement to our program of earthquake rehabilitation and expansion when they passed the $17 million dollar bond issue with a 16,178 to 2,031 vote. All of us are most grateful for this support. We can proceed now in a sound orderly manner with the building program. Every effort must be made to plan efficiently and well to the end that a fine quality of high school and community college education may continue to be offered the youth of this area. Many individuals and organizations assisted in the work of acquainting the people with the needs of our schools.

I am sure our entire staff joins me in expressing a sincere thanks to all of them. To you, the staff, may I say "thanks" for a job well done. Throughout the period prior to the bond election, you responded to every request and your combined efforts really brought the issue to a successful conclusion.

Now we have a job to do. The overwhelming support in the election came because the people recognized the problems facing our schools and had confidence in our total program. It is now up to us to carry on the instructional as well as the building program in a manner that will continue to merit this confidence.

In the Board meetings that took place that spring and on into the summer, hardly a one passed without some action taken on the building program. In fact, within the next five years, the physical appearance of the District was to take on a radical change.[36]

Following the Earthquake

New College Takes Shape

Of course plans were already underway for the new Bakersfield College site, the "campus on the hill", which Grace Bird had visualized. In fact, in the spring of 1951, the Board had authorized the purchase of 150 acres from the Kern County Land Company on Panorama Drive at $625 per acre.[37] The plot included Bluebell Canyon, which was to be the site of a new football stadium. The architectural firm of Wright, Metcalf, and Parsons had been selected before the earthquake of 1952 and had already begun some initial planning on the buildings. In addition, some funds had been earmarked for the beginning construction of the buildings, but there is no question that the quake and the urgency it gave to passing the bond issue facilitated the financing of the campus. Actually, however, the time schedule may have been deterred because of this natural disturbance. In the news media and on the street corners, whenever talk turned to the new college, much was said about the stadium being the first part of the institution to be constructed. Former Chancellor Edward Simonsen recalls the debate generated by this move.

> The first facility completed about which we took some criticism was the stadium. Theron Taber, Theron McCuen and the Board all told the same story to the public, which was valid. As the leveling on the upper part of the canyon was done, the dirt was moved down into the stadium, which was called Bluebell Canyon. This soil then from the upper part of the campus became a part of and enhanced the natural bowl itself. This was all a part of the engineering plan and resulted in the stadium being built first. Some of the more academically oriented people felt that this was a mistake and that, perhaps the library should have come first in the building plans."[38]

After the groundbreaking ceremonies on November 12, 1953, construction moved on the new college campus site with action on some part of the new campus on the agenda of most Board meetings.[39] It must be remembered that this planning and construction took place along with that occurring on other campuses of the District as a result of the devastation of the earthquake. Finally, during Easter vacation of 1956, the campus moved permanently to the new site having been on the location that it had occupied with the Kern County Joint Union High School since 1913. According to Ray Chism:

> During the Easter recess of 1956, Bakersfield College ceased its operation on the campus of Bakersfield High School and reopened in its new quarters up on the hill with no interruption in class work being reported. The new campus had 1400 students and 89 faculty members, and there were expectations that enrollment would increase by 30 per cent by the next fall. There were no inauguries at the time of the move at Easter time. The official dedication was on October 16, 1956, and it was performed by Robert Gordon Sproul, President of the University of California. Miss Bird was present at the ceremony.[39]

At last, then, Grace Bird's "campus on the hill" was a reality."[41]

200

Other Post-Earthquake Building

The damage caused by the earthquake to District facilities and the ensuing success of the 1953 bond issue perpetuated a flurry of construction activities that was to last through the greater part of the 1950's. The building programs consisted of two kinds: The first were those which would have been done whether or not the earthquake occurred and were occasioned by the growth and the need for expansion within the district system; second, of course, was the repair of damages caused to existing structures. The construction of Bakersfield College on its new campus would, of course, have occurred regardless of the earthquake. Two other school plants were constructed during the 1950's that were needed for growth. They were the North of the River School and the new high school in the south part of Bakersfield.

North of the River High School

Mention has already been made of the location of this school and the fact that the land purchased before World War II was exchanged for that in a slightly different location. The March, 1952, Kern High School District <u>Bulletin</u> carried this banner story regarding activities in the North of the River location:

> It was a dramatic moment during the Board of Trustees meeting recently when, in the presence of contractors and numerous sub-contractors, bids for construction of the new North of the River High School were open and read by Deputy Superintendent Theron S. Taber, Jr. There was a bid of $2,934,248 and another of $2,999,000, and a final one in the amount of $2,748,157. A list of sub-contractors in relation to the lowest bid was then read.
>
> The bids were referred to the architects for study, analysis and recommendations, and they left the room. After a time, the architects returned, and Architect C. B. Alford of the architectural firm of C. B. Alford, Architect, and W. J. Thomas, reported the low bid was in order and recommended that the contract be awarded to the lowest bidder, Guy E. Hall, General Contractor, on his bid of $2,748,157. Upon motion by Mr. O'Neill, seconded by Mr. Baldwin and unanimously carried, the Board awarded the contract to Mr. Hall.

Thus, a new high school in the district is about to be constructed.[42] Classes are expected to begin in the fall of 1953.

The school did open in the fall of 1953, and on October 6 of that year the school held an open house and dedication ceremony.[43]

The beginning enrollment was just over 600 and as was the custom in the district in the opening of schools, North of the River High School began with two classes. The four-year course of study was approved in the winter of 1955, and in the fall of the next year the school became a full-fledged four-year institution.[44]

During the summer of 1951 the Board had selected Jack M. Hill to be Principal of the new school. Mr. Hill was, at the time, Principal of Shafter High School and had formerly been on the staffa at East Bakersfield and Bakersfield High Schools. During the 1952-53 school year some seventeen district faculty members were selected to serve with Principal Hill at the new high school. These included: Jack Hilton, Assistant Vice-Principal; John Harp, Dean of Boys; Joy Robinson, Dean of Girls; Betty Lund, Allen Gruman, Gerald Hedden, Marlene Keach, Robert McLean, Wilbur Turney, Stanley Francis, Beulah Woodruff, Jack Bowles, H. B. Gelatt, Jordan Eliades, Ernest Graf, Richard Heber, and Charles Rhoads. Additional staff members from outside the district were added before the opening of the school in September of 1953. George Williamson became the second Principal of the school at the beginning of the 1955-56 school after the untimely death of Mr. Hill.

South High School

In the meantime, the metropolitan Bakersfield area was stretching southward and the need for a new school in that part of Bakersfield became apparent. Early in 1954, the architect for the new school, Ernest L. McCoy, presented a plans to the Board for the new plant which was to be built on a 50-acre plot on the south side of Planz Road between Chester Avenue and 'H' Street.[45] This location had been selected by the Board upon the

202

recommendation of the District administration. After satisfying the concerns of the State Department of Education and the Kern County Planning Commission regarding oil and gas rights and easements for canal, highways and railroads, the site was authorized for purchase in April, 1954, for the sum of $104,000.[46] Plans for the new school were developed during the ensuing two years with Grant W. Jensen selected to be the Principal. Mr. Jensen had been a member of the faculty at East Bakersfield High School and most recently had been Principal at Shafter High School.[47] In the spring of 1956 the planning was completed for the school and the contract was awarded to Tumblin and Company Construction Company at just under three million dollars.[48]

As construction on the buildings proceeded, Principal Jensen was busy drawing up plans for instruction and selecting a staff. The school opened in September of 1957 with a student body numbering some 800 and a faculty of 38 members. In addition to Principal Jensen, Gerald Hedden was Vice-Principal; Ann Dunstan and Henry Moroski, Deans; Gene Hartley, Coordinator of Student Activities; and Peter Algra, Attendance Officer. Among other staff members that first year were Elaine Avila, Spanish teacher; Milton Clift, social studies and coaching; Robert Douglas, art; Sally Briggs, business chairperson; Stanley Godecke, journalism; Robert Milliken, woodshop; Robert Coombs, mathematics and science chairman; Kenneth Fahsbender, fine arts chairman; Wayne Nunes, science; Bruce Pfutzenreuter, social studies and coaching; Genieve Magruder, English and social studies chairperson; Jack Towery, woodshop and coaching; Hal Williams, mathematics; and Tom Pettus, industrial arts chairman.[49] Dedication ceremonies took place on November 14, 1957.[50]

New Administration Offices

Plans had been laid before the earthquake to build new district administration offices to be located away from the Bakersfield High School campus. In fact, in the summer of 1949 the district had purchased property fronting on Twenty-fourth Street from the Kern County Land Company for the establishment of these offices. The property was located between 'D' and 'G' Streets and was purchased at a cost of $18,000.[51] It will be recalled that the earthquake forced the removal of the offices to a temporary location on Bernard Street and in December, 1953, Architect Robert N. Eddy was employed to draw plans and supervise the construction of the new buildings on Twenty-fourth Street.[52] Almost a year later plans were completed and a contract to construct the new buildings was awarded to D. M. Biggar.[53] In the summer of 1955 the building was completed and District headquarters were officially moved from the temporary location on Bernard Street. 2000 Twenty-fourth Street became the nerve center of the district.[54]

During the process of building the new District headquarters, it was decided to look at another location for a warehouse and maintenance facility. The property on Twenty-fourth Street would not accommodate such a facility and besides it seemed desirable that this structure be located elsewhere. Therefore, in January of 1955 the District made an agreement with Republic Steel Company to purchase a building just off the traffic circle on North Chester Avenue to be used for this purpose. Later District cafeteria facilities were located nearby.[55]

Bakersfield High School

As might well have been expected, the most damage to any of the district plants in the summer of 1952 would have been incurred on the "mother" campus, Bakersfield High School. Practically all of the buildings with the exception of the new auditorium facility would have to be rebuilt or razed and reconstructed. After extensive surveys it was determined that a new administration building would be built adjacent to Elm Grove and attached to the old Junior College Building. In 1956, the latter was renamed Warren Hall in honor of the school's most distinguished alumnus, Chief Justice of the United State Supreme Court, Earl Warren, after it was renovated.[55] In the location of the old Administration Building, a new cafeteria was also constructed and, just to the south, a new gymnasium. The Agriculture Building was razed and the agricultural program was incorporated into classrooms in the Science Building. The latter, along with Ludden Hall, the Library Building and the Industrial Arts Buildings were all deemed worthy of restoration.

Open house was held at the new administration facility in November of 1954 and construction continued on the rehabilitation of the other campus structures into the 1956-57 school year. When the renovation of the Library Building was completed, it was named Spindt Hall in honor of one of the long-time Superintendent/ Principal of Kern County Union High School, Herman A. Spindt.[59]

Further Changes

Other campuses were undergoing change because of growth during this period and abetted by the two successful bond elections in 1947 and 1953. At East Bakersfield High School construction was proceeding on a new study hall and thirteen classrooms, among other facilities. At Kern Valley High School, work on the gymnasium and three classrooms was under way. While at Shafter High School, plans for construction of a new administrative unit, library, study halls and classrooms were proceeding. On the latter campus in 1955, a contract was let for the building of the auditorium/music facility which was dedicated in the spring of 1957. In the March, 1955, issue of the District Bulletin, a listing of construction entitled "Here's How We Stand" included the following information:

> Bakersfield College; Wright Metcalf and Parsons, Architect: Group 1; Six Buildings, utilities, 28 per cent completed; Group II; Library, Campus Center, construction started; Group III; Speech, Arts, Agriculture, Residence Halls, Open Air Theater - plans at State Division of Architecture, perhaps to bid in April; Men's and Women's Physical Education and Health Center - 33% completed. Concentration on dressing, locker, shower rooms for September; Stadium and related site improvement 81 per cent completed, probably ready by May.

Arvin High School; Ernest L. McCoy, Architect: Auditorium, Music Unit - working drawings virtually complete, should go to the Division of Architecture at the State this month.

Bakersfield High School; C. B. Alford, Architect and W. J. Thomas: Cafeteria, 66 per cent completed - construction may be finished in six weeks; Boys and Girls Gymnasium, 56 per cent completed - ready for fall semester; rehabilitation, Ludden Hall, 27.8 per cent completed - ready for fall semester.

Kern Valley High School, Wright, Metcalf and Parsons, Architects: Gymnasium, Classroom additions completed.

Shafter High School; Wright, Metcalf and Parsons, Architects: Homemaking Unit and Classroom additions - construction started; Auditorium and Music Unit - working drawings nearing completion.

District Administration Building, Robert N. Eddy, Architect: Construction 25 per cent completed - expect it to be occupied in August.

New high school - Ernest L. McCoy, Architect: Property purchased, architect appointed. Site utilization plans prepared and now awaiting approval of Office of Schoolhouse Planning. Preliminary plans next step after site utilization plans approved.

Note: these facilities are included in the $17 million bond issue passed in January, 1953, as outlined to the voters.[58]

The "new high school" mentioned here is South High School.

Relocation of Burroughs High School

Out on the desert at China Lake a request was made by the District to the Commander of the Naval Ordnance Test Station for space for the relocation of Burroughs High School. Eventually, the new location was arranged with an access road which would allow access to the high school without entering officially the Naval Base proper. In 1957, approximately $1.4 million was allocated in federal funds for construction of the new school. The architectural firm selected for the project was Alford and Thomas and the contract was let for the construction in May of 1958.[59]

In spite of the funds provided by the voters in the bond issue of 1953, it became apparent that additional financing would be needed by the 1960's. In fact, an enrollment projection made in 1957 indicated that, by the school year 1964-65, the enrollment figures would be well over the 15,000 mark.[60] Because the trends showed that most of this excess in population would be in the metropolitan area, the Superintendent reported to the Board that a new campus in Bakersfield would be needed by the fall of 1961. Immediately, plans were set to raise these funds through a bond election and after one failure at the polls, a bond issue of just over $5.5 million was passed in February, 1960. This bond enabled the district to move ahead with building programs to take care of the growth of the 1960's.[61]

School Operations in the Post-War Days

Some of the activities of the new Director of Instruction, John W. Eckhardt, have been recorded earlier in this chapter. It soon became evident that there was need for the expansion of the duties of this new position to other areas of administration, most of which had been the responsibility of the Superintendent. A primary area of responsibility, that of staffing, was in need of additional attention because of the growing shortage of qualified teachers.

The Recruitment Program

Prior to 1950, teacher recruitment was not a major problem as far as quantity of staff was concerned and it was possible to visit a few teacher training institutions in California and secure qualified staff members. Up until this time the selection of teachers had been centralized through the Superintendent's Office with interviewing done by Principals and the Superintendent. After being assigned the responsibility of personnel in 1950 and taking on a new title of Assistant Superintendent for Instruction and Personnel, Mr. Eckhardt began developing a District Personnel Office with centralized responsibilities in that office. In the words of the new Assistant Superintendent:

> It took a little time to gain the cooperation of the Principals, but it did work out and soon the procedure got going on a large scale. Office procedures, forms, staff, secretaries, were set up in order to handle the volume. By 1954 the shortage of teachers really became acute and we wouldn't begin to find teachers to take the assignments in California that were available here in Bakersfield, so the out-of-state recruitment began in earnest, about the year 1954. I think the first actual out-of-state trip was taken by Mr. McCuen, who went to Oregon and, after that, I picked up these responsibilities.
>
> I felt the necessity of having more than one judgment on people, and in all the recruitment I ever did, I took another person with me, usually a Principal; often times more than one Principal went along. The peak years of the recruitment need were 1957, 1958, 1959, and out-of-state recruitment became almost our only source of personnel. This program was needed for more than a decade. The peak number of vacancies was about 200 and again, during the middle and latter Fifties, almost all of these people were to be brought in from other states. At one time we recruited as many as forty universities, colleges in some thirty different states. This occurred over a four month period of time and it meant that about three-fourths of my time was taken up with the personnel responsibility.
>
> The Board was very supportive of this program. They met the people we brought in and felt good about the quality of staff we were recruiting. It was suggested that we would probably need to interview at least ten applicants for every assignment made, which meant that there needed to be from 1,000 to 2,000 persons interviewed during some of those years. Usually there were at least three of us on the recruitment trips, a Principal, the President of Bakersfield College, and myself. This meant that we could compare our evaluations of the persons interviewed and have two to three judgments involved in each decision.[62]

In addition to the Board consensus that this program of recruitment of staff was a good idea, the other factor which supported quality in the personnel program was the willingness of the Board to keep salaries in the upper twenty per cent in comparison to other districts. Former Trustee M. Glenn Bultman recalls that the Board was unanimous in support of both of these programs and that while the attraction of the salary schedule and the presentation of the representative of the District attracted people of other states to the Kern High School District, they usually stayed here because of the quality of the District's program and the friendliness of the people in Bakersfield.[63]

Improvement of Instruction

Although much of Mr. Eckhardt's time was taken with personnel responsibilities, the instructional program did not lie dormant. In 1955 two members were added to the District instructional staff: Wilson Stone in reading supervision and Allen Cannon, in curriculum and research. Prior to that time an accreditation program had been introduced, called the Evaluative Criteria, and was pioneered at Bakersfield High School in the spring of 1952, and then in the fall of 1952 was used at East Bakersfield High School. Visiting committees were comprised of representatives from the University of California, State Department of Education, the local District administration and faculty, local elementary administration, P.T.A. and the County Superintendent of Schools staff. Reports were made to the faculty and to the District administration at the conclusion of the committees' visitation.[64] The program of accreditation was a broader one than that which had been experienced through the University of California and was a forerunner of the statewide accreditation which began under the Western Association of Schools and Colleges some five years later.

Because so much of the Board's meeting time had been taken up with the building programs and the tangible needs of the District, it was the feeling of the District administration that Board members should be kept better informed on the instructional program. Therefore, in the late 1950's, a series of reports was made on instructional programs in the District including English, science, social studies, vocational studies, industrial arts among others. It was at about this time at Bakersfield High School, that an accelerated program for gifted students was begun, allowing extremely capable students to complete the four year high school program in three years. Although the acceleration part of the program was discontinued, special classes for gifted students, including an advanced placement program at Bakersfield College, were established at Bakersfield High School and later at East Bakersfield and South High Schools.

During the 1957-58 school year an extensive study was made of pupil control problems, and in August, 1958, a pupil control program was adopted, "...to maintain proper standards of pupil behavior, to enforce greater academic effort."[65] It was also during these years that the driver's training and education programs were expanded and extended. Allen Cannon, the District Director of Curriculum and Research, remembers that a great deal of pressure was put on the school districts by outside interests in the community and students to make sure that there was a good, effective driver's instruction and driver's training program in the schools. Mr. Cannon also recalls the Elementary and Secondary Education Act which was passed in the Sixties during the Johnson administration. The result of this Federal involvement in instruction was that the schools were flooded with money for specific education projects. One instance related by Mr. Cannon shows the extent to which money was available:

> One of the Federal representatives from San Francisco called me and asked if I could use a million dollars under the Neighborhood Youth Corps. It seems he had an extra million dollars that he needed to spend and he thought that this would be a good place to spend it. Now we already had a Neighborhood Youth Corps and were already spending Federal money, but I went to the Board and asked for their approval. The reception I got was less than enthusiastic and when I called the man back in San Francisco, he said, "Well, that's all right, there has been a riot in Pittsburgh and I had to send it there."

Moneys also became available during this time under the National Defense Education Act and in 1959 there is a record in the Board minutes of such an application which yielded approximately $30,000 for counseling, foreign language, science and mathematics instruction.[66] The positive effects of the

National Science Foundation programs upon students and teachers alike should be noted in this era of education in the District.

In the 1950's, the District's adult education program was expanded. Although there had been Evening School for adults in the District since 1918, it was at this time that a District Director of Adult Education was appointed as now required by law; he was H. Parley Kilburn.

Personnel Changes in the 1950's

In the minutes of the July 2, 1954, Board meeting, special mention was made of the resignation of Dwight M. Griffith, who was leaving the district after forty-six years of continual service. Thirty-eight of these years were as head football coach at Kern County Union High School, later to be named Bakersfield High School.

Succeeding Grant Jensen at Shafter High School in 1956 was Arthur Johnson, coming from the Principalship at McFarland. Edwin DeMello succeeded him at the latter school. Upon the retirement in 1956 of Kenneth Rich, the first Principal at East Bakersfield High School, Assistant Principal Irving Lane became head of the school in the fall of 1956. Beginning the 1957-58 school year Robert M. Hoagland headed Kern Valley High School and Wallace B. Webster was appointed to the Principalship at Bakersfield Adult School. Another Adult School appointment earlier was to a position that attracted much attention from the public. The Board minutes of November 25, 1955 show that Wylie Logan Jones, Bakersfield College economics professor, was selected for the role of Director of the Open Forum, an educational program for the community at large.

At Bakersfield College, Ralph Prator resigned January of 1958 to accept the presidency of the new San Fernando Valley State College to be effective immediately. Edward Simonsen took over as President on February 1, 1958 Mr. Simonsen had been with East Bakersfield High School prior to World War II and had been Dean of Students at the college upon his return from the Marine Corps.

District Moves Ahead into the Sixties

New School on Morning Drive

The passage of the bond issue in 1960 left the District free to accommodate the growing student needs of the 1960's. High on the priority list of the accommodations of this growing population was a new campus on Morning Drive at the eastern extremities of the Bakersfield metropolitan area. Early in 1960 Architects Eddy and Paynter contracted to begin drawing plans for the new school.[67]

In 1961 Gerald Hedden was appointed to the Principalship and in accordance with a long standing policy was given a year to make plans for the opening of the new school.[68] In the fall of 1962 the new Morning Drive school, now named Foothill High School, was opened and Principal Hedden had with him a staff which included a mixture of veteran Kern High School District administrators and teachers, and a component of staff members new to the district. Assistant Principal was Wesley R. Anderson; Director of Curriculum, Richard Hause; Dean of Boys, Charles Gates; Dean of Girls, Yvonne Milliken; other administrators included Robert Town, Richard Regedal and John Ludeke. Included among the other staff members who helped open the school were Douglas Collins, English teacher and coach; Joe Fontaine, science; Freda I. Hamilton, girls' physical education; James B. Inskeep, U. S. history; Raymond P. Juhl, industrial arts; Laddie J. Kumelos, English; Peggy L. Lautenschlager, drama and speech; Norris W. Miller, band and orchestra; Betty J. Mulvana, girls' physical education and counseling; Keith Osborn, physical education; Clinton R. Osthimer, English and coaching; Dale E. Permenter, physical education; Tom Pettus, industrial arts; Harvel Pollard, physical education and coaching; Patricia Rowe, business; Pobert M. Petker, vocal music; Elmer Scritchfield, industrial arts; Allen R. Slate, mathematics; Edwin A. Tischbirek, agriculture; Glenn B. Wheeler, biology; Bill Williams, mathematics; and, Dorothy Wood, mathematics.

The College Becomes a Separate District

For some years, plans had been laid by the District moving towards a separation of the junior college into a district of its own. During 1960 the Board appointed a citizens' committee to determine the facts involved in the formation of a separate District for the junior college with boundaries to be the same as the present high school District. The election was set for November 8, 1960.[69] Such a strong case for this move was presented to the community that the election passed by a five to one margin, and plans were presented to the Board for the organization of the District in the spring of 1961.[70]

Elected President of the new Board was Albert S. Gould; Clerk, M. Glenn Bultman. It was officially named the Kern Joint Junior College District and Superintendent McCuen remained Superintendent of the new District. In addition, many of the other District administrators continued for several years in a joint capacity with a portion of their time assigned to the junior college District. The Board itself was augmented by two more members to the five high school trustees serving in a dual capacity with the two new board members. Although, originally, the boundaries of the junior college District were coterminous with those of the high school District, that soon changed as other high school districts petitioned to join, including those in the Wasco, Delano and Porterville areas.

Retirements and Other Personnel Matters

With the building program underway spurred on by the passage of the bond action in 1960 and the landmark change of organization of the District with the separation of the junior college as a separate entity, it seems an opportune time to make note of some changes in personnel who had primary responsibilities within the district. Foremost among these was the retirement of Howard K. Dickson at the close of the 1959-60 school year. We have had opportunity to recount some of Mr. Dickson's achievements in his more than forty years as head of the agriculture program, at Kern County High School and in the

District. The educational program in agriculture and the strength of the Future Farmers of America Chapter were well-recognized throughout the state. He was succeeded as head of the agriculture program at Bakersfield High School by Harvey Brockmeyer, a seasoned agriculture teacher and FFA advisor.

At Burroughs High School at the close of the 1959-60 school year, Earl Murray resigned as Principal and was followed by Kenneth Westcott. Mr. Murray had been Principal of the school since the second year of its operation and for some time had also been Superintendent of China Lake Elementary School District.

Another change in the ranks of principals was at Arvin High School. Clyde Dawald, the first Principal of the school passed away suddenly during the winter of 1960, and Edwin DeMello was named to fill the vacancy at the beginning of the 1960-61 year. Mr. DeMello had been Principal at McFarland High School. Thomas B. Henley followed Mr. DeMello at McFarland High School.

At Bakersfield High School in the spring of 1962, an event took place which that year's Oracle described as "a changing of the guard." On March 1, Leslie W. Hedge, who had been the Principal of the school for a period of 22 years, resigned and Vice Principal J. S. Wallace was selected as his replacement. The executive board of the school submitted a resolution honoring Mr. Hedge, detailing his many accomplishments at the school, statewide as president of the California Association of Secondary School Administrators, and, in the community, with such organizations as the Young Men's Christian Association and Rotary. This resolution was presented to the retiring Principal on February 22, 1962, in a ceremony in Harvey Auditorium, on "Les Hedge Day".

Across town at East Bakersfield High School in the fall of 1962, E. C. Mills became Principal upon the retirement of Irving Lane. Mr. Lane had been with the school in various capacities since its beginning in 1938. The new Principal at East Bakersfield

High School had been a Vice Principal at Bakersfield High School, and for a several years previously, had served as head of the Kern Valley High School.

On the school Board, a man who had served in this volunteer capacity for more than 21 years, most of that time as President of the Board, and had given immeasurably of his wisdom and guidance during the difficult post-World War II building programs, retired in June, 1960. He was Harold E. Woodworth.

Another Bond Election Needed

It became apparent in 1962 that, if the enrollment needs of the district were to be met, another bond issue must be passed to finance continued construction. The Board established a citizens' study committee under the leadership of Thomas P. Jarvis, District Manager of Pacific Telephone. With the final report of the committee presented in early 1963, the bond election was set to raise nearly seven million. After two months of campaigning and citizen involvement, the election passed in May of 1963 by a three to one vote. This then set the stage financially for the continued improvement and enlargement of the existing schools and for a new campus which was to be located in southwest Bakersfield.

A New School in the District

Whitney Biggar was to be the architect appointed to supervise construction of the new school and he worked together with District staff and teachers appointed by Superintendent McCuen in developing educational specifications for the construction of a modern high school. This time it was not necessary to purchase land for the new location since the school was to be built on 50 acres of the District-owned farm laboratory. In the spring of 1964 Edwin J. DeMello, Principal of Arvin High School, was appointed to head the new school. The organization of the new school took place during the 1964-65 school year when Mr. DeMello had released time to prepare the ground work. In the summer of 1965, he and Thomas B. Henley, a former Principal of McFarland High School, the newly appointed Assistant Principal and Doris Stowe, School Secretary, took up professional residence at the school which was still under construction. Other key administrators and counselors included John Cissne, Curriculum Director; Carl Wells, Dean of Students; Genivieve Magruder, Head Girls' Counselor; Claire Larsen, Librarian; Elizabeth Clarke, Counselor; Betty J. Mulvana, Counselor and physical education; Clifford Tucker, Counselor and attendance; Douglas Carroll, Counselor; and, Ray Hearon, Dean of Student Activities. Among others included on the new staff were Robert Nestor, English Department Chair; Anthony Drafth, English; Beverly Bonsall, English; Jim Wren, English and civics; Pat Church, English; Ivan Pfeffer, business head; Linda Cairns, vocal music; A. Coke Smith, instrumental music; Katherine L. Burdick, homemaking head; Forrest Bingham, industrial art head; Ray Juhl, industrial arts; Sebastian Lamb, industrial arts; Loyd P. Wollen, industrial arts; Darrell Meaders, mathematics head; Bert Rowe, mathematics and head football coach; Walter E. Pederson, Language Department Head; Charles Switzer, foreign language; Wayne Nunes, science; Bruce Curtis, science; Fred Laningham, science and varsity baseball coach; Tom Jones, Social Studies Chairman; Robert Himes, social studies; Hazel McCuen, social studies; George R. Pinheiro, social studies; Richard Tucker, boys' physical education head; Floyd Thionnet, physical education and coaching; Elsa J. Kominitsky, physical education; Betty Jo Ozanich, physical education and coaching.

The new campus, now called West High School, was opened in the fall of 1965. The October 1 enrollment showed slightly more than 1400 students attending West High School in the freshman, sophomore and junior years.[71]

Tax Proposals and Voter Resistance

After an era of goodwill expressed by the voters in a form of passing tax and bond election increases, the district encountered two rejections at the polls in 1965. As noted in an article prepared by Edwin J. DeMello in the <u>Bakersfield Californian</u> Centennial Edition in 1966: "During the sixteen year period from May 7, 1947 through May 21, 1963, six out of seven special elections were approved by the voters of the district."[72] However, when the District proposed an increase of fifty cents in the tax rate in an election held in April of 1965, the measure was killed with a vote of three to one. A number of local tax economy organizations opposed the increase led by the Kern County Property Owners Association and joined by the Kern County Taxpayers Association, and even by the Chamber of Commerce.[73]

Seeing that a more conservative approach was needed, the Board came back with another election try in July of that year, this time asking for only a twenty cent increase. This time the vote was more favorable, but still the measure was rejected by a margin of some 2,500 votes. An editorial in the Californian following this rejection entitled "Voter's Reject the Tax Increase Plan", pointed out that the election results sent out the word that, "...Kern County, long a bastion of support for public education, has capitulated to a small group whose awareness of the responsibility of the community for the education of its youth has been blunted by elements known only to the group, but secure in its myopic strength against the facts."[74]

During this period of time, after the first tax failure in April and prior to the subsequent tax election in July, it was necessary for the Board to make some budget decisions regarding the 1965-66 school year. Based upon the current income available, it was decided that there would be a reduction of thirty-two staff positions. The expectation was that there would need to be no dismissals and that class sizes would remain the same, but this would cause some limitation of elective subjects available to students. Another decision was made that Class A, or varsity, athletics only would be in operation and that swimming would be eliminated from the program completely. A reduction of seventy five per cent was authorized in the purchase of instructional and operational equipment. The textbooks and library budget would be cut in half and the preschool counseling program would be eliminated, as would the summer school program. Further, to save expenses, a tax shelter annuity program was also established in lieu of salary increases for certificated employees. After the tax election defeat in July, proposed salary increases for classified employees were eliminated.

During this time there were many communications from concerned citizens regarding the District's financial situation. Some of the organizations which had resisted the tax election proposals now had suggestions, as well as did individual citizens and groups of people or patrons from the various schools.[75] Finally, in the fall of 1965 after the school year was underway with the curtailed instructional and athletic programs, members of the local Chamber of Commerce approached individual Board members with an offer of assistance from that body. This offer materialized into a Chamber of Commerce sponsored study committee called Focus, "a fact-finding organization of citizens for an unbiased study." The committee was chaired by a prominent Bakersfield attorney, George A. Brown.[76]

In the spring of 1966 the Focus Committee chairman presented a report to the Board in which it was recommended that a twenty six cents tax override election be scheduled for the June primary election.[77] The committee worked in close cooperation with the Board of Trustees and the latter announced a declaration of intention that, if the proposed election override passed, the following action would occur: a) salaries of employees would be brought back to a competitive level; b) there would be a restoration of B and C class athletics; c) the preschool counseling program would be restored; and, d) there would be an improvement in the teacher-student ratios at the schools. Arthur Boehning, local manager of a J. C. Penney department store, chaired the campaign committee, with positive results - the election passed by a margin of some 3,000 votes. The campaign was so successful that even the Kern County Property Owner's Association gave a limited endorsement.

Building Funds Secured

On the heels of a successful tax election there appeared on the horizon a new financial need, this time for funds for the construction of a new high school in northeast Bakersfield, among other needs. Again, the Board turned to the community for assistance and advice, and, in August, 1967, a final report of a Citizens' Committee on School Building Needs chaired by Ray

Dezember was presented to the Board. The recommendation was for an election to be set at the ten million dollar figure and the Board was urged by the committee to establish plans for an election.[78]

Actually the Board trimmed back some of the recommendations of this committee and the election was scheduled for October, 1967, with a money total of just short of nine million dollars. The election issue was divided into two propositions and both passed by the required two-thirds majority.[79] An interesting side note of this election is that two future Board members were active in the citizen group which supported the election cause. One was Mr. Dezember, who has already been mentioned as Chairman of the Citizens Planning Committee; the other, Dr. George Ablin, who chaired the campaign committee to get out the vote on the bonds. Superintendent McCuen and Board President Albert S. Gould both publicly thanked the citizens involved and the District Faculty Association, whose members supported the bond in an organized manner.[80]

Other District Concerns

While financing the District's operation and building program was high on the list of priorities for Board consideration and action during this period of the 1960's, there were other District-wide concerns that were given attention. One of these certainly was the unification effort that was going on at the time. The Kern County Committee on School District Organization, which was the local legal arm of the state in carrying out unification efforts, was most active during these years. Several plans were presented for possible unification of school districts in Kern County and the Kern High School Board of Trustees supported a proposal which did not encroach on the central area.[81] A series of public hearings were held on these unification plans to hear points of view in the various areas of the District, and the Board was continually evaluating the prospects for change in the school district organization and the resulting effects on students. A change in the District's boundaries occurred in 1962 with the annexation of the Randsburg and Johannesburg Elementary School Districts to the Kern County Union High School District and Kern County Junior College District bringing in some added real estate, but not many pupils from the Antelope Valley area.[82]

Personnel relationships were somewhat tenuous in the midst of the financial problems encountered in the mid-Sixties, and Assistant Superintendent Eckhardt reported to the Board that the resignations at the close of the 1964-65 school year reached an all time high of 122. Whether this record was directly related to the financial problems and the cutbacks in positions might be conjectural, but some saw a relationship. An official change in the personnel relationships of the district came about in the mid-Sixties with the enactment of the Winton Act, which required that certificated employees be allowed to organize and present their requests to management in a structured form. This arrangement, called "meet and confer" was engaged in officially by the District for the first time in 1965, but it was a similar process to that already in use for a number of years. Representatives of the District Faculty Association met directly with administration and Board members in these meet and confer sessions to discuss salaries and other working conditions. Former Board member, Don Ruggenberg, in reflecting back on the operations under the Winton Act as contrasted with the later collective bargaining structures imposed on the Board by the Rodda Act, calls attention to the harmonious relationships that the former produced. It is his opinion that the Winton Act procedures operated "without adversary relationships," and that the change to the collective bargaining procedures brought division and worked to the disadvantage of the school systems.[83] This view was shared by many administrators and Board members when collective bargaining procedures were installed some ten years later.[84]

A report from an outside management study organization, the prestigous firm of Lybrandt, Ross Brothers and Montgomery was presented to the Board in the summer of 1967. Although no action was taken immediately on the report, the recommendation served as a springboard for changing and reshaping the management organization of the District in years to come.[85]

Reference has been made earlier to the Elementary and Secondary Education Act and the National Defense Education Act funding sources which provided moneys for certain programs at the various schools. These Federal funds continued to have a marked influence on the instructional programs at the schools and this influence was viewed with mixed emotions by educators who saw it as an unwelcome instrusion of the Federal government on the instruction in classrooms, while others looked at it as a welcome source of revenue from the arm of government that had the greatest taxing ability.

Continuation School

Continuation education had been underway in the District for a number of years, at first as a Saturday program for students to keep them from dropping out of school entirely. In 1965 State legislation was enacted mandating that each district with a high school graduating class of more than 100 students establish regular programs. The next year, H. R. Donald Cornett, Vice Principal at McFarland High School, was designated the first Continuation School Principal for the District. In his words:

> In the summer of 1966, I was selected to head up the continuation program. We established our first school on the East Bakersfield High School campus in the industrial arts wing. The program ran from 2:30 p.m. to 6:30 p.m., and we had a peak enrollment of 210 students that first year. The following year we moved to our new campus on Second and 'P' Streets in November of 1967. A church on South 'H' Street housed the program for the first three months of the school year until the new campus was ready.

Open house on the new campus was held on December 15, 1967. [86] The continuation program was eventually to expand to as many as eight campuses and enrolled 1,200 students with nearly seventy staff members involved.

Special Education

It was in the Sixties that special education, as we know it today, really got its impetus, although instructional programs for mentally retarded students had been organized earlier in the Fifties. Actually, according to Jack Schuetz, veteran special education administrator in the District, a State law was passed in 1956 allowing compensatory programs on a permissive basis for mentally retarded students and there were several such programs at the individual schools in the District which had started up at that time. Special funding was available for these programs, but they were not mandatory and there was little definition, really, as to the purpose and objective of this instruction.

Mr. Schuetz came to East Bakersfield High School in 1959 with a master's degree in special education and set up a program there under the State guidelines that was the first bonafide special education program in the District. Later when new laws were passed to make education for these students mandatory up through "school age", the instruction began to take on some definition District-wide. During this time, the District defined "school age" as being sixteen and students were dismissed from school at that time. To quote Mr. Schuetz:

> In 1962-63, the law was changed to say that the retarded youngster must have a program commensurate with the regular student. I was called in by the District administrators and asked to make our program "legal", and was designated at this time as District Supervisor of Special Education on a half-time basis. This, then, was the beginning of the District program as such and I continued to serve as half-time supervisor, teaching my four special education classes at East Bakersfield High School for some six years.[87]

In a few years, special education gained momentum and workshops were set up for teachers. More and more the District Supervisor was called in by the principals to assist with these programs on campus. Specialized instruction within the special education area was set up in the later Sixties including curricula for the educationally handicapped, the physically handicapped, and the aurally handicapped students. These specialized programs were centered at the various schools. In 1968 Mr. Schuetz was given full-time assignment as Director of Special Education and the program in the District had finally come of age.

Employment Concerns

The summer of 1962, Superintendent McCuen made a report to the Board on the employment of minorities District-wide. The report came as a result of an employment survey which had been requested by a local agency called "The Citizens in the Community for Good Government". The concern of this group was primarily related to employment of Blacks. The Superintendent related that there had been, over the years, few minority applicants, particularly Blacks and, as a result, few had been employed. This was the beginning of concerns raised by citizens in the community, state and national government agencies, and by the District itself, which was to result in an affirmative action program some ten years later.

Meanwhile - At The Schools

In telling the story of an educational system such as a large school district, there is an unfortunate tendency to dwell on the somewhat superficial factual happenings, such as tax election, building programs, district organization, and neglect accounting for instructional programs in the classrooms. This writer recognizes that he has fallen victim to this weakness because the type of information just mentioned is more easily accessible through Board minutes, newspaper accounts, and the like. In a District such as the Kern High School District, which is made up of schools with highly individualistic programs taking care of diverse school populations in widespread geographical areas, some many miles distant from the others, the story of education in the classroom is most difficult to relate. Fortunately, a study was made in 1964 entitled, "Status Report: Kern County Joint Union High School", which contains some summary information about curriculum and instruction.[88]

According to this document, the curriculum development in the District in the mid-Sixties was planned to accomplish several goals. In summary:

>   1) To encourage a critical evaluation of the contents and methods of the present course offerings in all the high schools....2) To encourage experimentation and

planning in teaching courses with new organization, content and methods...3) To help administrators and teachers keep abreast of projects being developed nation-wide by professional organizations in curriculum and subject matter fields...4) To encourage the study and investigation of new curriculum practices in other school systems and to bring a knowledge of these practices to the administrators and teachers in the subject areas concerned."

District-wide curriculum activities were listed as follows:

1. A study of how to teach basic principles of the American way of life;

2. A study of policy regarding reading lists and required reading;

3. A biology workshop dealing with the idea of the "American Institute of Biological Science";

4. Preparation of a uniform course outlines for the senior government course;

5. A study of the teaching of controversial issues within the classrooms;

6. Three workshops and methods of teaching foreign language under the new audiolingual approach;

7. Participation with the statewide curriculum committees in an evaluation of new ideas and practices in the areas of English, social studies, fine arts, science, mathematics, and the applied arts;

8. A study of the comparative course offerings in social studies;

9. The preparation of a report of the District framework committee;

10. Preparation of a pamphlet on the teaching of economics;

11. Preparation of a pamphlet on the teaching about communism.

Mention was made that District moneys had been appropriated for summer projects to develop these curriculum themes. For example, at Bakersfield High School, a study team had looked at procedures used in conducting large group lectures with small section laboratories dove-tailed together in chemistry classes. At East Bakersfield High School, teachers of U. S. History and music had worked together to correlate strands of these two subject areas into presentations in the classrooms, while at Foothill High School, remedial English was set in a laboratory situation. Art history and appreciation were developed into an enrichment program at North High School, and simultaneously teachers had updated courses in biology. A study of team teaching for academically unsuccessful students was continuing at South High School, a program which stressed basic skills of reading, writing and speaking developed around social studies centered on city, county and state government.

Since one of the problems of improving curriculum is finding money to provide adequate facilities, equipment and materials, the District had worked to coordinate projects for obtaining federal funds under Title III of the National Defense Education Act.

Again quoting from the document:

> During the past year, twelve project applications were filed under this act totalling $28,000. The money on a matching funds basis is meant to improve instruction in mathematics, foreign language and science. Generally the projects are for the purchase of foreign language laboratories, overhead projectors for mathematics classes, science electronic materials, reconstruction of science laboratories, microscopes and books for biology, and physics equipment.

Mention of the foreign language laboratories is a reminder that this new teaching procedure and the physical makeup revolutionized the foreign language classrooms, starting in the mid-Sixties.

The account goes on to tell of the curriculum development at the individual schools. At Arvin High School, revolutionary changes were reported in mathematics and new materials were developed for slow learners. As an example, the biology course for slow learners was described in detail and mention was made of new approaches to learning in the industrial arts. In fact, some ten examples were given of revolutionary types of program changes at Arvin High School in English, mathematics, business, programs for the outstanding students, foreign language, social studies, and special reading programs. At Bakersfield High School the emphasis was on developmental reading and writing instruction in English classes for the college-bound students. Also, in senior English, in a world literature and composition course, the team-teaching approach was being used with the large- lectures presentations alternating with laboratory sessions. In American history and U. S. Government the lecture type courses were being used to give students experience in note taking and listening in preparation for later college experiences.

Three developments were detailed at Burroughs High School. The first was the expansion of the foreign language program, including an introduction to Russian. Second, forensics, particularly debate, was introduced as a class in the curriculum. This innovation allowed students to take debate as an elective course rather than an extra-curricular activity. And third, at Burroughs, the State required instruction in federal, state and local government was organized into a new course. Ten curriculum innovations were noted at East Bakersfield High School. The major subject-type programming in use for many years for college preparatory students had been changed to a broader field approach; a certificate for proficiency was introduced for subject areas of a terminal nature; team teaching in English, U. S. History, geometry, and chemistry was being used; a co-education health program had been introduced. In addition, changes had also been made in industrial arts, while new programs in mathematics and sciences had been developed, and a reading laboratory had been instituted. Community resources were continually called upon to enrich subject areas. At Foothill High School, which had been in operation only two years, the subtleties of developing the curriculum in a new institution were briefly described.

Change in the curriculum had not been overlooked at Kern Valley High School with revisions made in the required and college preparatory courses, the industrial arts field, agriculture, mathematics for non-college bound students, biology and in English. At McFarland High School, a seven-period day was installed, thus allowing students more access to elective courses.

The sequence of experiences in industrial arts had been modified, and an experimental, ungraded offering in English for slow learners was underway. Community interest in the curriculum at North High School resulted in the addition of various courses to the schedule. For example, a pre-school class in orchestra was offered, and a course in preparatory algebra had developed primarily as a result of parental concerns over youngsters' difficulties in this latter discipline. A pre-school class in physical education had been established and changes in industrial science, electricity, and the addition of large group instruction in chemistry were noted. Community interest resulted in additional classes in foreign language and an experimental change in the traditional sequence of mathematics courses had occurred.

At Shafter High School, some fifteen different curriculum changes were enumerated. Among them were the establishment of bilingual instruction in foreign language; the addition of new science programs; the introduction of modern mathematics to the curriculum; the expansion of the government program; the addition of a course in reading improvement; the use of special clinic sessions in English; the development of a more comprehensive auto shop program; the extension in the home making curriculum; increased use of community resources in business; and the introduction into many classes of the new audio-visual techniques.

At South High School, it was noted that a serious study had been made of national trends in the modernization of classroom programs. As a result, important changes occurred in the school programs at South. For example, in the foreign language instruction, the use of the audiolingual methods has developed through the use of National Defense Education Act funds; in mathematics, materials developed by the School Mathematics Study Group at Yale University were being used; in physics, materials formulated by the Physical Science Study Committee at Massachusetts Institute of Technology were instituted; and in chemistry, classes were using materials developed by the Chemistry Study Group at the University of California. Other improvements were noted in instruction as a result of local school efforts in geography, world history, a core program for slow learners, physical science, fine arts, and history among others. In addition, course revision had occurred in physical science, which resulted from participation by staff in the District summer workshops.

This, then, will give a glimpse of what was going on in curriculum development District-wide certainly with a direct effect upon students in the classrooms.

Benchmark Events of the Sixties

Two staff members with long careers in the District, both of whom had a hand in shaping the course of events at the District level retired during the Sixties. In the field of transportation, Harold Pauly, resigned in 1965 after 46 years in the District. It will be remembered that he was hired in 1919 when the transportation system was in its embryo stage and presided over the development of a complex and expansive system, which was used as a model by many other districts in the West. John Hazzard, long-time employee in the District transportation system, was selected to head this part of the District's operations.

In the next year, J. B. "Cap" Haralson left his post as District Director of Physical Education and Commissioner of Athletics. Coming to the District in 1924, Mr. Haralson had coached a number of sports at Kern County High School, but had given particular attention to track and field while supervising the development of physical education programs District-wide. He had brought national attention to Kern County in his position with the Amateur Athletic Union of America (AAU) as national chairman of men's track and field. As a result of this activity, he was able to bring several AAU track and field events to Bakersfield. Gil Bishop, Director of Athletics at Bakersfield College and former staff member of East Bakersfield High School, succeeded Mr. Haralson in his District responsibilities for athletics.

Changes in personnel continued to occur at the school level and the principal's ranks. With the retirement of George Williamson from North High School, Jack Hilton, Assistant

Principal, took over the reins in 1964. The next year, Arthur Johnson, Principal at Shafter High School became the new head at Foothill High School with the resignation of that school's first Principal, Gerald Hedden. At Shafter, Harold Corrie became the new Principal, succeeding Arthur Johnson. Mr. Corrie had been an administrator at South High School. Other school leadership changes included: Kern Valley, where in 1964, Jack O. Schulze took on that responsibility left vacant when Robert Hoagland resigned. In 1964 at Arvin, Wesley R. Anderson became Principal after Edwin DeMello had been chosen to head the new West High School. One year later, in 1965, Jordon Kanikkeberg came to McFarland High School as Principal following Thomas Henley who moved to an administrative role at West. Later, in 1968, Mr. Schulze was to move to Arvin from Kern Valley when Wesley R. Anderson was selected for the lead role at the new Highland High School. Donald Lucas was the new Principal at Kern Valley High School in the Fall of 1968.

Retirements at the Top

In the fall of 1967, a double change in the two top administrative positions at the District was announced to take place at the end of the 1967-68 school year. Both Superintendent McCuen and Deputy Superintendent Theron S. Taber announced their retirements at that time. It will be recalled the careers of these two men were closely intertwined since their college days at Stanford. Mr. Taber came to the District in 1928 and encouraged his friend from college, Theron McCuen, to join the district in 1929. Between these two men, they had spent a total of nearly eighty years in teaching and administrative roles in the school District.

The Board did not wait long to appoint the new superintendent. In fact, at the next Board meeting, two weeks from the time the two top administrators announced their retirement, Assistant Superintendent John W. Eckhardt was appointed to take over the top leadership position in the District.

Mr. Eckhardt's recollection of the selection procedure used is interesting in view of nationwide searches and other modern selection techniques. He recalls that a few days after the announcement of Mr. McCuen's retirement, two of the Board members, Mark Raney and M. Glenn Bultman, met him in the hall, tapped him on the shoulder, and said, "John, you're it." The resignation of the two top administrators in the District effective July 1, 1968, sparked a series of domino-effect personnel changes at a time when these particular positions were expected to be filled from the inside.

The Superintendent-elect recommended a change in the organization of the top district administrative positions, including three assistant superintendents in the areas of personnel, instruction, and business. This change had been recommended by the management survey report made by Lybrandt, Ross Brothers and Montgomery mentioned earlier. The additional top management positions recommended by the report, the controller, was put on hold for the time being and eventually combined with the responsibilities of the Assistant Superintendent for Business. Later in the fall of 1967, upon the recommendation of Superintendent-elect Eckhardt, these personnel were appointed as Assistant Superintendents: Instruction, Grant W. Jensen, Principal of South High School; Personnel, J. S. Wallace, Principal, Bakersfield High School; and Business, Harry J. Ward, Jr., District Director of Research.[88]

It should be noted that, at this time, the dual responsibilities of the top District administration for the Kern Community College District were eliminated and the complete separation of the college District from that of the high school was a reality. Thus, Mr. Eckhardt became Superintendent only of the high school district, and Edward Simonsen, who had been President of Bakersfield College became the new Superintendent of the junior college District.[89] Burns Finlinson was named the new Bakersfield College President. He had come to the college in 1946 because of the influence of Allen Cannon whom he had known at Cedar City, Utah, where they had taught together. Mr. Finlinson was the first Dean of Records at Bakersfield College and, at the time of his new appointment, was Vice-President of the College. Former Superintendent McCuen, looking back over his tenure as head administrator of the Kern High School and Junior College Districts for 23 years, has this to say on reflection:

> No Superintendent could have had better support and understanding from the boards I served under. It was my feeling that a school board should be made up of people who are representative of the most respected and successful members in the community. They are the people who can rise above petty matters. They are the people who would be more apt to attend to policy making, which is the real function of the board, and not get involved in matters of administration.
>
> I regret to say that, in too many instances over the state as a whole, board members tend to get involved in administrative functions. When they do that, they get into trouble because they are stepping out of their role and that is to hire administrative staff and permit them to develop reommendations for policies. The board does not have to accept all of the recommendations. They can ask for revisions, but they should not get involved in the day-to-day administration of the district. For the most part, happily, this is the way that the Kern High School District was operated during the years of my superintendency.[91]

Also retiring in 1968 was Avery Allen who had developed the public information program in his 28 years with the District.

A New Administrative Regime for the District

The District newsletter, now called <u>Report</u>, the successor to the old Kern High School District <u>Bulletin</u>, headlined in October of 1968: "Enrollment Hits New High." More than 18,000 students were in the classrooms of the total District on opening day with excess of 14,000 in the schools of greater Bakersfield. This included: 3,173 at Bakersfield High School, 2,450 at East Bakersfield High School, 2,329 at Foothill High School, 1,834 at North High School, 2,094 at South High School, and 2,255 at West High School. At Arvin High School, the opening day enrollment was just in excess of 1,300, 1,554 students showed up at Burroughs High School, 304 at Kern Valley High School, and 350 at McFarland High School. All of these schools showed a growth in enrollment, the only school in the district with fewer students than the previous year was Shafter High School with 919.[92] Because of the District administrative changes, it was necessary for new principals to be assigned to Bakersfield and South high schools. Kenneth Robesky was the choice for Bakersfield High School. Mr. Robesky had been Director of Personnel at the District. Don Murfin was selected to succeed Grant Jensen at South High School. Mr. Murfin had also been on the District staff in the Compensatory Education Division.

Other members of the District administrative team under the new regime included:

>Dale Acree, Supervisor - Buildings and Grounds
>Carl Berra, Director - Athletics, Attendance and Drivers' Training
>Berniece Braddon, Supervising Librarian
>Cecil D. Briscoe, Project Director, ESEA
>Kenneth Brown, Supervisor, Public Information
>E. Ben Evans, Director, Instructional Materials
>Ben Cole, Purchasing Agent
>Allen Cannon, Director, Classified Personnel
>John Hazzard, Director, Transportation
>Herbert L. Martin, Director, Vocational Education
>Wayne Ridley, Supervisor, Data Processing
>Jack L. Schuetz, Supervisor, Special Education
>Donald E. Soelberg, Director, Specially Funded Programs
>Valentina Valena, Food Services Director
>James L. Waterman, Director, Pupil Personnel Services
>Wallace Webster, Director, Adult Education
>James C. Young, Supervisor, Research

The new district regime faced some ongoing problems in the fall of 1968. Although a tax override had been passed some two years previously, the need for new funds for the operation of the District were already apparent.

A New School on the Horizon

Actually the Principal for the new school had been selected in the fall of 1967, although the school did not open until 1970. He was Wesley R. Anderson, Principal of Arvin High School. Since the new school was to be located in the northeast section of Bakersfield on one of the higher elevations of the metropolitan area, it was actually named Highland High School, which gave the student body access to the Scottish tradition in the nomenclature connected with the school. Mr. Anderson had been a student of newer approaches to learning, stressing an individualized approach to classroom study, and had already introduced some of these ideas in his tenure at Arvin. The new school, then, embarked on an innovative approach to learning with a tie-in of the Model School's Project, under the leadership of the noted educator, Lloyd Trump.[93]

Finally then in 75 years, the District had come a long way insofar as numbers of students were concerned, insofar as geographical locations of schools were concerned, and insofar as educational expenditures were concerned. However, little had changed insofar as the objectives of the instruction since the beginning of the District in January, 1893, when a high school was established in a cast-off building of the elementary district because concerned educators and community members felt that more should be done for the education of the County's greatest resource, its young people.

REFERENCES

CHAPTER V - THE END OF WORLD WAR II AND THE FIFTIES

1. The Bulletin, Kern County Union High School District, (Bakersfield, California), October, 1945.

2. Minutes, Kern County Union High School District (Bakersfield, California), March 26, 1945.

3. Taped interview with Theron L. McCuen.

4. Taped interview with John W. Eckhardt.

5. Bulletin, March, 1947.

6. Facts Sheet, Kern County Union High School District Scrapbook, March 7, 1947.

7. The Bakersfield Californian, April 29, 1947.

8. Taped interview with Avery Allen
    Since construction costs had risen during World War II, the contractor believed that there would be some increase in bid price of the building of the auditorium. The meeting was called to satisfy the legal demands of public approval.

9. Minutes, November 12, 1945.

10. Minutes, November 30, 1945.

11. Taped interview with Gerald Smith.

12. Chism, Ray A., A Preliminary History of Bakersfield College, unpublished manuscript (Bakersfield, California), 1981, p. 12.

13. Ibid., p. 14.

14. Taped interview with Edward C. Simonsen.

15. Minutes, October 14, 1949.

16. Bulletin, November, 1949.

17. Minutes, March 13, 1950 and, Bulletin, October, 1950.

18. Taped interview with John Collins.

19. Bulletin, January, 1947.

20. Laurion, Yearbook of Shafter High School (Shafter, California), 1947.

Reference - Chapter V (Continued)

21. *Bulletin*, March, 1947.

22. Ibid, October 1952.
    Also see *Minutes*, December 12, 1949; March 12, 1951; February 11, 1952; April 12, 1952; May 12, 1952; May 15, 1952; and, July 18, 1952.

23. *Bulletin*, October, 1946, and July, 1947.

24. Ibid., October, 1946.

25. *Minutes*, November 19, 1946 and December 23, 1946.

26. Ibid., June 17, 1948.

27. *Bulletin*, February, 1949.

28. *Minutes*, January 31, 1949.
    Also see October 11, 1948, March 14, 1949, April 11, 1949, and, September 12, 1949.

29. McCuen interview.

30. *Minutes*, November 13, 1950.

31. Ibid., December 11, 1950.

32. *Facts Sheet*, March 7, 1947.

33. *Minutes*, July 25, 1949.

34. *Next Steps in the Development of the Kern County Union High School District*, Office of the District Superintendent, (Bakersfield, California), March 13, 1950, pp. 24-25.

35. *Minutes*, August 7, 1952, and August 15, 1952.

36. Ibid., August 25, 1952; September 8, 1952; September 22, 1952; October 13, 1952; November 10, 1952; Deember 8, 1952; February 8, 1953; March 9, 1953; May 11, 1953; and, May 22, 1953.

37. Ibid., March 12, 1951.

38. Ibid., June 13, 1953, and Simonsen interview.

39. *Minutes*, October 26, 1953.

40. Chism, p. 16.

Reference - Chapter V (Continued)

41. Minutes, April 13, 1953; May 22, 1953; June 22, 1953; July 13, 1953; October 26, 1953; May 8, 1954; July 12, 1954; January 10, 1955; April 25, 1955; April 29, 1955; August 8, 1955; September 12, 1955; April 23, 1956; and, February 25, 1957.

42. Bulletin, March, 1957.

43. Minutes, September 28, 1953.
    Also see September 14, 1953, and May 22, 1953, and Bulletin, January, 1953.

44. Ibid., February 28, 1955.

45. Ibid., March 22, 1954.

46. Ibid., April 26, 1954.

47. Ibid., February 13, 1956.

48. Ibid., April 23, 1956.

49. Merrimac, Yearbook of South High School (Bakersfield, California), 1957.

50. Minutes, October 14, 1957.

51. Ibid., July 1, 1949, and August 10, 1949.

52. Ibid., December 14, 1953.

53. Ibid., November 8, 1954.

54. Ibid., August 8, 1955.

55. Ibid., December 20, 1954 and January 10, 1955.

56. Ibid., November 12, 1956.

57. Ibid., May 10, 1954; August 13, 1954; November 8, 1954; November 22, 1954; October 24, 1955; April 9, 1956; and, November 12, 1956.

58. Bulletin, March, 1955.
    Also see Minutes, February 14, 1955; September 12, 1955; February 13, 1956; February 25, 1957; March 25, 1957; and, May 3, 1957.

59. Minutes, September 26, 1956; April 8, 1957; July 22, 1957; and, May 12, 1958.

60. Ibid., October 28, 1957.

Reference - Chapter V (Continued)

41. Minutes, April 13, 1953; May 22, 1953; June 22, 1953; July 13, 1953; October 26, 1953; May 8, 1954; July 12, 1954; January 10, 1955; April 25, 1955; April 29, 1955; August 8, 1955; September 12, 1955; April 23, 1956; and, February 25, 1957.

42. Bulletin, March, 1957.

43. Minutes, September 28, 1953.
    Also see September 14, 1953, and May 22, 1953, and Bulletin, January, 1953.

44. Ibid., February 28, 1955.

45. Ibid., March 22, 1954.

46. Ibid., April 26, 1954.

47. Ibid., February 13, 1956.

48. Ibid., April 23, 1956.

49. Merrimac, Yearbook of South High School (Bakersfield, California), 1957.

50. Minutes, October 14, 1957.

51. Ibid., July 1, 1949, and August 10, 1949.

52. Ibid., December 14, 1953.

53. Ibid., November 8, 1954.

54. Ibid., August 8, 1955.

55. Ibid., December 20, 1954 and January 10, 1955.

56. Ibid., November 12, 1956.

57. Ibid., May 10, 1954; August 13, 1954; November 8, 1954; November 22, 1954; October 24, 1955; April 9, 1956; and, November 12, 1956.

58. Bulletin, March, 1955.
    Also see Minutes, February 14, 1955; September 12, 1955; February 13, 1956; February 25, 1957; March 25, 1957; and, May 3, 1957.

59. Minutes, September 26, 1956; April 8, 1957; July 22, 1957; and, May 12, 1958.

60. Ibid., October 28, 1957.

Reference - Chapter V (Continued)

61. Ibid., May 13, 1958; July 1, 1958; December 8, 1958; October 26, 1959; November 23, 1959; and, February 16, 1960.

62. Eckhardt interview.

63. Taped interview with M. Glenn Bultman.

64. Bulletin, April, 1952, and November, 1952.

65. Minutes, August 25, 1958.

66. Ibid., May 25, 1959.

67. Ibid., March 14, 1960.

68. Ibid., March 13, 1961.

69. Ibid., October 10, 1960.

70. Ibid., May 8, 1961.

71. Ibid., March 25, 1963; August 5, 1963; June 18, 1964; October 22, 1964; December 17, 1964; April 8, 1965; and, August 26, 1965.

    Also see: DeMello, Edwin J., Highlights of West High School, unpublished manuscript, (Bakersfield, California), May, 1980.

72. DeMello, Edwin J., The Bakersfield Californian, Centennial Edition, May 21, 1966, p. 8C.

73. Californian, April 21, 1965.

74. Ibid., July 29, 1965.

75. Minutes, May 17, 1965.

76. Ibid., December 23, 1965.

77. Ibid., March 18, 1966.

78. Ibid., August 3, 1967.

79. Californian, November 1, 1967.

80. Ibid., November 14, 1967.

81. Minutes, May 27, 1963.

82. Ibid., September 10, 1962.

83. Taped interview with Don Ruggenberg.

Reference - Chapter V (Continued)

84. *Minutes*, October 21, 1964; January 26, 1967; March 23, 1967; and, April 27, 1967.

85. *Ibid.*, August 3, 1967.

86. *Ibid.*, August 4, 1966; December 14, 1967; and Taped interview with H. R. Donald Cornett.

87. Taped interview with Jack Schuetz.

88. *Status Report, Kern County Union High School District*, publication of the Office of the Superintendent, (Bakersfield, California), December, 1964, pp. 55-72.

89. *Minutes*, September 21, 1967; October 4, 1967; September 9, 1967; November 27, 1967; and, January 11, 1968.

90. *Ibid.*, October 4, 1967.

91. McCuen interview.

92. *Report, Kern High School District*, publication of the District Office (Bakersfield, California), October, 1968, pp. 1 and 4.

93. *Minutes*, November 27, 1967; February 8, 1968; March 3, 1969; November 3, 1969; May 4, 1971; and, November 4, 1971.

KERN COUNTY UNION HIGH SCHOOL

AND JUNIOR COLLEGE DISTRICT

BOARDS OF TRUSTEES

I. THESE GROUPS SERVED AS THE COUNTY BOARD OF EDUCATION - ALSO HIGH SCHOOL BOARD EX-OFFICIO

    1893-1894   J. H. Berry, Chairman
Mrs. M. L. Miller
F. M. Graham
Alfred Harrell, County Superintendent and Secretary of the Board

    1894-1895   J. H. Berry, Chairman
Mrs. E. V. Taylor
F. M. Graham
D. W. Nelson
Alfred Harrell, County Superintendent and Secretary of the Board

    1895-1896   Mrs. E. V. Taylor
R. L. Stockton
D. W. Nelson
F. M. Graham - Succeeded by Leo G. Pauly, July, 1896
Alfred Harrell, County Superintendent and Secretary of the Board

    1896-1897   D. W. Nelson, Chairman
Mrs. E. V. Taylor
R. L. Stockton
Leo G. Pauly
Alfred Harrell, County Superintendent and Secretary of the Board

    1897-1898   D. W. Nelson, Chairman
Mrs. E. V. Taylor
R. L. Stockton
Leo G. Pauly
Alfred Harrell, County Superintendent and Secretary of the Board

    1898-1899   D. W. Nelson, Chairman
Mrs. E. V. Taylor
Leo G. Pauly
W. C. Doub
Alfred Harrell, County Superintendent and Secretary of the Board

1899-1900	D. W. Nelson, Chairman Mrs. E. V. Taylor E. A. McGee Mrs. Charles H. Fox W. C. Doub, County Superintendent and Secretary of the Board
1900-1901	D. W. Nelson, Chairman Mrs. E. V. Taylor Leo G. Pauly Mrs. Charles H. Fox W. C. Doub, County Superintendent and Secretary of the Board
1901-1902	Leo G. Pauly, Chairman Mrs. E. V. Taylor D. W. Nelson R. L. Stockton W. L. McGinn W. C. Doub, County Superintendent and Secretary of the Board
1902-1903	Leo G. Pauly, President D. W. Nelson W. A. McGinn F. S. Benson R. L. Stockton, County Superintendent and Secretary of the Board, January, 1903
1903-1904	Leo G. Pauly, President D. W. Nelson F. S. Benson W. A. McGinn R. L. Stockton, County Superintendent and Secretary of the Board
1904-1905	Leo G. Pauly, President D. W. Nelson F. S. Benson W. A. McGinn R. L. Stockton, County Superintendent and Secretary of the Board
1905-1906	Leo G. Pauly, President D. W. Nelson F. S. Benson W. A. McGinn R. L. Stockton, County Superintendent and Secretary of the Board
1906-1907	Leo G. Pauly, President D. W. Nelson F. S. Benson W. A. McGinn R. L. Stockton, County Superintendent and Secretary of the Board

1907-1908	Leo G. Pauly, President D. W. Nelson F. S. Benson Daniel Gunderson R. L. Stockton, County Superintendent and Secretary of the Board
1908-1909	Leo G. Pauly, President D. W. Nelson F. S. Benson Daniel Gunderson R. L. Stockton, County Superintendent and Secretary of the Board
1909-1910	Leo G. Pauly, President D. W. Nelson F. S. Benson Daniel Gunderson R. L. Stockton, County Superintendent and Secretary of the Board
1910-1911	Leo G. Pauly, President D. W. Nelson F. S. Benson Daniel Gunderson R. L. Stockton, County Superintendent and Secretary of the Board
1911-1912	Leo G. Pauly, President D. W. Nelson F. S. Benson J. E. Dyer R. L. Stockton, County Superintendent and Secretary of the Board
1912-1913	Leo G. Pauly, President F. S. Benson J. E. Dyer Daniel Gunderson R. L. Stockton, County Superintendent and Secretary of the Board
1913-1914	Leo G. Pauly, President F. S. Benson J. E. Dyer Daniel Gunderson R. L. Stockton, County Superintendent and Secretary of the Board
1914-1915	Leo G. Pauly, President F. S. Benson J. E. Dyer Daniel Gunderson R. L. Stockton, County Superintendent and Secretary of the Board; L. E. Chenoweth, County Superintendent and Secretary of the Board, January, 1915.

1915-1916   Leo G. Pauly, President
            F. S. Benson
            J. E. Dyer
            Mrs. Jean A. Durnal
            L. E. Chenoweth, County Superintendent
            and Secretary of the Board

II. GROUPS NOW SERVED AS KERN COUNTY UNION HIGH
    SCHOOL DISTRICT BOARD OF TRUSTEES

1916-1917   Leo G. Pauly, President
            F. S. Benson
            Erwin W. Owen
            W. W. Kaye, Succeeded Mrs. Durnal
              November 6, 1916
            J. E. Dyer, Clerk

1917-1918   W. W. Kaye, President
            Leo G. Pauly
            Erwin W. Owen
            -- Henderson
            J. B. McFarland, Succeeded Leo G.
              Pauly, February 4, 1918
            D. H. Bitner, Clerk

1918-1919   W. W. Kaye, President
              Resigned July 24, 1918
            Erwin W. Owen, President; Succeeded
              W. W. Kaye
            G. M. Voll
            B. R. Fitzgerald
            W. J. Walters
            D. H. Bitner, Clerk

1919-1920   Erwin W. Owen, President
            B. R. Fitzgerald
            G. M. Voll
            W. J. Walters
            D. H. Bitner, Clerk

1920-1921   B. R. Fitzgerald, President
            D. H. Bitner
            Erwin W. Owen
            George M. Voll
            Ernest Tyler, Succeeded George M.
              Voll - October 4, 1920
            W. J. Walters, Clerk

1921-1922   Erwin W. Owen, President
            Ernest Tyler
            John Stroud
            W. J. Walters, Clerk
            B. R. Fitzgerald, Clerk; June, 1922

1922-1923	Erwin W. Owen, President Ernest Tyler W. J. Walters John Stroud B. R. Fitzgerald, Clerk
1923-1924	Erwin W. Owen, President, Resigned June 4, 1923 W. J. Walters, President; Succeeded Erwin W. Owen Ernest Tyler David E. Urner B. R. Fitzgerald, Clerk
1924-1925	W. J. Walters, President Ernest Tyler David E. Urner H. J. Brandt B. R. Fitzgerald, Clerk
1925-1926	B. R. Fitzgerald, President W. J. Walters Ernest Tyler H. J. Brandt David E. Urner, Clerk
1926-1927	B. R. Fitzgerald, President W. J. Walters Ernest Tyler H. J. Brandt David E. Urner, Clerk
1927-1928	Boyce R. Fitzgerald, President T. N. Harvey C. A. Melcher Ernest Tyler David E. Urner, Clerk
1928-1929	Boyce R. Fitzgerald, President T. N. Harvey, President; Succeeded Boyce R. Fitzgerald, February 7, 1929 C. A. Melcher A. C. Dimon A. D. M. Osborne David E. Urner, Clerk
1929-1930	T. N. Harvey, President A. D. M. Osborne A. C. Dimon C. A. Melcher William Gleason, Succeeded David Urner, September 28, 1929 W. B. Robb, Succeeded A. C. Dimon, September 28, 1929

1930-1931   T. N. Harvey, President
             A. D. M. Osborne
             C. A. Melcher
             W. B. Robb
             William Gleason, Clerk

1931-1932   T. N. Harvey, President
             A. D. M. Osborne
             C. A. Melcher
             W. B. Robb
             Harry West; Succeeded C. A. Melcher,
               November 2, 1931
             William Gleason, Clerk

1932-1933   T. N. Harvey, President
             W. B. Robb
             Harry West
             William Gleason, Clerk; (Leave of
               absence for three months, August
               1, 1932)
             A. D. M. Osborne, Clerk - in
               William Gleason's absence
             Marvin J. Davis, Clerk; Succeeded
               William Gleason, November 7, 1932

1933-1934   T. N. Harvey, President
             A. D. M. Osborne
             W. B. Robb
             Marvin J. Davis, Clerk
             Harry West

1934-1935   T. N. Harvey, President
             A. D. M. Osborne
             W. B. Robb
             Harry West
             W. J. Walters; Succeeded W. B. Robb,
               December 3, 1934
             M. J. Davis, Clerk

1935-1936   T. N. Harvey, President
             A. D. M. Osborne
             W. J. Walters
             Harry West
             M. J. Davis, Clerk
             C. F. Moore, Clerk; Succeeded M. J.
               Davis, February 28, 1936

1936-1937   T. N. Harvey, President
             W. J. Walters
             Harry West
             A. D. M. Osborne
             C. F. Moore, Clerk

1937-1938	T. N. Harvey, President A. D. M. Osborne W. J. Walters Harry West C. F. Moore, Clerk
1938-1939	T. N. Harvey, President A. D. M. Osborne W. J. Walters Harry West C. F. Moore, Clerk H. E. Woodworth, Clerk; Succeeded C. F. Moore, December 14, 1938
1939-1940	T. N. Harvey, President A. D. M. Osborne W. J. Walters Harry West H. E. Woodworth, Clerk
1940-1941	T. N. Harvey, President A. D. M. Osborne W. J. Walters Harry West C. W. O'Neill; Succeeded W. J. Walters, October 15, 1940 H. E. Woodworth, Clerk
1941-1942	T. N. Harvey, President A. D. M. Osborne Harry West C. W. O'Neill H. E. Woodworth, Clerk
1942-1943	T. N. Harvey, President A. D. M. Osborne C. W. O'Neill Phil Ohanneson H. E. Woodworth, Clerk
1943-1944	T. N. Harvey, President A. D. M. Osborne C. W. O'Neill Phil Ohanneson H. E. Woodworth, Clerk
1944-1945	T. N. Harvey, President A. D. M. Osborne C. W. O'Neill Phil Ohanneson H. E. Woodworth, Clerk
1945-1946	T. N. Harvey, President A. D. M. Osborne C. W. O'Neill Phil Ohanneson H. E. Woodworth, Clerk

1946-1947   T. N. Harvey, President
            A. D. M. Osborne; Died July 22, 1946
            William T. Baldwin; Succeeded A. D. M.
              Osborne, October 28, 1946
            C. W. O'Neill
            Phil Ohanneson
            H. E. Woodworth, Clerk

1947-1948   T. N. Harvey, President
            C. W. O'Neill
            Phil Ohanneson
            William T. Baldwin
            H. E. Woodworth, Clerk

1948-1949   T. N. Harvey, President;
            H. E. Woodworth, President; Succeeded
              T. N. Harvey, October 22, 1948
            William T. Baldwin
            A. H. Warner
            Phil Ohanneson
            C. W. O'Neill, Clerk

1949-1950   H. E. Woodworth, President
            William T. Baldwin
            Phil Ohanneson
            A. H. Warner; Resigned March 27, 1950
            A. S. Gould; Succeeded A. H. Warner,
              May 28, 1950
            C. W. O'Neill, Clerk

1950-1951   H. E. Woodworth, President
            William T. Baldwin
            Phil Ohanneson; Resigned January 5, 1951
            Emil Bender; Succeeded Phil Ohanneson,
              February 12, 1951
            A. S. Gould
            C. W. O'Neill, Clerk

1951-1952   H. E. Woodworth, President
            William T. Baldwin
            A. S. Gould
            Emil Bender
            C. W. O'Neill, Clerk

1952-1953   H. E. Woodworth, President
            William T. Baldwin
            A. S. Gould
            Emil Bender
            C. W. O'Neill, Clerk

1953-1954   H. E. Woodworth, President
            William T. Baldwin
            A. S. Gould
            Emil Bender
            C. W. O'Neill, Clerk

1954-1955	H. E. Woodworth, President William T. Baldwin A. S. Gould Emil Bender C. W. O'Neill, Clerk
1955-1956	H. E. Woodworth, President William T. Baldwin A. S. Gould Emil Bender C. W. O'Neill, Clerk
1956-1957	H. E. Woodworth, President William T. Baldwin Albert S. Gould Emil Bender; Resigned February 11, 1957 Donald E. Ruggenberg; Succeeded Emil Bender, February 11, 1957 C. W. O'Neill, Clerk
1957-1958	H. E. Woodworth, President William T. Baldwin Albert S. Gould Donald E. Ruggenberg C. W. O'Neill, Clerk
1958-1959	H. E. Woodworth, President William T. Baldwin M. Glenn Bultman, President; Succeeded William T. Baldwin, February 9, 1959 Albert S. Gould Donald E. Ruggenberg C. W. O'Neill, Clerk; Resigned June 30, 1959
1959-1960	H. E. Woodworth, President Resigned June 30, 1960 M. Glenn Bultman, Clerk Albert S. Gould Donald E. Ruggenberg Willard C. Myers; Appointed July 27, 1959 to succeed C. W. O'Neill
1960-1961	Albert S. Gould, President M. Glenn Bultman, Clerk Donald E. Ruggenberg Willard C. Myers Mark G. Raney; Appointed July 1, 1960 to succeed H. E. Woodworth

MAY 1, 1961:   Junior College District Board
               Organized with same President,
               Clerk, and Board Members

JULY 1, 1961: Junior College District Board
               Officialy Operates:

               "KERN JOINT JUNIOR COLLEGE
               DISTRICT"

1961-1962   Albert S. Gould, President
               M. Glenn Bultman, Clerk
               Donald E. Ruggenberg
               Willard C. Myers
               Mark G. Raney

1962-1963   Albert S. Gould, President
               M. Glenn Bultman, Clerk
               Donald E. Ruggenberg
               Willard C. Myers
               Mark G. Raney

1963-1964   Albert S. Gould, President
               M. Glenn Bultman, Clerk
               Donald E. Ruggenberg
               Willard C. Myers
               Mark G. Raney

1964-1965   Albert S. Gould, President
               M. Glenn Bultman, Clerk
               Donald E. Ruggenberg
               Willard C. Myers
               Mark G. Raney

1965-1966   Albert S. Gould, President
               M. Glenn Bultman, Clerk
               Donald E. Ruggenberg
               Willard C. Myers
               Mark G. Raney

1966-1967   Albert S. Gould, President
               M. Glenn Bultman, Clerk
               Donald E. Ruggenberg
               Willard C. Myers
               Mark G. Raney

1967-1968   Albert S. Gould, President
               M. Glenn Bultman, Clerk
               Willard C. Myers
               Mark G. Raney
               Donald E. Ruggenberg

As of July 1, 1968, the Kern Joint Union High School District and the Kern Junior College District (now named the Kern Community College District) separated totally, including the Board of Trustees.

1968-1969	M. Glenn Bultman, President Donald E. Ruggenberg, Clerk W. E. Davis W. C. Myers Mark G. Raney
1969-1970	M. Glenn Bultman, President Donald E. Ruggenberg, Clerk George Ablin W. E. Davis W. C. Myers
1970-1971	M. Glenn Bultman, President Donald E. Ruggenberg, Clerk George Ablin W. E. Davis Rayburn S. Dezember
1971-1972	Donald E. Ruggenberg, President W. E. Davis, Clerk George Ablin Rayburn S. Dezember Timothy Lemucchi
1972-1973	Donald E. Ruggenberg, President W. E. Davis, Clerk George Ablin Rayburn S. Dezember Timothy Lemucchi
1973-1974	Donald E. Ruggenberg, President George Ablin, Clerk Rayburn S. Dezember J. Craig Jenkins Timothy Lemucchi
1974-1975	Donald E. Ruggenberg, President George Ablin, Clerk Rayburn S. Dezember J. Craig Jenkins Timothy Lemucchi
1975-1976	George Ablin, President J. Craig Jenkins, Clerk Rayburn S. Dezember Donald E. Ruggenberg Mrs. Mary M. Vaughan

1976-1977   George Ablin, President
            J. Craig Jenkins, Clerk
            Rayburn S. Dezember
            Donald E. Ruggenberg
            Mrs. Mary M. Vaughan

1977-1978   Rayburn S. Dezember, President
            J. Craig Jenkins, Vice President
            Mrs. Mary M. Vaughan, Clerk
            George Ablin
            Donald E. Ruggenberg

1978-1979   Rayburn S. Dezember, President
            J. Craig Jenkins, Vice President
            Mrs. Mary M. Vaughan, Clerk
            George Ablin
            Donald E. Ruggenberg

1979-1980   J. Craig Jenkins, President
            George Ablin, Vice President
            Rayburn S. Dezember, Clerk
            Terry Moreland
            Mrs. Carol J. Wilcox

Note: Board election date changed to November and reorganization meeting held December 13, 1979.

1980-1981   Rayburn S. Dezember, President
            Mrs. Carol J. Wilcox, Vice President
            Terry L. Moreland
            George Ablin
            J. Craig Jenkins, Clerk

1981-1982   Fred L. Starrh, President
            Kenneth E. Secor, Clerk
            Muril Clift
            Earle J. Gibbons; Appointed to replace
              Muril Clift, June 2, 1982
            Mrs. Carol J. Wilcox, Vice President
            Terry Moreland

1982-1983   Fred L. Starrh, President
            Kenneth E. Secor, Clerk
            Earle J. Gibbons
            Mrs. Carol J. Wilcox, Vice President
            Terry Moreland

1983-1984   Kenneth E. Secor, President
            Brent P. Casper
            Earle J. Gibbons, Vice President
            David B. Stanton, Clerk
            Fred L. Starrh

1984-1985	Kenneth E. Secor, President Brent P. Casper Earle J. Gibbons, Clerk David B. Stanton, Vice President Fred L. Starrh
1985-1986	David B. Stanton, President Brent P. Casper, Vice President Earle J. Gibbons, Clerk Kenneth E. Secor Fred L. Starrh
1986-1987	David B. Stanton, President Brent P. Casper, Vice President Earle J. Gibbons, Clerk Kenneth E. Secor Fred L. Starrh
1987-1988	Fred L. Starrh, President Brent P. Casper, Vice President Earle J. Gibbons, Clerk Kenneth E. Secor David B. Stanton

KERN COUNTY UNION HIGH SCHOOL
AND
JUNIOR COLLEGE DISTRICT

SUPERINTENDENTS

1893-1894	Philip Eden, Principal January, 1893 to May, 1893
	E. F. Goodyear, Principal Beginning May, 1893
1894-1895	E. F. Goodyear, Principal
1895-1896	E. F. Goodyear, Principal Resigned December 7, 1895
	J. B. Newell, Principal Beginning December 7, 1895
1896-1897	J. B. Newell, Principal
1897-1898	A. B. Martin, Principal
1898-1899	C. C. Childress, Principal
1899-1900	C. C. Childress, Principal
1900-1901	C. C. Childress, Principal
1901-1902	Leroy B. Peckham, Principal
1902-1903	Leroy B. Peckham, Principal Released January 2, 1903
	C. C. Childress, Principal Beginning January 2, 1903
1903-1904	C. C. Childress, Principal
1904-1905	C. C. Childress, Principal
1905-1906	C. C. Childress, Principal
1906-1907	C. C. Childress, Principal
1907-1908	C. T. Conger, Principal
1908-1909	C. T. Conger, Principal
1909-1910	B. F. McComber, Principal
1910-1911	B. F. McComber, Principal

Superintendents (Continued):

1911-1912	B. F. McComber, Principal
1912-1913	B. F. McComber, Principal
1913-1914	B. S. Gowen, Principal
1914-1915	B. S. Gowen, Principal
1915-1916	B. S. Gowen, Principal Resigned May 29, 1916
	A. J. Ludden, Principal July 1, 1916
1916-1917	A. J. Ludden, Principal
1917-1918	A. J. Ludden, Principal
1918-1919	A. J. Ludden, Principal
1919-1920	A. J. Ludden, Principal
1920-1921	A. J. Ludden, Principal
1921-1922	A. J. Ludden, Principal Deceased January, 1922
	H. A. Spindt, Principal Effective March 6, 1922
1922-1923	H. A. Spindt, Principal
1923-1924	H. A. Spindt, Principal
1924-1925	H. A. Spindt, Principal
1925-1926	H. A. Spindt, Principal
1926-1927	H. A. Spindt, Principal
1927-1928	H. A. Spindt, Principal
1928-1929	H. A. Spindt, Principal
1929-1930	H. A. Spindt, Principal
1930-1931	H. A. Spindt, Principal
1931-1932	H. A. Spindt, Principal
1932-1933	H. A. Spindt, Superintendent
1933-1934	H. A. Spindt, Superintendent

Superintendents (Continued):

1934-1935	H. A. Spindt, Superintendent
1935-1936	H. A. Spindt, Superintendent
1936-1937	H. A. Spindt, Superintendent
1937-1938	H. A. Spindt, Superintendent
1938-1939	T. L. Nelson, Superintendent Elected May 13, 1938
1939-1940	T. L. Nelson, Superintendent
1940-1941	T. L. Nelson, Superintendent
1941-1942	T. L. Nelson, Superintendent
1942-1943	T. L. Nelson, Superintendent
1943-1944	T. L. Nelson, Superintendent
1944-1945	T. L. Nelson, Superintendent Resigned June 20, 1945
1945-1946	Theron L. McCuen, Acting Superintendent, July 2, 1945
1946-1947	Theron L. McCuen, Superintendent
1947-1948	Theron L. McCuen, Superintendent
1948-1949	Theron L. McCuen, Superintendent
1949-1950	Theron L. McCuen, Superintendent
1950-1951	Theron L. McCuen, Superintendent
1951-1952	Theron L. McCuen, Superintendent
1952-1953	Theron L. McCuen, Superintendent
1953-1954	Theron L. McCuen, Superintendent
1954-1955	Theron L. McCuen, Superintendent
1955-1956	Theron L. McCuen, Superintendent
1956-1957	Theron L. McCuen, Superintendent
1957-1958	Theron L. McCuen, Superintendent
1958-1959	Theron L. McCuen, Superintendent
1959-1960	Theron L. McCuen, Superintendent

Superintendents (Continued):

1961-1962	Theron L. McCuen, Superintendent
1962-1963	Theron L. McCuen, Superintendent
1953-1964	Theron L. McCuen, Superintendent
1964-1965	Theron L. McCuen, Superintendent
1965-1966	Theron L. McCuen, Superintendent
1966-1967	Theron L. McCuen, Superintendent
1967-1968	Theron L. McCuen, Superintendent
1968-1969	John W. Eckhardt, Superintendent
1969-1970	John W. Eckhardt, Superintendent
1970-1971	John W. Eckhardt, Superintendent
1971-1972	John W. Eckhardt, Superintendent
1972-1973	John W. Eckhardt, Superintendent
1973-1974	John W. Eckhardt, Superintendent
1974-1975	John W. Eckhardt, Superintendent
1975-1976	John W. Eckhardt, Superintendent
1976-1977	John W. Eckhardt, Superintendent
1977-1978	Gerald S. DeGrow, Superintendent
1978-1979	Gerald S. DeGrow, Superintendent
1979-1980	Gerald S. DeGrow, Superintendent
1980-1981	Gerald S. DeGrow, Superintendent
1981-1982	Don L. Murfin, Superintendent
1982-1983	Don L. Murfin, Superintendent
1983-1984	Don L. Murfin, Superintendent
1984-1985	Don L. Murfin, Superintendent
1985-1986	Don L. Murfin, Superintendent
1986-1987	Don L. Murfin, Superintendent
1987-1988	Don L. Murfin, Superintendent

(Information through the 1987-88 School Year)

KERN COUNTY UNION HIGH SCHOOL DISTRICT
HIGH SCHOOLS AND PRINCIPALS

ARVIN HIGH SCHOOL
Address: 900 Varsity
   Arvin, CA 93203
Opened: 1949
Yearbook: Praeterita
Colors: Red & White
Team: Bears

From		Through	Principal
1949-1950	-	1959-1960	Clyde Dawald
1959-1960	-	1959-1960	Carl Bee, Acting Principal
1960-1961	-	1963-1964	Edwin DeMello
1964-1965	-	1967-1968	Wesley R. Anderson
1968-1969	-	Present	Jack O. Schulze

BAKERSFIELD ADULT SCHOOL
Address: 501 So. Mt. Vernon Avenue
   Bakersfield, CA 93307
Opened: 1918; school held in various places.
   No principal until 1926

From		Through	Principal
1926-1927	-	1953-1954	Guy Gerrard
1954-1955	-	1956-1957	Gerald Hedden
1957-1958	-	1981-1982	Wallace Webster
1982-1983	-	1983-1984	Donald Soelberg
1984-1985	-	Present	Clinton Osthimer

BAKERSFIELD HIGH SCHOOL
Address: 1241 'G' Street
   Bakersfield, CA 93301
Opened: 1893
Yearbook: Oracle
Colors: Blue and White
Team: Drillers

Bakersfield High School - CONTINUED:

From		Through	Principal
1893-1894	–	May, 1893	Philip Eden
1893-1894	–	December, 1895	E. F. Goodyear
1895-1896	–	1896-1897	J. B. Newell
1897-1898	–	1897-1898	A. B. Martin
1898-1899	–	1900-1901	C. C. Childress
1901-1902	–	January, 1903	Leroy B. Peckham
1902-1903	–	1906-1907	C. C. Childress
1907-1908	–	1908-1909	C. T. Conger
1909-1910	–	1912-1913	B. F. McComber
1913-1914	–	1915-1916	B. S. Gowen
1916-1917	–	1920-1921	A. J. Ludden
1921-1922	–	1036-1937	Herman Spindt
1937-1938	–	1938-1939	Thomas Nelson
1939-1940	–	1961-1962	Leslie Hedge
1962-1963	–	1967-1968	J. S. Wallace
1968-1969	–	1976-1977	Kenneth Robesky
1977-1978	–	1979-1980	James R. Fillbrandt
1980-1981	–	Present	William Lacey

BURROUGHS HIGH SCHOOL

Address: French Street
         Ridgecrest, CA 93555
Opened: 1945
Yearbook: El Burro
Colors: Green and White
Team: Burros

From		Through	Principal
1945-1946	–	1945-1946	F. R. Wegner
1946-1947	–	1959-1960	Earl Murray
1960-1961	–	1968-1969	Kenneth Westcott
1969-1970	–	1972-1973	John Cissne
1973-1974			Harold Reid, Acting Principal

Unified in 1974

CONTINUATION SCHOOLS

Vista Continuation High School
Address: 200 'P' Street,
  Bakersfield, CA 93304
Opened: 1966

Vista East Continuation High School
Address: 815 Eureka Street
  Bakersfield, CA 93305
Opened: 1974

Vista West Continuation High School
Address: 7115 Rosedale Highway
  Bakersfield, CA 93308
Opened: 1986

Summit Continuation High School
Address: 5105-A Lake Isabella Road
  Lake Isabella, Ca 93240
Opened: 1984

Nueva Continuation High School
Address: 8600 Palm Avenue
  Lamont, CA 93241
Opened: 1970

Central Valley Continuation High School
Address: 730 E. Lerdo Highway
  Shafter, CA 93263
Opened: 1971

From	Through	Principal
1966-1967 - Present		H. R. Donald Cornett

H. R. Donald Cornett was the first principal of Vista Continuation School (1966). In 1977, he was named Principal/Director of all continuation schools.

EAST BAKERSFIELD HIGH SCHOOL
Address: 2200 Quincy Street
  Bakersfield, CA 93306
Opened: 1939
Yearbook: Sierran
Colors: Red and White
Team: Blades

From	Through	Principal
1939-1940	1955-1956	Kenneth Rich
1956-1957	1961-1962	Irving Lane
1962-1963	1973-1974	E. C. Mills

East Bakersfield High School - CONTINUED:

1974-1975 - 1982-1982   James Waterman
1982-1983 - Present   Jean Philippe

FOOTHILL HIGH SCHOOL
Address: 501 Park Drive
         Bakersfield, CA 93306
Opened: 1962
Yearbook: Aurora
Colors: Black and Gold
Team: Trojans

From	Through	Principal
1962-1963 -	1964-1965	Gerald W. Hedden
1965-1966 -	1972-1973	Arthur Johnson
1973-1974 -	1986-1987	Jordon Kanikkeberg
1987-1988 -	Present	Bill Bruce

HIGHLAND HIGH SCHOOL
Address: 2900 Royal Scots Road
         Bakersfield, CA 93306
Opened: 1970
Yearbook: Regalia
Colors: Blue and Green
Team: Scotsmen

From	Through	Principal
1970-1971 -	1974-1975	Wesley R. Anderson
1975-1976 -	1975-1976	Robert G. Milliken, Acting Principal
1976-1977 -	1983-1984	Wesley R. Anderson
1984-1985 -	Present	Dr. Anne Scott

HORIZON HIGH SCHOOL
Address: 7115 Rosedale Highway
         Bakersfield, CA 93308
Opened: 1975

From	Through	Principal
1975-1976 -	1982	Robert Amenta, Director

KERN VALLEY HIGH SCHOOL
Address: 3280 Erskine Creek Road,
         Lake Isabella, CA 93240
Opened: 1941, as Kernville High School
         for ninth and tenth grade students

         1947, as Kern Valley High School
         for grades nine through twelve

From		Through	Principal
1941-1942	-	1942-1943	Manville Pettys
1943-1944	-	1943-1944	Lawrence Wiemers
1944-1945	-	1946-1947	Thomas Merson
1947-1948	-	1952-1953	E. C. Mills
1953-1954	-	1956-1957	James I. Van Fossen
1957-1958	-	1960-1961	R. M. Hoagland
1961-1962	-	1961-1962	Earl Murray
1962-1963	-	1963-1964	R. M. Hoagland
1964-1965	-	1967-1968	Jack O. Schulze
1968-1969	-	1977-1978	D. E. Lucas
1978-1979	-	1983-1984	Clinton Osthimer
1984-1985	-	Present	Bruce Farmer

MCFARLAND HIGH SCHOOL
Address: 259 Sherwood Avenue
          McFarland, CA 93250
Opened: 1928
Yearbook: Recuerdos
Colors: Red and White
Team: Cougars

From		Through	Principal
1928-1929	-	1929-1930	Information not available
1930-1931	-	1931-1932	E. P. Janes
1932-1933	-	1938-1939	Leslie Hedge
1939-1940	-	1944-1945	J. H. Porterfield
1945-1946	-	1947-1948	Clyde Dawald
1948-1949	-	1950-1951	Grant W. Jensen
1951-1952	-	1955-1956	Arthur Johnson
1956-1957	-	1959-1960	Edwin DeMello

McFarland High School - CONTINUED:

1960-1961 -	1964-1965	Thomas Henley
1965-1966 -	1968-1969	Jordon Kanikkeberg
1969-1970 -	1979-1970	Charles Gates

Joined McFarland Unified District, July 1, 1980

NORTH HIGH SCHOOL
Address: 300 Galaxy Avenue
 Bakersfield, CA 93308
Opened: 1953
Yearbook: Galaxy
Colors: Scarlet and Gray
Team: Stars

From	Through	Principal
1953-1954 -	1954-1955	Jack M. Hill
1955-1956 -	1964-1965	George Williamson
1965-1966 -	1968-1969	Jack Hilton
1969-1970 -	1972-1973	Harold Corrie
1973-1974 -	1983-1984	Richard Brown
1984-1985 -	Present	Warner Brooks

REGIONAL OCCUPATIONAL CENTER
Address: 501 So. Mt. Vernon Avenue
 Bakersfield, CA 93307

Joined the Kern Union High School District in the 1980-81 School Year.

From	Through	Principal
1980-1981 -	Present	Cecil D. Briscoe, Principal/Director

SHAFTER HIGH SCHOOL
Address: 526 Manuel Avenue
 Shafter, CA 93263
Opened: 1928
Yearbook: The Laurion
Colors: Gold and Blue
Team: Generals

Shafter High School - CONTINUED

From	Through	Principal
1928-1929 -	1928-1929	Herman Spindt
1929-1930 -	1935-1936	Elmer J. Peery
1936-1937 -	1942-1943	E. P. Janes
1943-1944 -	1944-1945	"Pat" Kelly
1945-1946 -	1950-1951	Jack Hill
1951-1952 -	1955-1956	Grant W. Jensen
1956-1957 -	1964-1965	Arthur Johnson
1965-1966 -	1968-1969	Harold Corrie
1969-1970 -	1972-1973	Jordon Kanikkeberg
1973-1974 -	1978-1979	Neal W. Olsen
1979-1980 -	January,1983	Evan Jones
1982-1983 -	Present	Herb Neufeld

SOUTH HIGH SCHOOL
Address: 1101 Planz Road
         Bakersfield, CA   93304
Opened: 1957
Yearbook: Merrimac
Colors: Blue and Gray
Team: Rebels

From	Through	Principal
1957-1958 -	1967-1968	Grant W. Jensen
1968-1969 -	1977-1978	Don L. Murfin
1978-1979 -	Present	Ms. Jeannine Thompson

WEST HIGH SCHOOL
Address: 1200 New Stine Road
         Bakersfield, CA   93309
Opened: 1965
Yearbook: Valhalla
Colors: Green and White
Team: Vikings

From	Through	Principal
1965-1966 -	1974-1975	Edwin DeMello
1975-1976 -	1981-1982	Thomas N. Jones
1982-1983 -	Present	Ms. Ann Cierley

KERN COMMUNITY COLLEGE DISTRICT
CHANCELLORS, PRESIDENTS, AND BOARDS OF TRUSTEES
1968 to 1987

CHANCELLORS:

1913 - 1915	G. E. Congre, Principal
1915 - 1916	B. S. Gowen, Principal
1916 - 1922	A. J. Ludden, Principal
1922 - 1938	Herman Spindt, Principal/ Superintendent
1938 - 1945	T. L. Nelson, Superintendent
1945 - 1968	Theron L. McCuen, Superintendent
1968 - 1978	Edward E. Simonsen, Chancellor
1978 - Presdent	James C. Young, Chancellor

PRESIDENTS:

Bakersfield College:
Opened: 1913
1801 Panorama Drive
Bakersfield, CA 93305

1913 - 1950	Grace Van Dyke Bird Vice Principal and Dean of College
1950 - 1958	Ralph Prator Vice Principal and Dean of College
1958 - 1968	Edward E. Simonsen President
1968 - 1972	Burns Finlinson President
1972 - 1983	John Collins President
1983 - Present	Richard Wright President

Cerro Coso Community College
Opened: 1972
3000 College Heights Boulevard
Ridgecrest, CA 93555

1972 - 1975	Richard Jones President
1975 - 1978	Richard Meyers President
1978 - Present	Raymond McCue President

Porterville College
Opened: 1927
900 So. Main Street
Porterville, CA 93257

1927 - 1928	Benjamin Grisemer Vice Principal and Dean of College
1928 - 1930	Francis Gault Vice Principal and Dean of College
1930 - 1955	B. E. Jamison Dean of College
1955 - 1978	Orlin Shires President
1978 - President	Paul Alcantra President

BOARDS OF TRUSTEES:

1968-1969	M. Glenn Bultman Edward Cornell Albert S. Gould W. C. Myers Mark G. Raney Donald Ruggenberg Loren Voth
1969-1970 through 1970-1971	M. GLenn Bultman Edward Cornell Albert S. Gould Angus Marchbanks Mark G. Raney Donald Ruggenberg Loren Voth

Boards of Trustees - Continued:

1971-1972 through 1972-1973	Cecil Bailey M. Glenn Bultman Edward Cornell Albert S. Gould Angus Marchbanks Mark G. Raney Loren Voth
1973-1974 through December, 1983	Cecil Bailey M. Glenn Bultman Edward Cornell Angus Marchbanks Gilbert Plain Mark G. Raney Loren Voth
December, 1983 to Present	Cecil Bailey Rose Marie Bans M. Glenn Bultman Edward Cornell Angus Marchbanks Gilbert Plain Mark G. Raney

GRAMMAR SCHOOL GRADUATION QUESTIONS

The following is the final examination taken by Eighth Grade Grammar School Graduates to get into Kern County High School - June, 1914.

Arithmetic

1. If 5/8 of a pound of tea cost 50 cents, how much will 251 3/4 pounds cost?
2. A man spent 1/6 of his salary for clothing, 1/20 for rent, 1/4 for food, and had $640.00 left. What salary did he receive?
3. A flag pole is 125 feet high. Another pole on the opposite side of the street, 60 feet wide, is 75 feet high. What is the distance between the tops of the poles? Draw a diagram.
4. Find the simple interest of $3,840.00 from October 13, 1908 to May 5, 1910, at 5%.
5. A note of $4,500.00 dated May 15, 1908, bearing 5 1/2% interest has the following indorsements:
    May 15, 1909, $600.00
    June 10, 1909 $50.00
    December 24, 1909, $150.00
   What is due June 10, 1910?
6. At $2 5/8 (two dollars and five-eighths) a cubic foot, what is the cost of a block of marble 8 ft. 2 in. long, 4 ft. 8 in. wide and 2 ft. 6 in. thick?
7. A house is worth $6,480.00. It is insured for 2/3 of its value at 3/4%. What is the premium?
8. A man sold an article for $24.00 and lost 25%. If he had sold it for $34.00, what per cent would he have gained or lost?
9. The property valuation of a town is $8,100,000.00. The tax to be raised is $91,500.00. What is the city rate if there are 1000 polls at $1.50 each? What is Mr. Brown's property tax if he is assessed for $2,500.00?
10. (a) Divide 1. by .02
    (b) Divide 7/8 by 3/4
    (c) Find the product, sum and difference of 31 and 279.

Grammar

1. Write a telegram, a formal note of invitation, and a description of some person you know.
2. Give one or more stanzas from some poem, and tell what pictures you see in these stanzas.
3. Write five paragraphs telling what your State does for you.
4. Name and define the parts of speech. Give the parts that are inflected.
5. Use correctly in sentences: lie, lay, laid, lain, sit, set, rise, raise, teach, learn.
6. Name and define the tenses. Illustrate the uses of shall and will in sentences.
7. Write sentences illustrating the different modes.
8. Analyze or diagram:
    (a) Books (is are) a proper noun.
    (b) Either John or Hames (have has) gone.
    (c) Every chair and table (were was) broken.
    (d) Each day and hour (pass passes) swiftly.
    (e) The jury rose to (its their) feet when the judge came in.
    Give reasons for your choice of words.
9. Define and illustrate complement, clause, infinitive, participle, collective noun.

Grammar School Graduation Questions - CONTINUED

Spelling

convenient	lieutenant	erosion	iodine
genuine	deceit	automobile	massacre
separate	metaphor	disguise	enormous
grammar	antecedent	behavior	adjective
cashier	bureau	leisure	celluloid
geranium	disappoint	contagious	schedule
delicious	declarative	strychnine	macaroni
gauntlet	morphine	privilege	villian
bouquet	souvenir	pyramid	emulate
digestion	chloroform	porcelain	musician
dynamite	rheumatism	auxiliary	hideous
suffrage	prairie	assurance	luxury
attorney	psalm		

History

1. Give a brief history of the Declaration of Independence.
2. Name the first three presidents of the United States and the principal events during this time.
3. Give an account of the Lewis and Clark Expedition.
4. What were the causes of the War of 1812? The results?
5. Connect the following names with U. S. History: Captain Perry, Robert Fulton, Henry Clay, Daniel Webster, Lafayette, General Pickett.
6. Tell how a president is elected. Can a candidate be declared elected president without receiving a majority of the popular vote?
7. Give a brief account of causes which led to the Civil War. Name four battles and the opposing generals in each.
8. Tell all you can of the events of McKinley's administration.
9. Give a brief account of the acquisition and construction of the Panama Canal.
10. Explain the effects of the European War on commerce of the U. S. On the revenue of the U.S. What remedies have been applied?

Geography

1. Describe the climate, vegetation and animals of the different zones.
2. Name the states bordering on the Great Lakes and give their capitals.
3. Trace a water route from Kansas City to San Francisco.
4. What parts of the U.S. are noted for the production of each of the following: corn, cotton, lumber, gold, coal, iron, silver, copper, wheat, and livestock.
5. Describe the physiography and climate of Canada.
6. Name and locate five of the principal ocean currents and give their effect on the adjacent countries.
7. Compare and contrast Germany with Russia as to physiography, government, education, and industries.
8. Compare and contrast the physiography and production of Asia with Africa.
9. Tell about the surface, climate, native animals, and industries of Australia.
10. Draw an outline map of the U.S. locating the principal bodies of water, mountains, and ten large cities.

THE HIGH SCHOOL GRADUATION EXAMINATION QUESTIONS

Copied from The Morning Echo, Bakersfield, California,
Sunday, May 29, 1904

LATIN: VERGIL'S AENEID.

I. Translate book VI, ll. 390-404,

"Umbrarum hic locus est, Somni Noctieque soporae;
Corpora viva nefas Stygia vectare carina.
Nec vero Alciden me sum laetatus euntem,
Accepisse lacu nec Thesa Perithoumque.
Dis quamquam geniti atque invicti vincla petivit
Tartareum ille manu custodem in vinela petit
Ipsius a solio regis taraxitque trementem;
Hi dominam Ditis thalaine deduere adorti.
Cuae contra breviter fata est Amphrysia vates;
Nullae hic insidiae tales, (abiste moveri);
Nie vim tela ferunt: licet ingens ianitor antro
Aeternum latraus exsangues terreat umbra,
Casta licet patrui servet. Proserpina limen,
Throrus Aeneas, uietate insignis et armis.
Ad genitorem imas Erebi descendit ad umbras."

II. Translate book VII, ll. 509-519.

"Ad quae Priamides; Nihil Otibi amice, relictum;
Omnia Deiphobo solviste et funeris umbris,
Sed me fata mea et scelus exitiale Lacaenae
His mersere malis; illa haec monumenta reliquit;
Namque ut supremam falsa inter guandia noctem
Equrimus, notsi; et nimium meminisse necesse est.
Cum fatalis equus saltu super ardua venit
Pergama et armatum peditem gravis attulit alvo,
Illa, chorum simulans, evantes orgia circum
Ducebat Phrygias; flammam media insa tenebat;
Ingentem, et summa Danaos exarce vocabat.

III. Translate book VI, ll., 845-853

"Tu Maximus ille es."
"Unus qui nobis cunctando restituis rem.
Excudent alii spirantia mollius aera,
Credo equidem, vivos ducent de marmore vultus,
Orabunt caucas melius, caelique meatus
Describent radio et surgentia sidera dicent;
Tu regere imperio populis, Romane mememto:
(Hae tibi etunt artes), pacisque imponere morem,
Parcere subjectis, et debellare superbos."

IV. Explain all historial and literary references in ll. 845-853.

V. (1) Comment on the force of ille (l.845); give principal parts of mememto (l.851); two possible translation of meminisse; explain the derivation of nefas (l. 391); distinguish in meaning between ius and fas
(2) Scan ll. 851, 852.

The High School Graduation Examination - CONTINUED

Physics

1. Is the focal strength of a bi-convex glass lens the same in water as in air? Is the focal strength the same for light of different colors?
2. How may a real image be distinguished from a virtual image? Give diagrams which will illustrate the formation of (a) real image, (b) a virtual. Will the image of an object viewed in a plane mirror be shifted as the eye is moved from place to place? Illustrate your answer by a diagram.
3. How may the velocity of light be determined?
4. How should you measure the magnifying power of a lens?
5. An object under water appears to be elevated above its true position. Explain. Would the object appear displaced if the eye were likewise immersed?
6. How many 50-volt lamps can a 2000-volt machine run in series, when one-tenth of the voltage is lost in the leading wires?
7. How many watts are used by an arc lamp that requires 45 volts and 9.5 amperes? How many such lamps can be run by a 30-H.P. engine provided 90 per cent of the energy of the engine is used in the lamps?
8. The hot resistance of a 100-volt, 16-candle-power lamp is 192 ohms. How many amperes are required to burn such a lamp? How many watts per lamp? How many watts per candle power?
9. A dynamo, when run at a certain speed, showed a potential difference of 125 volts at its terminals and sent a current of 24.5 amperes through a motor circuit. What was the resistance of the circuit?
10. What is the resistance of an arc lamp that requires a 9-ampere current and a potential difference of 45.8 volts to burn it properly?

U. S. Civil Government

I.
1. Give the genealogy of state governments.
2. How many houses have state legislatures in general? California?
3. In California what are the names of the houses; how are the members chosen; term of office, salaries, and qualifications?
4. Is there any restriction placed on the origin of bills in the numerous states; in California?

II.
1. How many sets of courts has every state and what are they?
2. Is there any limit on the jurisdiction of state courts? Explain.
3. Name the disadvantages in the present method of appointing state judges, in the length of their term of office, and their small salaries.
4. What checks exist in our state to counter balance the faults of this system?

III.
1. Name the general divisions of the constitution of the United States.
2. Of what does each article treat?
3. Give an example of an inherent, created, and delegated power.

IV.
When and what was the occasion of the first ten amendments;
Why the eleventh;
When and Why the twelfth?

V.
Mention all the clauses in the constitution of the United States that deal or might be construed to deal with the slavery question.

The High School Graduation Examinations - CONTINUED:

VI. What is Vergil's theory of a past and future spiritual life, as shown in Book VI? What earlier philosopher had given this theory to the world? In what modern poems have you found the expression of similar views?

VII. What purpose of Vergil in writing the Aeneid is shown especially in Book VI?

Senior English

I.
1. What are the duties of youth as shown in Browning's "Rabbi Ben Ezra?"
2. What compensation has age?
3. Explain the figure of the potter and the clay.
4. Why was the grammarian in "The Grammarian's Funeral" buried on the mountain top?
5. What lesson do we learn from "Justan's Tyrannus?"
6. Compare the types of women in "Evelyn Hope," "A Woman's Last Word," "A Pretty Woman," and, "Oeone."
7. What are the characteristics of Shelley's poetry?
8. Name four things with which Shelley compared the skylark.
9. What things does Wordsworth point out in "Intimations of Immortality?"
10. Compare his view of the progress of the soul through life with Browning's conception.

II.
Explain the following quotations and tell from what poem each is taken:

1. "Peace hath her victories no less renowned than war."
2. "That orbed maiden with white fire laden whom mortals call the moon."
3. "The soul that rises with us, our life's star, hath had elsewhere its setting."
4. "And God fulfills himself in many ways lest one good custom should corrupt the world."
5. "Those hadst one aim, one business, one desire; else wert thou long since numbered with the dead."
6. "There lies a vale in Ida, lovelier than all the valleys of Ionian hills."
7. "Learned him great language, caught his clear accents; made him our pattern to live and to die."
8. "God's in his heaven; all's right with the world."
9. "All that is, all all, lasts ever, past recall."
10. "To me the meanest flower that blows can give thoughts that do often lie too deep for tears."

Trigonometry

1. If secant x equals 7 and tangent x is negative, find the numerical value of sine x.
2. Express cosine (-200 degrees) in terms of the functions of a positive angle less than 45 degrees.
3. Find the numerical value of the tangent of 350 degrees.
4. Draw a unit circle and shade the sectors in which the value of x in the expression sine x-cosine x is negative.
5. Express cotangent of (x-180 degrees) in functions of x.
6. Find sine 3x in terms of sine x.
7. Prove that the cotangent of 1/2 x equals sine x divided by (1- consine x).
8. Find the numerical value of the sine of the angle whose tangent is 5-12.
9. State and prove the Law of Sines.
10. State, without proof, the Law of Tangents.

COUNTY TEACHERS EXAMINATION

Copied from The Morning Echo, Bakersfield, California
May 6, 1904

Physics

1. Give some experiments in physics which you would perform or have the pupils perform in the elementary schools.
2. Define atom, molecule, matter, specific property, hydrostatics, pneumatics, pulley, volt, osmose.
3. Give the four laws of the pendulum.
4. Explain the steam engine.
5. Explain the syphon; give two of its practical uses.
6. How far would a body fall in five seconds in a vacuum?
7. What effect has salt in solution on the freezing point in water; on the boiling point? What effect has pressure?
8. Name and explain a recent invention in electricity.
9. Name the prismatic colors in the order of their reflection.
10. Explain how a rainbow is formed.

History

1. Give a brief account of the discovery of America; of the discovery of the Pacific Ocean.
2. How did the following affect subsequent history: The expedition of Cortez, La Salle, Hudson, Cabrillo, Lewis and Clarke?
3. Tell briefly of the settlement of Virginia, Massachusetts, Pennsylvania, Georgia.
4. What was the decisive battle of the French and Indian War? What effect did it have on the colonial question?
5. What causes led to the Revolutionary war? Name two important battles of that war and the results of each battle.
6. Discuss briefly three acts of congress relating to slavery.
7. Write a brief account of the Spanish-American war.
8. How are the following officials elected: President of the United States, United States senator, member of the lower house of congress?

Geography

1. Give a brief description of the general air circulation.
2. Account for the location of the lake regions of the United States.
3. How do plans and animals affect the soil?
4. How do the glaciers of Alaska compare with those of the Swiss Alps?
5. What country leads the world in the production of wheat? Cotton?
6. Name five of the leading manufacturing countries of the world.
7. Tell what you can of Japan, using these topics: Physiography, products, government, education, commerce.
8. Discuss fully the climate of the western coast of North America.
9. What and where are the following: Everest, Liverpool, Dardanelles, Milan, Seine, Dresden, Port Arthur, Corsica, Hong Kong, Luzon.

# # # # # # # #

County Teachers Examination - CONTINUED

Copied from The Morning Echo, Bakersfield, California
         May 4, 1904

English and American Literature

1. Mention three writers of the colonial period of American literature and give a work of each.
2. Characterize the work of Emerson with reference to subject matter and expression.
3. Name five patriotic poems in American literature and give author of each.
4. Name five authors whose works help to give California an honorable place in the literary ranks of the country.
5. Compare and contrast the writings of Longfellow and Tennyson.
6. Chaucer. (a) When did he live? (b) What did he write? (c) What has been the influences of his writings on the English language and literature?
7. Name the author and give briefly the subject matter of each of the following: Utopia, The Dunciad, The Hind and the Panther, Sartor Resartus, Comus.
8. Who were the Lake poets? Why were they so called? What is remarkable as to this school of poets?
9. Write briefly of the life and works of Herbert Spencer.
10. What is meant by the "Elizabethan period" in English literature? Name five writers of this period and give one production of each.

Arithmetic

1. A boy having a number of marbles gives to one schoolmate one-fifth of them; to another one-eighth of the remainder, loses one-fourth of what then remains and sells 2 1-7 times as many as he loses, when he has but 6 marbles left. How many had he at first?
2. What amount is due July 3d, 1904 on a note dated June 15th, 1902, for $448.50, interest at 7 per cent, and endorsed with the following payments: April 19th, 1903, $125; January 25, 1904.
3. What is the edge of a cubical box whose solidity is equal to that of a bin whose length, breadth and height are respectively 144, 36 and 9 inches.
4. What will it cost to fence at $2.35 per rod diagonally across a rectangular piece of land whose length is to its breadth as 2 is to 1, and which contains 5 acres of land.
5. How shall I mark a package of collars which cost me $4 each, so that I may fall 20 per cent from the marked price and yet gain 25 per cent on the purchase price?
6. A stone immersed in a cylindrical vessel 10 inches in diameter raises the water in the vessel 5 inches. What are the contents of the stone?
7. A person has just 2 hours spare time. How far may he ride in a stage which travels 12 miles per hour so as to return in time, walking back at the rate of 4 miles per hour?
8. Bought sugar for refinery: 6 per cent is wasted in refining, 30 per cent becomes molasses which is sold at 40 per cent less than the same weight of sugar cost. At what per cent advance on the first cost must the clarified sugar be sold to yield a profit of 14 per cent on the investment?
9. A, B and C do a piece of work in 10 days, A and C in 12 days and B and C in 15 days. In what time can each do it working alone.
10. A commission merchant sold cloth on a 1 3-5 per cent commission and invested the proceeds in cotton on 2 1/2 per cent commission. His commission amounted to $241.40. What did he receive for the cloth and what did he give for the cotton?

LIST OF TAPED INTERVIEWS

Name	District Relationship
ALLEN, Avery	District Staff 1940-1968, Office of Public Information
ASHE, Mary Ann	Graduate, Kern County High School, 1908
BALDWIN, William T.	Graduate, Kern County High School, 1933 Board Member 1946-1959
BREWER, Harold	Graduate, Kern County High School, 1929
BOHNA, Marianna	Graduate, Kern County High School, 1906
BULTMANN, M. Glenn	Graduate, Kern County High School, 1931 Graduate, Bakersfield College, 1933 Board Member, Kern County High School, 1959-1971 Board Member, Kern Community College Board 1971 to present
CANNON, Allen	Teacher, Bakersfield High School, 1939-1955 District Office, 1955-1969, Instruction and Personnel Offies
CORNETT, H. R. Donald	Teacher, Bakersfield High School, 1959-1965 Teacher, McFarland High School, 1965-1966 Principal, Continuation School, 1966-present
COLLINS, John	Teacher, Bakersfield High School and Bakersfield College, 1947-1966; President, Bakersfield College, 1972-1983;
DRENNAN, Harry	Graduate, Kern County High School, 1922 District Transportation Department, 1922-1929; Teacher/Professor, Kern County High School/Bakersfield College, 1929-1956; Chair, Industrial Arts Department, Bakersfield College, 1956-1968
ECKHARDT, John W.	Head of Instruction and Personnel Departments, Kern County High School District, 1946-1977 Superintendent, Kern County High School District, 1968-1977
EVANS, Dorothy	Graduate, Kern County High School, 1927

EVANS, E. Ben	Graduate, Kern County High School, 1927 Graduate, Bakersfield College, 1929 Head of Library/Instructional Services, Kern County High School, 1933-1972
FINLINSON, Burns	Dean of Records, Vice-President, President, Bakersfield College, 1946-1972
HART, Don	Graduate, Kern County High School, 1933
HART, Leo B.	Teacher, Counselor, Kern County High School, 1925-1939
HILTON, Jack	Graduate, Kern County High School, 1934 Teacher, East Bakersfield High School, 1938-1941; Dean/Coach, Bakersfield High School, 1946-1953; Vice Principal / Principal, North High School, 1953-1969 Director of Personnel, Kern County High School District Office, 1969-1973
KELLY, H. W. (Pat)	Attendance Supervisor, Kern County High School, 1939-1943 Principal, Shafter High School, 1943-1945
McCUEN, Theron L.	Teacher, Kern County High School, 1929-1936 Business Manager, Kern County High School District, 1936-1945 Superinendent, Kern County High School District, 1945-1968
PAULY, Harold	Director of Transportation, Kern County High School District, 1919-1966
PHILIPPE, Jean	Graduate, East Bakersfield High School,
RANEY, Mark	Board Member, Kern County High School District, 1960-1969; Board Member, Kern Community College District, 1969-present
ROBESKY, Donald	Graduate, Kern County High School, 1924 Teacher/Department Head, Kern County High School/Bakersfield High School, 1934-1972
ROBESKY, Margo	Teacher/Counselor, Bakersfield High School, 1942-1980
ROBESKY, Thomas	Graduate, Kern County High School Teacher/Counselor, East Bakersfield High School, 1958-1981

RUGGENBERG, Don	Board Member, Kern Community College District, 1957-1979
SCHUETZ, Jack	Teacher, East Bakersfield High School, 1959-1963 Chair, Special Education Department, Kern County High School Distrct, 1963-1968 Director, Special Education Department, Kern Union High School District, 1968 to present
SIMONSEN, Edward	Teacher, East Bakersfield High School, 1938-1941 President/Chancellor, Kern Community College District, 1946-1978
SMITH, Gerald	Graduate, Kern County High School, 1926 Teacher/Manager, Harvey Auditorium, Kern County High School/Bakersfield High School, 1930-1972
STIERN, Senator Walter	Graduate, Kern County High School, 1932 Graduate, Bakersfield College, 1933
STUTZMAN, Ruth Heil Emerson	Teacher/Department Head, Kern County High School/Bakersfield High School, 1919-1957
SUMMERS, Christine Noriega	Graduate, Kern County High School, 1919
TANGEN, Louis	Graduate, Kern County High School, 1933 Graduate, Bakersfield College, 1936 Engineer, Bakersfield High School, 1945-1948; Kern Union High School District, 1948-1973
VEON, Frances Getchell	Graduate, Kern County High School, 1915 Graduate, Bakersfield College, 1916
WAGY, Philip	Graduate, Kern County High School, 1925
WEILL, Lawrence	Graduate, Kern County High School, 1906
WHEELER, Jeannette	Teacher, Shafter High School, 1944-1977

CHRONOLOGY OF EVENTS 1968-1980

Note: This outline of chronological events consists for the most part of actions of the Kern High School District Board of Trustees listed according to the dates of those actions. In a few cases events are listed by the effective date of the action. Selection of items was based entirely upon the author's judgement and is intended primarily to be of assistance to someone who might continue the narrative at a later date.

J. S. Wallace, Editor

1968-1969

September 26, 1968: Hearing of citizens on student safety at South High School.

October 24, 1968: Hearing of citizens regarding safety of students at Bakersfield and South High Schools.

November 14, 1968: Evaluation of tax override failure in election of November 5, 1968.

Confederate flag removed as symbol at South High School.

December 12, 1968: Albert Gould resigned as Trustee, will remain on Kern Community College Board.

William E. Davis of Ridgecrest appointed to fill in Mr. Gould's term.

February 19, 1969: Citizens' Committee formed to study student unrest.

Committee established to study graduation requirements.

March 3, 1969: Contract awarded for construction of Highland High School.

April 17, 1969: Notice of completion of Board and Conference Rooms at District Office.

John Cissne assigned Principal, Burroughs High School.

Harold Corrie assigned Principal, North High School.

May 29, 1969: Allen Cannon and Elmer Peery retire.

Chronology of Events, Continued:

June 19, 1969: Mark Raney resigned from Board of Trustees. Will stay on Board of Kern Community College District.

July 1, 1969: Charles O. Gates assigned Principal, McFarland High School.

July 8, 1969: Jordon Kanikkeberg assigned Principal, Shafter High School.

George Ablin welcomed to first meeting as member of Board.

M. Glenn Bultman elected President of Board.

1969-1970

October 7, 1969: Letter read from State Department of Education commending Vista High School.

November 3, 1969: Ken Croes, President of Chamber of Commerce, proposes a committee representing the Chamber to communicate on District matters.

Evaluation of tax override defeat in election held on October 28, 1969.

Review of necessary steps to establish a regional joint powers agreement for a vocational center.

November 20, 1969: Notice of completion of Shafter High School rehabilitation projects.

December 18, 1969: Notice of completion of McFarland High School administration/classroom building.

Approval of building of Bakersfield High School Student Center out of student funds.

February 5, 1970: Fourteen District plans for unification now under consideration at the County level.

March 5, 1970: Procedure for termination of 51 certificated positions adopted. Lottery conducted.

April 2, 1970: Notice of completion of Arvin High School Student Center.

May 14, 1970: Final termination notices sent to certificated staff.

1970-71

July 1, 1970: Resignation of W. C. Meyers as Trustee.

Chamber of Commerce Committee study of school District operations presented by Fred Morris.

July 17, 1970: Personnel who were sent termination notices are reinstated because of vacancies which occurred after the lottery.

August 6, 1970: New dress and grooming code adopted.

November 5, 1970: Letter from ACLU presented regarding student rights and the new dress code.

Notice of completion of Lecture Centers for Burroughs and Foothill High Schools.

December 2, 1970: Board meeting at Burroughs High School. First public meeting in new Lecture Center.

Board response to Chamber of Commerce Study approved.

January 8, 1971: Tax and bond election set for April 20, 1971, $.48 tax increase; $5,500,000 bond.

May 4, 1971: Failure of tax/bond election reviewed.

Budget adjustments needed as result.

Report on Highland High School participation in Model Schools Project received.

June 24, 1971: M. Glenn Bultman resigned after 12 years on Board. Will remain on College Board.

County Superintendent presented "Statement of Fact" regarding potential conflict of interest by Board member, Timothy Lemucchi, whose wife is a teacher in the District.

1971-72

July 1, 1971: Don Ruggenberg elected President of Board.

New location for school farm approved.

October 7, 1971: Resolution honoring former Trustee H. C. Woodworth adopted.

November 4, 1971: Board members invited to attend meeting with Lloyd Trump of the Model Schools Project.

Recruitment report: Necessity for the continuance of out-of-state recruiting primarily for minority staff needs.

December 2, 1971: Meetings with minority advisory committee reported.

April 6, 1972: Notice of completion of West High School Lecture Center.

Reports on activities of Mexican-American Advisory Committee.

May 11, 1972: Recognition of retirees Berniece Braddon, E. Ben Evans, and Herbert L. Martin.

May 25, 1972 Letter of support for bond election received from Chamber of Commerce.

June 22, 1972: Failure of bond/tax election held on June 6, 1972 reviewed. $.48 tax increase/$6,425,000 bond proposal.

July 6, 1972: Ward at General Hospital to be used temporarily for career training center for handicapped students.

1972-73

August 3, 1972: Stull Bill Committee on teacher evaluation established. J. S. Wallace will chair.

September 14, 1972: Gasoline station to be leased temporarily for a branch of Career Training Center for Handicapped Students.

October 12, 1972: Management positions designated under the Dent Bill.

Proposed discipline code presented by a citizens committee. Superintendent suggested that members of this committee work with administration to review the discipline code now in use.

December 14, 1972: Board received proposal for unification of the China Lake/Ridgecrest area from the Kern County Committee on School District Organization.

January 11, 1973:	Trustee Ray Dezember presented a proposal for attendance boundary changes. Retirements: Arthur Johnson, Principal, Foothill High School; Jack Hilton, District Office, Classified Personnel.
January 22, 1973:	Consensus reach on Regional Occupational Center issues.
February 8, 1973:	Preliminary report on long-range attendance boundary and building programs resulting from the Dezember suggestions. Board proposed that a committee from the community make an in-depth study of the recommendations.
March 8, 1973:	Unification election in the Burroughs area reported. Attendance area set for May 1, 1973. Proposal received from Fred Harvey Company for work experience program in Grand Canyon. Would involve 700-800 District students.
April 12, 1973:	Kern County Taxpayer's Association challenges use of state-wide comparisons in setting salaries. Statement of personnel policy for affirmative action adopted. Administrative appointments: Jordon Kanikkeberg, Principal, Foothill High School Richard Brown, Principal, North High School
May 10, 1973:	Administrative appointments: Neal W. Olsen, Principal, Shafter High School James R. Fillbrandt, District Director, Instruction and Personnel. Superintendent reported that, because enabling legislation failed to pass, the District cannot continue with plans for the Grand Canyon work experience program.
June 14, 1973:	Report on Burroughs area unification now that election has passed. New district will become operative with the 1974-75 school year.

1973-1974

July 9, 1973: Don Ruggenberg elected Board President.

J. Craig Jenkins welcomed to his first official Board meeting as Trustee.

Guidelines of Stull Committee for 1973-1974 adopted.

Discipline Code updated as result of work of parents and staff.

July 19, 1973: Lengthy report on ROCK.

$.08 tax will continue to be allotted.

August 2, 1973: Request sent to Governor by Board to veto collective bargaining bill.

November 20, 1973: Report of Citizens Committee on long range planning received.

January 10, 1974: Ground breaking ceremonies for the new Special Education Career Training Center (later named the Ruggenberg Career Center).

February 14, 1974: Report on alternative schools given by Don Murfin. He recommends establishment of such a school in the District.

Resignation of E. C. ("Bus") Mills received.

March 14, 1974: Purchase of property for relocation of Nueva Continuation High School authorized.

April 18, 1974: Administrative appointments:
James Waterman, Principal, East Bakersfield High School
John Cissne, District Director, Pupil Personnel

Board petitioned for name change asking that "Joint" be eliminated because of loss of Burroughs High School, to be officially: Kern Union High School District of Kern County.

Robert Amenta appointed Director of the new alternative school.

June 13, 1974: Resolution passed to purchase property for Central Valley Continuation School on Lerdo Road.

282

1974-1975

July 18, 1974: Bond election slated for November, 1974. Set at $10,665,000.00.

October 3, 1974: Public hearing held on expulsion - first ever by this District. Disciplinary action taken by school was upheld.

October 14, 1974: Report on District Honor Orchestra Program.

November 14, 1974: Results of failure of November bond election received. Consensus of Board is to call another election in March, 1975.

December 12, 1974: Revenue limit increase election set for March 4, 1975. Bond election part of the election tabled.

February 13, 1975: Thomas N. Jones designated Acting Principal of West High School.

March 13, 1975: Mrs. Mary M. Vaughan welcomed as new Trustee.

Board expresses appreciation to public for passage of the revenue limit increase.

Sixth period load for students and 42 teaching positions restored.

April 10, 1975: George Ablin elected President of the Board.

Alternative school authorized to open in the Fall of 1975 after delay of one year because of funding problems.

May 13, 1975: Facility on 'K' Street leased for the alternative school.

Participation under California Educational Training Act approved (CETA).

1975-1976

July 17, 1975: Case settled with teacher at West High School after District lost its attempt to release her.

September 11, 1975: Appointment of Dr. Ruth Love Holloway as Superintendent of Oakland Schools reported. She is a noted graduate of Bakersfield High School.

September 16, 1975: Vista overflow facility leased; located on Flower Street.

November 13, 1975: Need for affirmative action policy reported.

Consensus reached by Board to participate in joint powers agreement to hire a private attorney as District counsel. Kern County Superintendent of Schools is providing leadership.

February 19, 1976: Unification hearings on Shafter and North of the River areas scheduled.

March 11, 1976: Resolution passed for election to raise revenue limit for June, 1976.

April 1, 1976: Faculty Association is proceeding to organize under the new collective bargaining legislation - the Rodda Bill. Will continue to operate under "meet and confer" procedures, however.

California School Employees Association recognized as exclusive representatives for classified employees.

April 22, 1976: Adoption of Affirmative Action Plan. Commendation from Faculty Association and community representatives.

May 27, 1976: Thomas N. Jones appointed Principal of West High School.

June 10, 1976: Tax election failure reviewed. Superintendent noted that need exists.

June 24, 1976: Ms. Fuchsia Ward appointed Affirmative Action Supervisor.

1976-1977

September 16, 1976: Impending retirement of Superintendent John W. Eckhardt announced.

Program of selection of his successor outlined.

October 14, 1976: Report by Grant Jensen of Fenton Project in Citizenship Education.

December 9, 1976: Building contracts awarded for: Shafter High School Applied Arts Building; McFarland High School classroom additions; East Bakersfield High School parking lot.

January 13, 1977: Restoration of Bakersfield High School Administration Building authorized. Damaged by fire on January 3, 1977. Principal Robesky reported that records are intact.

February 18, 1977: Gerald S. DeGrow appointed to succeed John W. Eckhardt as District Superintendent. New Superintendent introduced.

March 10, 1977: Physical Education Assessment Report presented.

April 14, 1977: Principal Kenneth Robesky had asked to be reassigned. Bill French appointed Acting Principal, Bakersfield High School, for remainder of year.

James R. Fillbrandt appointed Principal of Bakersfield High School beginning with 1977-1978.

May 26, 1977: Retiring Superintendent John W. Eckhardt presented a special commendation by the Board after 31 years of service to the District.

Session adjourned in memory of Kenneth Robesky, Principal, Bakersfield High School.

1977-1978

July 14, 1977: Superintendent Gerald DeGrow reported on his first two weeks on the job.

August 4, 1977: Mrs. Connie Pappas appointed District Supervisor of Food Services after the retirement of Ms. Valentine Valena.

September 8, 1977: Master Plan for Special Education explained by Jack Schuetz. Will double number of students served.

October 13, 1977: Lloyd Colvin appointed to new position of District Director of Research and Forward Planning.

Cecil Briscoe appointed District Director of ROCK.

Ron Fontaine appointed District Director of Specially Funded Programs.

November 17, 1977: Plan for Educational Excellence approved.

December 7, 1977: Revenue limit increase election set for March 7, 1978.

January 12, 1978: District negotiating team established.

Report on damage to facilities by December dust storm received.

February 9, 1978: Administrative staff evaluation instrument presented.

March 9, 1978: Failure of tax election reviewed.

April 6, 1978: Rayburn Dezember elected President of the Board.

Joint powers agreement approved for establishment of self insurance plan - SISK.

Revision of staff selection procedures approved.

Appointments:
Ms. Christina Mastaire, District Director, Instructional Services;
Herb Neufeld, District Director, Pupil Personnel Services

May 25, 1978: Don L. Murfin appointed Special Assistant to the Superintendent.

Early retirement incentive plan approved.

Lease of facilities for Horizon High School on 19th Street authorized.

June 15, 1978: Appointments:
Ms. Jeannine Thompson, Acting Principal, South High School

Clinton Osthimer, Acting Principal, Kern Valley High School

June 29, 1978: Superintendent reported on cuts needed to comply with results of passage of Proposition 13.

1978-1979

July 24, 1978: Budget cuts totalling $7,500,000 recommended by Superintendent.

Discussion about the place of ROCK program in a period of cutbacks. Motion to proceed with construction of ROCK center defeated.

Agreement reached to lease facilities for Horizon High School located on 17th Street.

September 7, 1978: Community Advisory Committee authorized for formation of Master Plan on Student Enrollment in metropolitan area.

Kenneth Brown, District Supervisor, Public Information, resigned.

November 7, 1978: Mrs. Ann Gutcher appointed District Supervisor, Public Information.

November 16, 1978: Carl Berra, District Director, Athletics, resigned.

December 14, 1978: Faculty Association presented first master contract proposal under collective bargaining procedures. Superintendent noted that this is the only "major school district" in the State without a contract.

January 1, 1979: Carl Berra, District Athletics Commissioner and Director of Drivers Education, retired. Succeeded by Don Harrison, Athletic Director, Bakersfield High School.

February 8, 1979: Resignation: Assistant Superintendent Grant Jensen; District Transportation Supervisor John Hazzard.

District certificated negotiation team with use of professional negotiator approved.

February 26, 1979: Contract with classified staff ratified. 110 hours needed at table, according to Assistant Superintendent, Personnel.

May 10, 1979: Don L. Murfin appointed Assistant Superintendent, Instruction.

Proposed new graduation requirements presented.

May 31, 1979: Tentative agreement with Faculty Association on contract reported by Superintendent.

Appointments:
Neal W. Olsen, Administrative Director, Instruction;
Benjamin Seykora, District Supervisor, Transportation.

June 14, 1979: New graduation requirements plan approved.

Contract with certificated staff ratified. Board members express reservations about collective bargaining process.

"Meet and Confer" procedures approved for counselors, management, and some part-time adult employees.

Master Plan Committee deliberation summarized.

June 28, 1979:   Evan Jones appointed Principal, Shafter High School.

Communications received from County Superintendent of Schools regarding Board elections in the newly unified McFarland District.

Board commended citizens who served on Master Plan Committee.

Board approves lease of site on Eureka Street for location of Vista East Continuation High School (formerly Lincoln Junior High School).

1979-1980

September 6, 1979: Final budget adopted. Reduced $2.4 million from that in 1977-1978.

Affirmative Action Supervisor Fuchsia Ward reported that affirmative action obligations were fulfilled.

October 11, 1979: Report on District Scholastic Aptitude Test scores showed students have made positive gains.

November 14, 1979: Recognition given retiring Trustees Mary M. Vaughan and Don Ruggenberg, latter had served 22 years.

New Board members Mrs. Carol J. Wilcox and Terry Moreland introduced.

December 13, 1979: J. Craig Jenkins elected President of Board.

January 9, 1980: J. S. Wallace, Assistant Superintendent for Personnel, resigned.

January 21, 1980: Rosedale property accepted from ROCK.

February 14, 1980: Superintendent received effects of Proposition 13 on operations of District.

A number of issues regarding operation of District raised by one Board member.

Harold Corrie, District Director, Classified Personnel, resigned.

March 21, 1980: Citizens heard in opposition to closing of handicapped senior program.

April 8, 1980: Assistant Superintendent Harry Ward explained tax revenue results because of unification of McFarland High School area.

May 15, 1980: Incident reported at Foothill High School in which Principal was held hostage.

James R. Fillbrandt appointed Assistant Superintendent, Personnel.

Committee established to develop a five-year program for Regional Occupational Program to be separated frm the Regional Occupational Center of Kern (ROCK).

May 29, 1980: Plan for ROP approved, to be separated from ROCK.

June 26, 1980: William Lacey appointed Principal of Bakersfield High School.

Sequence for filling administrative positions approved.

Lease with option to purchase Col. Baker School approved to house ROP Program.